Constitutions and Religious Freedom

Many of us take for granted the idea that the right to religious freedom should be protected in a free, democratic polity. However, this book challenges whether the protection and privilege of religious belief and identity should be prioritized over other rights. By studying the effects of constitutional promises of religious freedom and establishment clauses, Frank B. Cross sets the stage for empirical questions that examine the consequences of such protections. Although the case for broader protection is often made as a theoretical matter, constitutions generally protect freedom of religion. Allowing people full choice in holding religious beliefs or freedom of conscience is central to their autonomy. Thus, freedom of religion is potentially a very valuable aspect of society, at least so long as it respects the freedom of individuals to be irreligious. This book tests these associations and finds that constitutions provide national religious protection, especially when the legal system is more sophisticated.

Frank B. Cross holds a joint appointment as the Herbert D. Kelleher Centennial Professor of Business Law and Professor of Law at the University of Texas. His scholarship traverses several fields, including descriptive and normative studies of judicial decision making, the economics of law and litigation, and traditional policy and doctrinal issues in administrative and environmental law. Since 1998, he has published more than twenty articles in various publications, including the *Yale Law Journal*, *Cornell Law Review*, *New York University Law Review*, and *Columbia Law Review*.

Comparative Constitutional Law and Policy

Series Editors

TOM GINSBURG, *University of Chicago*
ZACHARY ELKINS, *University of Texas at Austin*
RAN HIRSCHL, *University of Toronto*

Comparative constitutional law is an intellectually vibrant field that encompasses an increasingly broad array of approaches and methodologies. This series collects analytically innovative and empirically grounded work from scholars of comparative constitutionalism across academic disciplines. Books in the series include theoretically informed studies of single constitutional jurisdictions, comparative studies of constitutional law and institutions, and edited collections of original essays that respond to challenging theoretical and empirical questions in the field.

Volumes in the Series

Comparative Constitutional Design edited by TOM GINSBURG (2012)

Consequential Courts: Judicial Roles in Global Perspective edited by DIANA KAPISZEWSKI, GORDON SILVERSTEIN, AND ROBERT A. KAGAN (2013)

Presidential Legislation in India: The Law and Practice of Ordinances by SHUBHANKAR DAM (2014)

Constitutions in Authoritarian Regimes edited by TOM GINSBURG AND ALBERTO SIMPSER (2014)

Social Difference and Constitutionalism in Pan-Asia edited by SUSAN H. WILLIAMS (2014)

Constitutionalism in Asia in the Early Twenty-First Century edited by ALBERT CHEN (2014)

Constitutions and Religious Freedom by FRANK B. CROSS (2014)

Constitutions and Religious Freedom

FRANK B. CROSS

University of Texas

CAMBRIDGE
UNIVERSITY PRESS

CAMBRIDGE
UNIVERSITY PRESS

32 Avenue of the Americas, New York, NY 10013-2473, USA

Cambridge University Press is part of the University of Cambridge.

It furthers the University's mission by disseminating knowledge in the pursuit of education, learning, and research at the highest international levels of excellence.

www.cambridge.org
Information on this title: www.cambridge.org/9781107041448

First published 2015

A catalog record for this publication is available from the British Library.

Library of Congress Cataloging in Publication Data
Cross, Frank B., author.
Constitutions and religious freedom/Frank B. Cross.
pages cm. – (Comparative constitutional law and policy)
ISBN 978-1-107-04144-8 (hardback)
1. Freedom of religion. 2. Freedom of religion – Social aspects. 3. Constitutional law. I. Title.
K3258.C76 2014
342.08′52–dc23 2014001850

ISBN 978-1-107-04144-8 Hardback

Contents

Foreword by Zachary Elkins *page* ix

1 Why Freedom of Religion? 1

2 Religious Freedom Around the World 34

3 Measuring Religious Freedom 58

4 Social Factors and Religious Freedom 78

5 Constitutions and Religious Freedom 105

6 The Constitutional Protection of Religious Freedom 153

7 Religious Freedom and Society 185

Bibliography 209

Index 235

Foreword

Frank B. Cross is known for his straightforward and direct approach to big questions, and this book is no exception. Indeed, this book launches a frontal attack on not one, but a *series* of weighty questions that have likely intimidated less ambitious scholars. In so doing, he unsettles conventional wisdom and opens productive avenues into the study of constitutions and religion that we will be traversing for years to come.

Many of us take for granted the idea that the right to religious freedom should be protected in a free, democratic polity. Not Cross, who wonders why we would protect and privilege a religious basis for beliefs and identity over any other. Cross's questions startle: Of how much social or material value is religious freedom, really? This is a provocative and arresting beginning, and it sets the stage for a set of empirical questions that he answers clearly and succinctly in subsequent chapters.

The empirical chapters unfold in a highly methodical and organized fashion as he builds the scaffolding for his core question: Does religious freedom, once it is promised in higher law, yield real de facto freedom? This question has been at the heart of constitutional analysis at least since James Madison's concern about mere parchment barriers. Cross is highly adept and resourceful in his analysis of relevant data on the question. He leads us through the meaning of religious freedom – which we may have thought we knew – and picks apart its various manifestations and observable attributes. In the end, the question is whether constitutional guarantees enhance religious freedom over and above a set of other predictors such as the country's prevailing religion, its relative level of democracy, its rule of law, and its per capita GDP. I know Cross's answer here, but there is no reason to spoil the ending.

For those new to the intersection of religion and constitutionalism, Cross's book is a comprehensive and discerning guide. The sad reality of scholarship is that many authors, because of either impatience or arrogance, read the existing scholarship with just enough attention to launch an idea. Cross, by contrast, seems to have devoured the last thirty years of empirical and theoretical work on the topic with gusto, and has left behind a beautifully curated tour that is anything but narrow and superficial. This is a book that requires a pencil for marginalia and, perhaps, a credit card or a library card handy: Cross leaves no question about where to go for further reading and provides ample inspiration for such.

Zachary Elkins, co-editor
Cambridge Comparative Law and Policy series

1 Why Freedom of Religion?

Although freedom of religion is often presumed, its protection is heavily disputed. Why should freedom of religion be constitutionally protected when other freedoms are not? Why not protect a broader freedom of conscience, which would shelter the religious and the nonbelievers? Although the case for broader protection is often made as a theoretical matter, constitutions generally protect freedom of religion. This book examines the consequences of such protections.

The original U.S. Constitution did not contain a guarantee of freedom of religion, but such constitutional protection was soon provided in the Bill of Rights. The constitutional protection was placed alongside freedom of speech in the very first amendment, ahead of property rights, the rights of criminal defendants, and other matters. As such, freedom of religion is considered foundational to Americans.

Special respect for religious freedom is not unique to Americans. Freedom of religion is widely protected by international law (Scolnicov 2011). The 1976 United Nations International Covenant on Civil and Political Rights declared that everyone should have the right to freedom of religion. The 1981 United Nations Declaration on the Elimination of All Forms of Intolerance and of Discrimination

Based on Religion or Belief proclaimed that religion or belief "is one of the fundamental elements in ... [a person's] conception of life" that "should be fully respected and guaranteed." It proceeds to lay out particular elements to be protected.

Few ask why religious freedom should be guaranteed constitutionally, but the question is a relevant one. It may be that religion is undeserving of special constitutional protection. Even if we deem freedom of religion to be worthy of such exalted status, the purpose of such protection should be relevant to the manner in which such a constitutional provision is interpreted and applied.

At the threshold one might want to define religion, so as to know what freedoms are protected. The definitional question has proven to be a challenge. Neither social science nor law has settled upon a clear definition. Many definitions "erect a canopy so large that atheism and most college sororities would qualify as religions" (Grim 2004, 7–8). Asad (1993) contends that there can be no universal definition of religion.

Leiter (2010) argues that religion has certain unique characteristics, such as the issuance of categorical (nonconsequentialist) demands on action and a reliance on faith, rather than reason or evidence, for beliefs. Feofanov (1994) employs a similar definition, as do many others. The most common definition typically relies upon a belief in the sacred or supernatural as fundamental, though some groups, such as Buddhists, have an ambiguous belief in the supernatural.

Koppelman (2010) takes issue with Leiter's definition but concedes that no definition of religion works very well. Much like pornography, he suggests that the definition of religion is simply that "[w]e know it when we see it" (Koppelman 2010, 976). If religion is to be protected (or limited), though, it must be defined. Some contend that prevailing definitions have produced only a mess or a quagmire (Feofanov 1994). But definition is dangerous. It risks excluding true beliefs as not qualifying as religious. Sullivan (2006, 924) contends that religion cannot "be defined in such a way that it can be legally protected and maintained as separate."

There may be no good definition of religion, but Sullivan's view is too gloomy, and the difficulty need not be a serious problem. Disputes tend to arise only at the boundary. Thus, Europeans debate whether

Scientology should be considered a religion or a cult. While this may be important – very important to some – the vast majority of religious freedom issues are not such boundary problems, so a precise definition is unnecessary for a general assessment of global freedom of religion. Lupu (1996, 358) notes that the "combination of cultural pluralism, pragmatism, and experience" suggests that the definitional problem is not great, as we have "conventional understandings of what constitutes religion."

The Justification for Protecting Religious Freedom

The right to choose one's religion is a constitutional protection not offered to other individual choices. There is no constitutional right to choose what one eats, for example, though that is undeniably important to people. Religion is an important area of individual autonomy, but so are choices of dress or vocation or countless other areas of personal autonomy. The privileged status of religion in constitutions may fairly be questioned. This is especially true when religious freedom appears to conflict with other freedoms, such as gender rights.

Brian Leiter is a legal philosopher and academic who has questioned the reason for privileging religion. He claims that no one has offered a credible principled argument for tolerating religion itself, as opposed to other personal choices. While there are ample philosophical justifications for tolerating personal differences, he says that religion may not be so special as to warrant a specific constitutional protection. He suggests that there is no principled reason for constitutions to single out religion for special legal protection.

While Leiter is especially vigorous in pursuing the point, he is not alone in the theory. Ronald Dworkin (1986) basically agrees. Christopher Eisgruber and Lawrence Sager (2007, 6) argue for "equal liberty" which denies that "religion is a category of human experience that demands special benefits and/or necessitates special restrictions." They suggest that any deeply held concern of persons should be given equal regard, though they recognize that the history of religious violence might cause constitutions to single it out.

Religion "may be no more important to a person's conception of who she is than other terms based on such diverse factors as personal relationships (mother, sister) profession (engineer, lawyer), race (Hispanic, Native American), political affiliation (Republican, Libertarian), special skills (violinist, gardner), socioeconomic status (yuppie, homeless), residence (New Yorker, Westerner), or individual habits, tastes activities, interests, or loyalties (vegetarian, Cubs fan)" (Smith 1991, 203). Religion would not be the primary identifier for many and does not plainly merit special status. Some argue that religious belief "cannot be qualitatively distinguished from other belief systems in a way that justifies special constitutional consideration (Marshall 1991, 320–321). Yet others arguing to the contrary contend that religion is of unique importance to people (Greenawalt 2008).

Leiter would not deny all legal recognition to religion. But he suggests that it merits tolerance rather than respect. As a consequence, religious freedom should be more readily compromised when it conflicts with other societal interests. Hamilton (2005), making a similar argument, notes that religion is not a particular good and that religious groups should not be generally exempted from secular laws. This notion is related to a concept known as *proportionality*, which will be discussed later in the book.

Some disagree with Leiter. They contend that "religion is special" and "more than simply a peculiarly form of freedom of speech and assembly, privacy, and autonomy" (Witte 2005, 250). Perhaps religion is a uniquely important aspect of human autonomy. It has been called a "defining feature of the human personality" (Boyle & Sheen 1997, 11). For many, religion is simply more important than other aspects of personal life (Greenawalt 2008). Traditionally, religious beliefs have been considered "important enough to die for, to suffer for, to rebel for, to emigrate for, to fight to control the government for" (Laycock 1996, 317). Other choices have not seen this response.

Religion could thus be justified as a matter of degree if not of kind. The choice of a theoretically organizing principle for one's life may transcend one's choice of food or clothing or other common individual daily choices (Eisgruber & Sager 1994). Thomas Jefferson declared that the constitutional freedom of religion was the "most inalienable and sacred of all human rights" (Smith 1991). Beliefs about religion are "often of extraordinary importance to the individual" (Laycock 2011, 951). Religious goods may be distinctive ones, more important than other material matters.

Finnis (2009) contends that religion is special in its direction of truths about humanity and the world. Religious freedom has long been justified as a "unique source of individual and personal identity" (Witte 2005, 250). But religion itself is not truly so unique as such a source of personal identity. Many people have no religious belief, but they are not without individual and personal identities; they simply find their identities in other sources, which may be constitutionally protected. Secularists have their own moral beliefs. One may find one's personal identity in a theory such as Marxism or even racism, for example, which is not generally considered a religion. Leiter notes that religion is not grounded in reason so much as in faith, and that religion has certainly been a source of societal "bads" throughout history. Desmond Tutu (1996, xv) has declared that religion "should produce peace, reconciliation, tolerance, and respect for human rights but it has often promoted the opposite conditions." As such, religion might not merit special protection.

The Historical Case for Freedom of Religion

The historical case for singling out religion for constitutional protection may be simply a pragmatic one. History has shown that religion has been a powerful force in the broad oppression of individuals, singling them out for death, among other sanctions. Perhaps we protect religious freedom merely because religious oppression has historically been a force of great harm and strife (Garvey 1996a). Throughout history, "governmental attempts to suppress religious views had caused vast human suffering" (Laycock 1996, 317). Because religious beliefs are so deeply felt, they lead to a particular risk of conflict (Lupu 1996). It is not accidental that religion is the oldest human right to be internationally recognized (Venter 2010). Historically, religion "is more likely to be a ground of persecution" (Nussbaum 2008, 165). Over two hundred million persons have been killed due to their religious affiliations throughout recorded history (Barrett & Johnson 2001). The same cannot be said about other personal choices, such as food and clothing. Most people are familiar with this history, and it is beyond the scope of this book to engage in a historical tour de force of oppression in the name of religion, but I will undertake a brief review.

The classic case of religious oppression is probably that of the Spanish Inquisition of the fifteenth century. At the outset, the Inquisition was an attempt to drive out Christian heretics, but it soon turned to the Jews, among others. Jews were arrested and tried, and hundreds or thousands were burned at the stake. Some were tortured. Many had their wealth confiscated, and large numbers fled Europe to avoid oppression. The Inquisition is a dramatic story of the consequences of a lack of religious freedom, but there are others. Pogroms against the Jewish religion are unfortunately common throughout the history of the Middle East and Europe. Russia has seen a series of anti-Jewish pogroms over the past two centuries.

Religious oppression arguably came to a head with Nazi Germany. The Holocaust saw the execution of millions of Jews, for no reason other than their religious faith. Before the killings, though, there was a steady pattern of persecution. The Nuremberg laws of 1935 prohibited, among other things, intermarriage among Jews and Christians. Jews were denied the right to vote and hold office. Jews were required to wear yellow badges when out and were confined to ghettoes. The oppression steadily escalated, of course, ultimately leading to death camps.

Historic religious oppression continues to this day, often unrecognized. In 1999–2001, inter-religious violence in Indonesia caused thousands of deaths and hundreds of thousands of internally displaced persons (Sidel 2006). The nation of India has seen spasms of violence directed at Muslims and Sikhs. Hindus, in turn, have suffered at the hands of Islamists. The former nation of Yugoslavia saw a civil war resulting from violence among Catholics, the Orthodox Christians, and Muslims. Islamic nations today engage in various acts to repress the beliefs of Christians, Jews, and disfavored Islamic sects. Various nations in Africa are seeing a struggle between Muslims and Christians.

Marty (1996, 2) suggests that the "monstrous totalitarian systems of the twentieth century, be they Fascist, Nazi, Communist, Maoist, or whatever, set out to suppress rights, beginning with those of religious people." If in earlier times, it was more typical for one religion to repress others, a more recent phenomenon is that of irreligious autocrats repressing religious believers. Because of the strong influence of religion on people and the potentially subversive organizing role of churches, the suppression of religious freedom may be particularly vital for would-be autocrats. Thus, religious freedom may be uniquely important to humans. One suspects that few would have suffered torture and death in order to continue their eating habits, unlike their religious beliefs. The Pilgrims fled across a dangerous North Atlantic to a dangerous American wilderness to avoid an official church and religious persecution. It has been said that tolerance "has been particularly difficult to achieve in the sphere of religion" (McClosky & Brill 1983, 103). Laycock (2011, 951) suggests that it was uncontroversial to claim that "attempts to suppress dissenting religious views had caused vast human suffering and social conflict."

Historically, the struggle for religious freedom has also been part of the fight for freedom more generally. There is a reason why freedom of religion, along with speech, is found in the very first amendment to the U.S. Constitution. "In the eighteenth century, as in preceding centuries, the efforts to gain religious liberty were central to the struggles for freedom of belief, paving the way, by argument and physical resistance, for the later struggles for democratic rights in general" (McClosky & Brill 1983, 103). Religious freedom was central to Enlightenment recognition of individual freedom (Scolnicov 2011).

In addition, religious disagreement has been a common source of conflict and death. Muslims and Christians today battle in Nigeria and other African nations. Conflict has occurred even within broadly defined religions. Protestants and Catholics fought a virtual civil war within Ireland. And, as I write this book, Sunnis and Shi'ites are engaged in a similar conflict in the Middle East. Can freedom of religious belief can help prevent such conflict?

Indeed, empirical evidence reveals that religious freedom promotes peace. The restriction of religious freedom correlates positively with involvement in armed conflict (Grim 2004). Religion is traditionally a source of conflict, which obviously continues in the present era. And religious conflicts may be more intractable, given the devoutness of believers. McClosky and Brill (1983, 103) suggest that tolerance has been "particularly difficult to achieve in the sphere of religion."

The historical case of freedom of religion depends on contingency, however. While religion has been used as a source of severe oppression in the past, this need not be so in the future. Some nations (though certainly not all) appear to have transcended religious oppression. Constitutional rights are not generally grounded in historical accidents. And it may be, as later evidence in this book will show, that legal protection of religion is unnecessary to protect against such oppression of individuals. Such oppression has typically occurred in autocracies. Perhaps democratic governance provides sufficient shelter for religious freedom, so constitutional protections are simply superfluous. In addition, the historical case does not counsel universal religious freedom. A very small minority group does not likely threaten strife, and fear of violence does not necessarily argue against its oppression.

Is Religion a Particular Good?

Religion might be specially singled out for protection simply because it is uniquely important (Engel 2011). Smith (1991, 149) argues that "the religious justification is also the most satisfying, and perhaps the only adequate justification for a special constitutional commitment to religious liberty." Conkle (2011) suggests that religious belief may be the only truly robust foundation for religious liberty's protection. For a believer, religion is quite important, probably the most important choice of his or her life. For many, eternity is at stake, which places religious choice considerably above other individual preferences in terms of importance.

The importance of religion can be a double-edged sword, however. If religious belief is such an enormous transcendental decision, it becomes all too easy for a person to want to impose his or her particular beliefs on others, to "save their souls." The strong moral belief that slavery is wrong commonly prevents people from choosing to practice human slavery. Likewise, a strong moral belief in the truth of one's religion, and the falsity of others, can readily lead to a decision prohibiting the following of the beliefs perceived to be false, which could condemn a soul to eternal damnation. Thus, the extreme importance of religious belief to many could easily form an argument *against* religious freedom, so that the "true" religion might be imposed on the people. History shows this tendency to be the case, from the Catholic Church of centuries past to Islam in some contemporary societies.

A separate case for religious freedom might be found in the claim that religious belief in general is pragmatically an affirmative good to be encouraged by the state, without the state's embracing any particular religious belief. This position does not rely on any intrinsic philosophical value of religion; it merely contends that a peoples' religious faith, in whatever religion, is good for those people and for society as a whole. Some have argued that, without religious belief to keep them in check, people will regress to a state of immorality. Dostoyevsky (1990, 589) warned that "... without god ... everything is permitted." Garvey (1996b, 49) argues that the "best reasons for protecting religious freedom rest on the assumption that religion is a good thing." Smith (1991) suggests that this was the foundation of the First Amendment right. Religious belief, whether true or not, could have functional value for a society.

Some conservative constitutional scholars have argued that the American First Amendment should be interpreted only to protect against discrimination among religious sects, while allowing government favoritism toward religion generally. Religion in general arguably should be encouraged. This actually parallels the law of freedom of speech. Government is free to encourage speech as a broad matter but to prohibit discrimination over the particular content of speech.

At first blush, the thesis that religion is good for society might argue against religious freedom. It might seem that, rather than religious freedom, the best way to promote religious belief in a society would be through the adoption of a compulsory and subsidized state religion, to which all citizens must belong. King Louis XIV compelled the inhabitants of Paris to attend mass or go to jail, which might seem an effective way of increasing religiosity. In 1646, Thomas Edwards wrote that religious toleration was "the greatest of all evils because it would bring skepticism in doctrine and looseness of life, then atheism" (Porter 2000, 105). But this position reflects a naïve vision of the role and power of government in society.

Greater religious belief may have various practical benefits for a society, calling for its encouragement. Economists have mused on the effects of religion, and Max Weber (1930) famously argued that Protestantism brought with it personal characteristics that fostered capitalist economic growth. Weber's theory is generally not supported by research (Iannaccone 1998); nevertheless, it is plausible that religious belief could have economic consequences, as certain faiths may encourage traits such as "honesty, work ethic, and thrift" (McCleary & Barro 2006a). Attitudinal studies have found that religion appears to be good for the development of attitudes that are conducive to economic growth (Guiso, Sapienza, & Zingales 2003).

Societies with freedom of religion may encourage entrepreneurship, while "[c]losed religious systems foul economic development and stunt growth" (Malloch 2008, 51). Conversely, resources devoted to religion may be drawn from economically more productive activities, so greater religiosity might have negative economic effects. Some religious practices, such as prohibitions on consumption of certain products, cannot help the economy. In addition, the social activities common to religions may facilitate networks that are useful for economic purposes.

McCleary and Barro (2006a) studied the association of religious belief and economic well-being. They found that greater levels of religious belief were associated with statistically significant positive effects on economic growth, while higher levels of church attendance were associated with statistically significant negative effects on economic growth. Of course, belief and attendance were associated, with the results separated out in a multiple regression. So the results mean that greater religious attendance was negative when levels of belief were held constant, not that greater religious attendance was a per se negative. Still, the results suggest that religious belief is good for economic growth and that more devout belief (as expressed in more frequent religious attendance) can undermine this effect. The authors took statistical steps to show that they had found an effect of religion on growth, not one of growth on religion. The evidence on religious belief and economic growth provides at least some mild grounds for encouraging religion.

Durlauf, Kourtellos & Tan (2005) have criticized these results. They reestimated the study with different control variables and found that none of the religiosity variables were statistically significant at the 0.05 level. The authors conceded that religion was potentially relevant to growth but argued that there was no evidence to suggest that any such effect was quantitatively important. The set of countries studied by Durlauf et al. was relatively small, though.

Various studies have considered the association of particular faiths with economic growth, but their results are quite conflicted. Some research has shown that Islamic belief is associated with economic growth. Others have reached different conclusions for Islam while finding a positive effect for Orthodox Christianity. The presumed positive effect of Protestantism has generally not appeared. A study within the United States found that Judaism and nonfundamentalist Protestantism were associated with higher income, while Catholicism and fundamentalist Protestantism were not (Heath, Waters, & Waston 1995). The research on religious belief and the economy is inconclusive, though there may be some positive effect.

Beyond the economy, religion may have a variety of positive societal effects on the lives of believers. Religion is said to "inculcate in citizens the moral character necessary to a democratic society" (Smith 1991, 199). Religious belief has been shown to increase altruistic behavior. For a Randian, this might not be such a positive, but most Americans consider charitable giving a very good thing. And the religious are more charitable. Brooks (2003, 41) found that religious people are 25 percent more likely to donate money and 23 percent more likely to volunteer their time in charitable work. The differences attributable to religion were strong even after using controls on ideology and income. Moreover, the religious were much more likely to give to nonreligious charities. Grim (2009) found a positive effect of religious freedom on numerous measures of social well-being.

The greater generosity of religious groups may be due to the commands of their religions to be generous. They may feel a moral obligation to be generous to the needy. Or perhaps this is a characteristic of group formation. Because religion is a community of sorts, the religious may be more communitarian in orientation and hence more likely to give. This is consistent with evidence that the religious are more likely to participate in all sorts of voluntary associations (Smidt 2008). Thus, an atheist has suggested that "[m]ore than any other institution, religion deserves our appreciation and respect because it has persistently encouraged people to care deeply – for the self, for neighbors, for humanity, and for the natural world – and to strive for the highest ideals humans are able to envision" (Sheiman 2009, ix–x).

The greater civic engagement of the religious may contribute valuable social capital to a society. It is religious life that purportedly "makes basic forms of civility and social restraint possible" (Smidt, 1999, 176). At least the outwardly oriented religious groups "foster the growth of bridging social capital by motivating their members to give and volunteer beyond their own communities of belief, through inclusiveness that brings together socially, economically, and ethnically diverse communities" (Brooks 2005, 167). Such social capital is generally considered a valuable feature of a society.

"Social capital" is commonly used as a general term for mutual trust and cooperation in a society. Putnam (2000, 319) argues that when "trust and social networks flourish, individuals, firms, neighborhoods, and even nations prosper." Greater social capital is associated with many goods, including economic growth, social order, and health (Cross 2005). Religion offers "regular opportunities for social activity and interaction and so provides fertile terrain for the cultivation of friendships" (Sherkat & Ellison 1999, 373). Members of religious congregations are also more likely than nonmembers to belong to a diverse range of voluntary organizations and to show higher levels of social trust (Norris & Inglehart 2004).

By fostering such social connections and contacts and facilitating organizational abilities, churches might be expected to enhance social participation outside the churches, an effect that has been well documented (Peterson 1992). An investigation of the United States and Canada found that religious tradition and church attendance played "an important role in fostering involvement in civil society" (Smidt 1999, 176). People develop greater secular volunteering activities from religious community sources (Schwadel 2005). African American churches have been found to be "vital sources of collective self-help and community development, moral reform, social service delivery, community leadership, and political mobilization" (Sherkat & Ellison 1999, 375). An international study found that for all beliefs, a higher attendance at religious services was associated with higher levels of trust (Guiso, Sapienza, & Zingales 2003). Religion is not a necessary condition for altruism or social capital, but it appears to provide a net increase, fostering social connectedness. Hence, greater religious belief may offer a broad benefit to society generally. Smidt (2008) documents how the more religious seem to have a greater civic morality on matters such as not evading taxes.

Religious belief may also offer benefits for individual believers. A study of black male youth found that church attendance favorably affected their school attendance and work activity and reduced the level of socially deviant activity (Freeman 1986). Studies show that crime rates are negatively associated with religious membership (Lee 2006, Bainbridge 1989). Iannaccone (1998) summarizes various studies indicating that religion tends to reduce various deviant behaviors, including divorce, drug and alcohol abuse, and suicide. It is difficult to establish causality here. It may well be that those who are genetically predisposed to engage in deviant behaviors are simultaneously predisposed not to be religious. But still, the association means something, as those with positive attributes commonly choose religion.

Religious belief appears to be positively associated with higher levels of personal life satisfaction. A large study in Europe, using numerous factors that could affect personal attitudes found that greater religiosity had a statistically significant association with greater life satisfaction (Greene & Yoon 2004). An earlier study in the United States reached similar conclusions (Ellison 1991), reporting that the religious consistently showed higher levels of life satisfaction, greater personal happiness, and fewer negative psychosocial consequences of traumatic life events. This is generally true for different religions (Cohen 2002).

Elliott and Hayward (2009) studied the interaction of religion, government regulation, and life satisfaction. Both religious belief and personal freedom tend to be associated with greater happiness or satisfaction. The study also found that the association between church attendance and life satisfaction "actually changes from positive to negative as government regulation increases" (Elliott & Hayward 2009, 301). A study in Sweden found that religious belief was associated with fewer divorces, fewer children born out of wedlock, and less nonpayment of debt (Berggren 1997).

Religious belief is also positively associated with mental health. One study reported that those diagnosed as mentally ill were far less likely to attend church (Stark 1971). Religion may be valuable in helping humans cope with stress and suffering and may psychologically benefit the believer. From a Freudian perspective, religion may offer people a tool to control the inherent natural destructiveness of their innate impulses. The evidence is not conclusive, and the religious may suffer different problems, but it appears that this may offers another benefit of belief (Ellison 1998).

Religion may also offer benefits in physical health. Religious belief appears to make alcohol abuse less likely (Koenig, George, Meador, & Blazer 1994). Iannaccone (1998) reports that hundreds of epidemiological studies, with precautions taken to avoid spurious correlations, have consistently found that religious belief was associated with a variety of health benefits, physical and mental. These effects may come from discouragement of unhealthy behavior, community support, or the enhancement of self-esteem and personal efficacy (Sherkat & Ellison 1999). Some caution is required, as the research does not use the sort of controlled tests employed in medicine, but the sheer bulk of the research provides strong evidence that religion may be beneficial. The "evidence generally indicates that religion is broadly beneficial for the individual, and that this relationship holds up across a variety of measures both of religion and of well-being (Elliott & Hayward 2009, 285). Hummer, Rogers, Nam, & Ellison (1999) report that religious belief in the United States is associated with lower mortality. Studies throughout the world have found that religious participation, including activities such as prayer and meditation, are associated with greater human well-being. Overall, the research is clear that greater religiosity is generally beneficial for human health and well-being (Lehrer 2004a). Even defenders of atheism acknowledge that the research shows religiosity to be associated with greater life satisfaction and psychological well-being (Zuckerman 2009).

Most of the research on the potential individual benefits of religion has been conducted in the United States, but the association does not appear to be limited to this country. A study of Venezuelan evangelicals indicated that religion could be a means to overcome addiction, violence, and other personal and social difficulties (Smilde 2005). And the global association of religious belief with greater life satisfaction demonstrates that the effect is not one unique to America.

One difficulty with the study of the individual benefits of religious belief, though, lies in a selection problem. These studies are not clinical tests in which individuals are assigned to religious beliefs or nonbelief. It may be that those who would benefit from religion choose religion, while those who do not choose religion would draw no benefits from faith. Or some unrelated third factor might explain the correlations. Perhaps some underlying environmental or even genetic factor tends to yield both religious belief and charitable action. If so, religious belief is not a cause of charity. These are only possibilities, though, and the general association of religious belief and human welfare, for some at least, suggests the benefits of belief. Freeman (1986, 373) addresses the difficulty of establishing causality but argues that the "pattern of statistical results suggests that at least some part of the churchgoing effect is the result of actual causal impact."

Economics of Religion

There is a growing movement viewing religion in economic terms. In this context, competition is productive. A single, state-directed religion, by contrast, would be inefficient and ineffective. The state can compel attendance at religious functions, but it cannot compel belief. A state-controlled religion may cause stagnation such that it produces less belief in the state religion than would exist if it were not the state religion (Iannaccone, Finke, & Stark 1997).

An official state church is in a monopoly position. Economics teaches us that monopolies have a tendency to take excess profits and underproduce goods or services, while becoming stagnant due to a lack of competition. A state church needs to make fewer efforts to appeal to people, and religion becomes intertwined with the state itself, causing resentment (Fox 2008a). Gill (1999) reported that the dominant Latin American Catholic Church serviced the wealthy and neglected the poor. These negatives do not require a formal state church, as any market power, such as could come from government favoritism, would have a similar, if lesser, effect. Adam Smith thus argued that religious freedom would produce religious competition, which would generate greater religious activity and produce higher-quality religious services, just as in any other market. The competition "generates religious 'products' that are high in quality and well-aligned with individual preferences" (McCleary & Barro 2006a, 50).

In addition, diversity by itself should promote religious belief. Just as different people prefer different products, they might be expected to prefer different religious beliefs. A creed that is more accepting of women's rights might be expected to attract more women. Some people are more conservative and traditional and would prefer such values in their religious doctrine, whereas others might prefer the opposite. A single religion with defined beliefs will be less able to adapt to different personal preferences than will a variety of different religions with distinct belief systems.

There is evidence to support this hypothesis. A study of early twentieth-century America found that cities with higher rates of religious diversity had higher rates of religious affiliation and practice (Finke & Stark 1988). Stark and McCann (1993) found that the religious activity of Catholics was greater in regions where they represented a smaller fraction of the population. An empirical analysis of answers on the World Values Survey found that religious pluralism was associated with religious belief (McCleary & Barro 2006a). It is also positively associated with monthly church attendance and belief in heaven and hell (Barro & McCleary 2003a).

North and Gwin (2004) used U.S. State Department reports to define the level of religious freedom in various countries. The authors found that an official state religion, registration requirements, and other scales of restrictions on religious freedom consistently associated negatively with religious attendance. This is consistent with the finding that greater government entanglement with religion, whether aimed positively or negatively, tends to undermine popular religiosity.

The association between pluralism and religious participation seems a logical one, but it is still sometimes disputed. Breault (1989) reanalyzed some of the results of Finke and Stark and found that including consideration of Catholic population made the relationship disappear. However, because Catholicism is a religion, the findings do not necessarily refute the hypothesis, absent evidence of identical Catholic participation in the presence of greater pluralism. Internationally, many nations without pluralism have higher levels of faith-based behavior (Norris & Inglehart 2004).

Gill (1999) examined the growth of Protestantism in Latin American countries that were traditionally Catholic. He tested the theory that religious freedom would be associated with increased religious diversity and participation in twenty nations. Using an index of state religious regulation for these countries, he consistently found strong statistical associations between religious freedom and broader religiosity.

Some research finds that the existence of a state religion is associated with lower rates of church attendance (Chaves & Cann 1992), though other research reaches the opposite conclusion (Barro & McCleary 2003a). Highly regulated religious economies, via state religions or subsidies, have been associated with reduced religious participation in Western Europe (Stark & Iannaccone 1994, Barro & McCleary 2003a). These studies do not show causation, and some evidence suggests that pluralism does not itself promote participation (Chaves & Gorski 2001). There is some evidence to support the theory that religious pluralism encourages greater religious belief. In general, there is a correlation between rates of religious diversity and overall religious participation (Iannaccone 1998).

A mathematical problem arose with much of this research, however, deriving from the calculation of diversity. For example, Voas, Olson, and Crockett (2002) demonstrated that, depending on the size distributions of religious denominations, there was likely to be a statistically significant positive association, even when pluralism has no effect on participation. The authors reviewed several large past datasets to show this effect.

Not all studies have used the pluralism variable that these authors found debatable. For example, Fox and Tabory (2008) studied the effects of state regulation of religion on religious participation and belief. They found that countries with greater levels of separation of church and state tended to have higher levels of religiosity. Practice was affected relatively more than belief, but the results confirmed the preceding economic hypothesis.

Less rigorous historical evidence also confirms the economic hypothesis. In America the deregulation of religion in the First Amendment increased the level of religious competition and mobilization and produced "dramatic increases in church adherence" (Finke 1990, 623). This nation's efflorescence of religious pluralism and belief may thus be traceable to the constitutional guarantee. The previously established religions (Episcopalian, Congregationalist, and Presbyterian) saw their "market share" decline dramatically under constitutional religious freedom (McConnell & Posner 1989).

In addition, a state religion is by definition state as well as religion. The decisions made will be motivated by the interests of the state as well as those of religious groups. The interplay between popes and kings in feudal Europe reveals that pragmatic negotiation required when state and religion overlap. Hirschl (2010) notes that the effect of a state religion is to co-opt religion on behalf of the interests of the state. With "state recognition and funding come state regulation and monitoring" (Hirschl 2010, 51). Thus, state support for religion may incidentally undermine religion itself.

There is ample reason to believe that religious freedom serves to encourage religious belief. If such belief is a good thing, that would justify the freedom. Leiter (2008) has suggested that religion may more systematically produce harms, because it may contain categorical commands that are divorced from evidence or reason. Religious wars have killed many in Africa and Asia and even Western countries such as Ireland. These extreme events might suggest that religion not be encouraged.

It would be a mistake, however, to extrapolate the generalized consequences of religious belief from such extreme cases. One must also consider the more typical effects of religious belief, and religious freedom by promoting religious diversity might well serve to counteract the religious extremes. Adam Smith claimed that the zeal of religious radicals could be dangerous only where religious diversity was limited (Iannaccone 1991).

It is the absence of religious freedom that may produce such dangerous extremism. And government involvement with religion may be associated with greater religious violence (Iannaccone & Berman 2006). Broad religious diversity and religious freedom in the United States is largely associated with pacific religious practice. The more government is involved in religion, the greater the need for believers to assume political power on behalf of their faith, which may include violence. The violence and terrorism sometimes associated with religious belief may be a function of a lack of religious freedom.

Politics and Religion

Religion may also serve a useful political function. Religious organizations are the original nongovernmental organizations (NGOs). As such, they can supplement government efforts and possibly resist government abuses, even those unrelated to religious liberty. Gill and Lundsgaarde (2004, 400) note that "religious organizations are often the creators and purveyors of important values, beliefs, and norms that affect how people behave politically." Religion is a competing power center. Religions can mobilize people for action, including political protest (Gill 2001). Globally, membership in religious associations is significantly associated with voting, signing petitions, attending demonstrations, and joining strikes (Norris & Inglehart 2004). Of course, some suggest that religion is an "opiate" for the masses that precludes their political activism, but this is not demonstrated empirically.

The 1980s saw a world democratization wave involving dozens of countries moving out of autocracy. In many nations, this transition was led by the religious, in particular the Catholic Church

(Philpott 2007). Unsurprisingly, this progressive effect was much more profound among religious groups that were not preferred by the state. National churches did not oppose authoritarian governments, or did so only weakly. The increasing competition that the Latin American Catholic Church was receiving from evangelical Protestantism may have helped drive them to push for democracy. Indeed, it appeared that the greater religiosity of a church community was associated with more pressure for democratization (Philpott 2007). Religion was central to both the downfall of Soviet communism and the development of democracy in former communist countries (Richardson 2006).

Within the United States, religion has played an important role in African-American politics. Rather than serving as an opiate, religion has inspired the community to activism. Harris (1994) describes how religion has served as a political resource for the community and as a catalyst for its mobilization. The church provides physical organizational resources and psychological forces for activism. Greenberg (2000) similarly reports that churches can be important networks for political activism, especially in the African-American community. Mattis (2001) explores the great importance of religion to black political action in the United States. She notes how biblical passages have provided great force in the struggle for racial equality and how black churches have strengthened this message.

The church, and religion generally, is commonly regarded as a "mediating institution" of society. Like other such institutions, it countervails against the power of government in society and may protect individual liberties of all sorts. James Madison himself recognized that independent religions could serve as a check on the tyranny of the majority. To repeat, religion may be the original NGO (nongovernmental organization) and as such beneficial.

Mediating institutions have various merits. Neuhaus and Berger (1977) argued that it was necessary to have such institutions standing between individuals and large institutions of public life in order to prevent tyrannical abuses. They claimed that their mediating structures were essential for a vital democracy and empowered people throughout society. The actions of such institutions may supplement or balance governmental interventions.

All private organizations may serve the function of mediating institutions, but religious groups may be especially valuable. Churches were the first major NGOs (Berger 2004). Churches can foster diversity and act as a buffer between the individual and the state (Marshall 1996). Religious affiliation can "serve as the base for group cohesion necessary to successfully challenge established institutions and practices" (Noland 2003, 1).

Putnam (2000), who has written extensively on the question, contends that religious organizations are uniquely important in American civil society. Religion is described as "the single most important repository of social capital in America" (Putnam 2000, 66). Churches provide numerous social activities unrelated to religion and may be an incubator for people developing their participatory skills. Religiosity is highly correlated to civic engagement, as previously discussed.

In U.S. history, religion was a particularly powerful force "in the struggle for African American civil rights – providing organizational and symbolic resources, leadership, a premobilized constituency embedded in dense social networks, and an indigenous source of funding" (Sherkat & Ellison 1999, 369). President Lincoln was openly motivated by religion in his antislavery position. In today's world, religious conservatives are quite active on other matters such as public policy toward abortion and gay rights, and religious liberals on matters such as war and the death penalty.

Any individual's view of the current political role of religious groups probably depends on that individual's ideology, though churches can be found on both sides of many major political issues. If one believes in individual rights, the political positions of religious groups are at best a mixed bag in this nation. Some religious beliefs are contrary to freedom and democracy. Historically, however, the progressive force of religion on behalf of civil rights probably overwhelms other more negative effects. Tocqueville believed that religion was necessary to the success of democracy, though it seems more likely that religious choice is the key (Fradkin 2000).

Some have argued that the net political role of religious belief is a positive one. Habermas (2006, 7) concluded that religion had value in "stabilizing and advancing a liberal political culture." There is a "growing literature which argues that religion can be used to support tolerance, reconciliation, and human rights" (Fox 2008b, 930), though religion may at times support the opposite ends. Tocqueville suggested that religion may be necessary "to sustain (as well as to moderate) individualism and material prosperity and thus may be doubly necessary to the future success of democracy" (Fradkin 2000, 88).

Religion has sometimes played a very important political role overseas. The Catholic Church played a significant role in the fall of Polish communism. The World Council of Churches had an important part in the fall of apartheid (Fox 2008b). In the Latin America of the 1970s, religious diversity played a role in defending human rights, perhaps to help attract followers (Gill 1994). When the state had established a religion, it tended to side with the oppressive state. But when a religion had to compete for followers, it tended to support human rights.

The net political effect of religion and religious freedom is surely uncertain. A strong fundamentalist group might stifle democracy and oppress opponents, but such a group is unlikely to encourage greater religious freedom. In a nation with broad religious diversity, fundamentalists are less likely to assume such oppressive power. The contemporary extremist tendencies of Islamic fundamentalism appear to be tamed by participation in a liberal democracy (Nasr 1995).

Moreover, one must consider why a state would deny its people religious freedom. In some cases, it may simply be religious fervor of national leaders or people who disrespect other faiths. But this cannot explain many cases. China, for example, is an atheist society that allows some religion but periodically cracks down on certain religious groups. It seems likely that an autocratic state views religious organizations as competing centers of power that could represent a threat.

Religion or Freedom

The identified benefits of religion to individuals should not be too surprising. In the United States, religious belief is an individual choice. Although people certainly make bad choices at times, we presume that their choices are more often than not in their self-interest. This is a presumption of freedom of all sorts. As such, it is reasonable to presume that individual choices tend to produce a net benefit to those individuals. In these circumstances, the religious beliefs of people should generally be a good thing. And what is best for individuals presumably will be best for the general society as well.

The case for protecting religion as an innate good is much shakier than the evidence might suggest, however. As already noted, religion has occasionally been the source of some very bad things historically. While the studies of individuals have shown benefits from religious belief, the evidence is much weaker on a state level, and many nonreligious people can attain these benefits.

The Gallup polling service has conducted measures of religiosity throughout the world and within this country. Individuals were asked: "Is religion an important part of your daily life?" The five countries with the highest rate of yes answers were Egypt, Bangladesh, Sri Lanka, Indonesia, and the Congo. Those with the fewest positive answers were Estonia, Sweden, Denmark, Norway, and the Czech Republic. The latter group had 21 percent of individuals or fewer answering yes. The highest rate of atheism is reportedly found in Sweden, which has a high standard of life by international standards. The more secular countries typically show higher levels of happiness, less crime, greater equality, and better health and education (Zuckerman 2009). They tend to have more freedom and be more prosperous.

Looking at the relatively more and less religious countries, one would be hard pressed to claim the societal benefits of religious belief. The less religious countries appear to be more functional and protective of the rights and interests of their people. They certainly are wealthier. Perhaps it is the greater wealth of the nations that makes them less religious, a prospect that will be discussed shortly. Regardless, it is clear that countries with high levels of religious belief may show considerable pathologies, including terrorism, while countries with low levels may be fine and healthy places to live. The international comparison makes it difficult to make the case that greater belief in religion makes societies better. Indeed, Paul (2005) performed this comparison for developed countries and found that greater religion actually correlated with higher rates of homicide, STD infection rates, teen pregnancy, and abortion. Homicide is highest among highly religious nations (Fajnzylber, Lederman, & Loatza 2002). Any claim that atheists are more likely to be immoral "has long been disproven by systematic studies" (Beit-Hallahmi 2007, 306).

Sundry studies have suggested that religious belief increases personal happiness, on average. Opfinger (2010, 8) conducted an international study that found the association was one of a "U shaped pattern." While especially high levels of national religiosity were associated with high levels of happiness, so were especially low levels of national religiosity. Relatively secular nations may be successful and happy. Of course, this study was based on national averages and not individuals. The author theorized that a common culture (whether religious or secular) was a key factor.

It is important to note that the studies showing the benefits of religious belief for individuals and communities generally exist in a climate of religious freedom. They may simply display the value of individual choice, not religion *qua* religion. Those who chose religious belief may simply have benefited because they perceived, perhaps implicitly, that it would be valuable to them. Others, who perceived no such benefits from belief, may have benefited from nonbelief, but this has not been studied. So even if religion itself is not a per se good, religious choice may be. Of course, it is this choice that is generally protected by freedom of religion, as addressed in the following segment of the book.

The positive effects of religious belief may simply be the effect of religious freedom. At the time of the drafting of the Constitution, many believed that "religious belief and practice are efficacious only when voluntary" (Laycock 1996, 324). While religion has been much studied, the effect of freedom with religion has not. One clear apparent benefit of religious belief lies in social capital. A recent study of European nations found that state support of religion did not increase its effect but significantly decreased the value of religion to society, whether measured in religious membership, volunteering, or donations (Traunmuller & Freitag 2011). While researchers have struggled to find an effect of religious belief on economic growth, one study found that religious freedom was positively associated with growth, even after controlling for economic freedom and other relevant variables (Alon & Chase 2005). And Elliott and Hayward (2009) found that it was religious freedom, not religion itself, that was associated with happiness. When religious activity is voluntarily chosen, "people will be more likely to adopt self- and other-stereotyping that enhance their psychological well-being" (Elliott & Hayward 2009, 290).

Fukayama's (2011, 37) world history declares that religion has been a "source of social cohesion that permits human beings to cooperate far more widely and securely than they would if they were the simple rational and self-interested agents posited by the economists." All historic societies, to our knowledge, have been religious. Pinker (1997) suggests that religion is built into the brain through evolution because of the cooperative benefits it supplies. Gioso, Sapienza, and Zingales (2003) report that religious affiliation and participation were associated with more cooperative attitudes.

Religion clearly has a great benefit for many people, and religious belief appears to offer certain societal benefits as well, over and above what intrinsic libertarian value is offered by religious freedom. The advantages of religious belief may only occur in societies that offer their citizens freedom of religion. If religion is forced on the people, or oppressed, those benefits may not arise. It is the virtue of freely chosen religious beliefs that is the value to be protected. Moreover, it is possible that freedom of religion may be of benefit to nonbelievers, addressed in the following section of this chapter.

Religious Freedom and the Irreligious

Leiter's argument seems grounded in opposition to the conservative constitutional position that religion is to be encouraged as special and greatly privileged. But this interpretation is not how the law has generally developed. Religious freedom has been used to protect the rights of nonbelievers against the demands of the religious. Under the U.S. Constitution, at least, secularism is often protected from religion, much as if it were a religion. Laycock (1996) contends that any coherent concept of freedom of religion must also protect the atheists, agnostics, and secularists.

Indeed, atheists may be particularly in need of constitutional protection. In the United States, a negative view of atheism is pervasive, and atheists may be at the top of the list of groups Americans dislike (Zuckerman 2009). The constitutions of South Carolina and Arkansas ban atheists from holding public office. There is evidence that the American people disfavor atheists and agnostics more than any other material minority group (Edgell, Gerteis, & Hartmann 2006). A majority of Americans reportedly would not vote for an atheist for president. None of this is apparently constitutionally based.

The U.S. Supreme Court has frequently used national constitutional religious provisions to advance the rights of atheists. Free exercise may be interpreted as the right not to exercise a religious belief. In *Torcaso v. Watkins* (1961, 495, n.11), Justice Hugo Black listed "secular humanism" as a First Amendment religion. The Court has held that the First Amendment protects the "conscience of the infidel or the atheist" (*Wallace v. Jaffree* 1985). In the salient decision in *United States v. Seeger* (1965), the Court reversed a conviction of a party who refused induction into the military services because of his conscientious objection, which was not grounded in traditional religious beliefs. While the case involved a statute and not the Constitution, the court held that "religion" simply meant a man's devotion to "the highest ideal that he can conceive" (*United States v. Seeger* 1965, 862). Belief in a "supreme being" or deity was not required, just a "belief and devotion to goodness and virtue for their own sakes (*United States v. Seeger* 1965, 854).

The U.S. Constitution is said to "neither advance nor inhibit religion" (*Board of Education of Kiryas Joel v. Grumet* 1994, 719). It merely ensures each individual the right of conscience, to follow a faith or not. The constitutional provision provides some additional protection for religion, though, as only beliefs rooted in religion are protected by the free exercise clause (*Frazee v. Illinois Dept. Employment Sec.* 1989). Thus, a Jew may have a right to wear a yarmulke, where an atheist may not have a right to particular headgear. For central, conscience-centered matters, though, the irreligious are protected. An atheist can object to the constitutionality of a compulsory school prayer.

Some have thus argued that the U.S. Constitution protects "freedom from religion" as much as "freedom of religion." The "right to free exercise of religion implies the right to free exercise of non-religion" (Sullivan 1992, 197). This effect is not limited to the United States. Gey (2007, 251) reports that the "religious liberty jurisprudence in most constitutional democracies recognizes the need to protect atheists and agnostics," though he recognizes it may at times marginalize them. However, before "the development of modern conceptions of religious liberty, atheists had no effective legal protection (Gey 2007, 252). The United Nations' standards for freedom of religion are explicit in the protection of atheist beliefs as well.

Miner (1998, 624) thus argues that religious freedom provides "one of the most vital elements that go to make up the identity of believers and their conception of life, but it is also a precious asset for atheists, agnostics, skeptics, and the unconcerned." The European Court of Human Rights has written that its expression of religious freedom was "a precious asset for atheists, agnostics, skeptics, and the unconcerned" (*Kokkinakis v. Greece* 1993). Interestingly, the study on the association of religion, government regulation, and personal satisfaction found that less government regulation of religion also increased life satisfaction among those who were not religious (Elliott & Hayward 2009).

Smith (1991) argues that the constitutional protection of the rule of law in America has become self-negating. He contends that the nation's commitment to religious freedom had a religious rationale borne of a religious world view. Yet the interpretation of the First Amendment, he suggests, has come to forbid governmental reliance on religious justifications, with a secularizing effect. Thus, in its development, religious freedom has come to have a secularizing consequence. While he is critical of this, others might find it beneficial.

There are three primary types of constitutional provisions relevant to religious freedom: (i) provisions creating or banning a state religion; (ii) provisions prohibiting the establishment of religion or calling for separation of church and state; and (iii) provisions guaranteeing individuals freedom of religious belief. Plainly, a constitutional provision barring a state religion benefits atheists and agnostics, who need not be subjected to contrary religious beliefs. A constitutional provision requiring the separation of church and state would have much the same effect. Theoretically, a constitutional provision guaranteeing the free exercise of religion could privilege religion, but it has been interpreted to guarantee the free exercise of nonreligious beliefs, so it too should benefit the irreligious. Thus, freedom of religion is not intrinsically pro-religion; it is fundamentally pro-choice for individual decisions of conscience. Freedom of secular belief is important (Boyle & Sheen 1997).

The irreligious are not equally protected by the Constitution, though, with one example being the ministerial exception to general legislation. Religious organizations are free to hire and fire clergy, without respect to antidiscrimination laws, for example, and courts generally do not even consider the possible presence of a contrary compelling state interest (Tebbe 2011). This is true even for decisions made for nontheological reasons. No comparable protection extends to the irreligious. Historically, there are various other decisions in which courts have allowed some discrimination against the irreligious (Tebbe 2011, 1150–1151). When the Supreme Court allowed the Amish the right to remove their children from school, it expressly said that this right would not extend to someone driven by "purely secular" motivations (*Wisconsin v. Yoder* 1972, 215–216). The constitutional protections for freedom of religion have provided material support to nonbelievers, but the protection is not fully as strong as for the religious. In other areas, though, such as government funding, the religious are more constrained by the Constitution than the irreligious.

John Rawls (1996) focuses on religion as a core freedom. He argues that such freedom is as important as respect for quality and notes that religion represents a comprehensive doctrine regarding the meaning of life, in which individuals typically engage. He argues for a doctrine of liberty of conscience, whether or not this involves a belief in an established religion. This is consistent with those who question the need for special protection of religion itself.

Nussbaum (2008) expands upon this Rawlsian interpretation. She notes that America's constitutional protection speaks of religion, not conscience, and that religion is thus legally privileged over some other personal beliefs. The American Constitution was written at a time when religious persecution was apparent, but nearly everyone ascribed to some sort of religious belief. Atheists and agnostics have grown in numbers and have suffered their own repression over more recent years. Nussbaum believes that the concept of religion, as protected by the constitutional freedom, should be viewed as extending to any matters of fundamental conscience. This approach is not dramatically unlike the result reached by the U.S. Supreme Court.

There is even an argument that constitutional freedom of religion favors the irreligious, in that it "implies secularism" (Engel 2011, 9). It precludes the state from imposing religious beliefs on its people. By its nature, religion governs the lives of believers, and it is a small step to using the government to govern the lives of all. Religious groups commonly involve themselves in politics, trying to make their values official ones, such as seen by America's religious right (arguing against abortion) and left (arguing for equality of rights). Freedom of religion necessarily allows such efforts, but it more fundamentally limits them, at least in the imposition of religious beliefs on others. Religious liberty puts political importance on nonreligious justifications for policy positions. The religious justification for the freedom may have been dominant in the creation of the First Amendment, but it is seldom heard by contemporary courts, which have secularized the right (Smith 1991).

The traditional liberalism associated with free-exercise guarantees arguably is secularist in nature (Liviatan 2011). Religion arguably contradicts the commitment to total human freedom of choice. Most religions favor some sort of social control that runs up against the tenets of classical liberalism. By fully embracing individual freedom of choice, even religious freedom limits religion.

The establishment clause surely respects the beliefs of those without religion. It essentially prevents religious values from being written into the nation's laws. Even seemingly neutral policies, such as a compulsory moment of silence in schools, may be invalidated, if adopted for a religious purpose (*Wallace v. Jaffree* 1985). The primary standard for applying the clause requires that to be constitutional a statute have a secular purpose and must not have a primary effect of advancing or inhibiting religion (*Lemon v. Kurtzman* 1971). The government has been "stripped of all power to tax, to support, or otherwise to assist any or all religions" (*Everson v. Board of Education* 1947, 11). The First Amendment not only protects religion from the state, it also exists to protect the state from religion. The establishment clause has been applied with some inconsistency, and it allows some actions seemingly favorable to religious beliefs, but it has frequently been used to protect the irreligious. Moreover, it gives the courts a path to protect the irreligious if the courts so choose.

Indeed, the establishment clause might not be considered freedom of religion, insofar as it prevents help given to religions. Of course, such a clause promotes freedom because it prevents a state religion. But by barring nondiscriminatory assistance to religion more broadly, while not constraining assistance to the irreligious, the clause is in some ways essentially antireligious. Thus, McConnell (2000) suggests that constitutional religious freedom is a necessary provision to balance out the antireligious effect of an establishment clause. In any event, such a provision should benefit the irreligious.

Hirschl (2010, 13) examines the application of constitutional protections of religion in various countries and concludes that "constitutional law and courts in virtually all such polities have become bastions of relative secularism, pragmatism, and moderation, thereby emerging as effective shields against the spread of religiosity and increased popular support for principles of theocratic governance." Raday (2009) argues that constitutionalism is intrinsically secular and that this is vital to the protection of human rights.

Constitutions themselves become objects of worship, perhaps competing with religion. In the United States, the Constitution and the Bill of Rights have become objects of religious fetish. But they are human-made, not divine. A bill of rights focuses on the individual and his or her rights, not the typical religious concern with obligations. Rights by nature tend to be value neutral, in contrast to religion. Constitutions may be cosmopolitan. By its nature, constitutionalism may be "attractive to antireligious interests" (Hirschl 2010, 72) and a convenient domain for the irreligious. Comparative analysis of constitutional law reveals a "growing reliance on constitutional courts and their jurisprudential ingenuity to block the spread of religiosity"

(Hirschl 2010, 103). The fact that religion is expressly mentioned in constitutions provides the courts with this ability, an ability they might lack if the constitutions did not recognize religious freedom. India, for example, shifted many religious questions to courts that were fundamentally secular-oriented (Goodman 2009) and advanced the interests of minority groups.

Even when there is a state religion, constitutional law and courts "have become bastions of relative secularism, pragmatism, and moderation, thereby emerging as effective shields against the spread of religiosity" (Hirschl 2010, 50). The state in various countries has used its influence over religion to tame the effects of growing fundamentalism. Hirschl (2010) documents a series of nations, including some from the Middle East, in which constitutions and courts have contained the influence of religion in law. The constitutional approach permits the state and its courts to "talk the religious talk without walking most of what they regard as theocracy's unappealing, costly walk" (Hirschl 2010, 247). In practice, freedom of religion becomes the broader freedom of conscience and plausibly discourages religion.

There is thus a strong argument that religious freedom may be especially valuable to atheists and agnostics. Secular humanists have written that the lack of freedom of religion is the most serious impediment to the practice of humanism (Gogineni & Gule 2004). Even if the protections of constitutional freedom were not extended to them, the irreligious could benefit from the existence of a diversity of competing religious choices, as opposed to a state imposing religious beliefs on the society. But freedom of religion has been interpreted by secularizing courts to include the freedom *not* to believe in religion. This provides direct benefits to the irreligious. I will examine this effect later in the book.

Conclusion

Free speech is sometimes justified by the benefits of providing a marketplace of ideas to draw upon, and freedom of religion might be justified in the same manner, with a marketplace of beliefs. This is something of an epistemic warrant – people are more likely to find the "correct" religious belief with more choices and information about alternatives. By "correct" I do not mean true but instead mean the faith that is most valuable to that individual under his or her circumstances. In an economic market, we let people choose their cars on the theory that, in general, they will select the brand best for them. Similarly, greater religious freedom should allow individuals to more functionally arrange their fundamental belief systems. And people may switch religions if they find a new one preferable.

While religious belief may not instrinsically be a good thing for everyone, considerable evidence shows that it is a good choice for many people, given their circumstances. Allowing people choice is always a recognition of personal autonomy, and being allowed full choice in holding religious beliefs or freedom of conscience is central to one's autonomy. Freedom of religion is thus potentially a very valuable aspect of society, at least so long as it respects the freedom of individuals to be irreligious. One need not embrace religion itself in order to embrace the importance of freedom of religion.

While this chapter has discussed the benefits of religion for individuals, some argue that religion creates negative effects at least for societies as a whole. Religion is not infrequently associated with suppression of women's rights. Under common interpretations of Islamic shari'a, for example, a woman's testimony counts as less than half a man's in court, women are disadvantaged in divorce, and they have little autonomy in various areas of their life, including the clothes they wear. Christians also have patriarchical doctrines that women are subordinate to men, and they may be denied certain religious offices. The Hindu Mahabharata suggests that women may be the root of evil. Buddhism has its own tradition of misogyny (Faure 2003). There are also social benefits to religion, but the balance is not clearly positive.

However, constitutional religious freedoms do not particularly promote religion or any of its disadvantages. Leiter (2008) is surely correct in understanding that constitutional recognition of religion to some degree exalts its importance, as a purely theoretical matter. But in practice these rights seem to have had an opposite effect. They promote individual freedom, but among the freedoms promoted is the opportunity to be irreligious and hence the ability to avoid the pathologies that may be associated with religion. The system uses constitutions, as Hirschl (2010) notes, to limit the power of religion in civil society.

Yet the perceived value of freedom of religion must be operationalized, and its effects may be tested. There are different forms of constitutional religious freedom, which may have different effects. It is an open question whether any of the forms truly offers much benefit in protecting religious freedom, or whether some other feature of government and society provides the shelter. This is the essential topic of the book – testing the determinants of religious freedom, with a focus on constitutional guarantees.

In future chapters, I will consider how constitutional protections of religious freedom relate to these theories. A threshold matter is whether expressed constitutional rights make any difference or whether they are simply window dressing for the sake of appearances. If they do matter, the final chapter will consider the relevance of religious freedom, advanced by constitutions, for religious faith, atheism, and other human goods. Before undertaking this analysis, though, I turn to a review of the status of religious freedom throughout the world.

2 Religious Freedom Around the World

This chapter examines the degree to which religious freedom is protected – or not protected – around the world. The most severe forms of religious repression are fortunately in the past, but considerable persecution remains to this day. Although numerous international agreements promise to protect freedom of religion, considerable restriction of this freedom occurs around the world. Twining (2009, 125) suggests that religious freedom in the world is "treading water at best, retreating at worst." Beyer (2003, 333) claims that no nation truly allows unfettered religious freedom and that all seek to manipulate the process to reinforce the hegemony of a religion or ideology. Still, there may be relative differences among the nations.

This chapter reviews the record of religious discrimination in today's world. There are some very comprehensive reviews of this practice (Fox 2008a, Marshall 2008, Boyle & Sheen 1997). This chapter is not meant to be a thorough review of global religious freedom but just a contextual background. Some understanding of the nature of restrictions on freedom is necessary to appreciate the quantitative analysis in subsequent chapters.

Restriction on religious freedom takes many forms, which I will place into several groups. The first, and most pernicious, is the direct oppression of minority religions, which may take the form of killing *in extremis* but more commonly places limits on religious belief or advocacy. Another form is the adoption of religious laws. While not directly favoring a religion, such laws may favor a belief and make the following of others more difficult. In some cases, there may be restrictions on religious political parties or public gatherings. These are laws applicable to all residents that are based on religious beliefs. They may include such things as restrictions on the sale of alcoholic beverages, placing institutions such as marriage or burial under religious control, restrictions on public dress, or blasphemy laws. Other restrictions on religion take the form of registration requirements that can be used to control religious organizations. Finally, there is the question of favoritism, through which government subsidizes a particular church.

Direct Oppression of Minority Religions

The most typical and commonly the most severe form of religious persecution is the oppression of disfavored minority religions, as was the case with the Nazis and the Jews. Today, there are numerous cases throughout the world of religious figures being arrested or officially harassed. Religious organizations and/or schools may be constrained by the state. This section reviews some contemporary practices.

In 2006, an Afghan man was arrested and prosecutors sought the death sentence for his conversion to Christianity. Resistance from the international community was extremely strong, and he escaped this fate, being released from prison and obtaining asylum in Europe after being held for several years. In 2011, though, another Christian convert was arrested and threatened with the death penalty. Even if the threat of execution is not carried out, the prospect of arrest and detention for a person's choice of religious beliefs is a considerable restriction on religious freedom.

The Middle East is commonly seen as the region of the greatest discriminatory religious repression. Kuwait has Islam as its state religion and refers to shari'a as the main source of the nation's law. The country bans any expression or publication that criticizes Islam. Muslim women may not marry non-Muslim men and Islamic religious instruction is mandatory in public schools, but Kuwait is far from the most oppressive of the Middle Eastern governments.

Algeria has adopted a law confining non-Muslim worship to buildings approved by the state, which gives the government a functional veto on their formal worship. The law also made proselytism a crime (Marshall 2008). Algeria is among numerous Middle Eastern nations that prohibit the distribution of some non-Islamic literature. Egypt has punished those who insult Islam and has been especially repressive toward Copts, who have even been subject to forced conversions, and it bans Baha'i institutions. Yemen prohibits some evangelistic activities by non-Islamic groups, and conversion away from Islam is potentially punishable by death. Places of worship may not be built without government approval.

Iran's state is largely theocratic with little religious freedom. Other religions are permitted to form societies, but only so long as they do not violate "the criteria of Islam" (Marshall 2008, 207). The Iranian constitution explicitly denies freedom of the press to writing that is "detrimental to the fundamental principles of Islam." Conversion away from Islam is punishable by death. A non-Muslim man may be sentenced to death for sex with a Muslim woman. Christians in the nation are said to "endure discrimination, harassment, constant surveillance, arrests, and imprisonment" (Marshall 2008, 209), and many have fled the country. Churches are prohibited from trying to convert Muslim believers. Minority Islamic sects, such as the Baha'I, are also persecuted with their property confiscated and some arrested and killed.

The U.S. State Department has flatly declared that in Saudi Arabia, "freedom of religion does not exist" (International Religious Freedom Report, Sec. II). It notes that non-Muslims are in danger of arrest, imprisonment, deportation, and even torture for engaging in their religious activity. Shari'a law forbids Muslims from changing their religion. It "offers limited toleration of some non-Muslim religions but vehemently opposes others, especially any religion, such as Baha'i, that recognizes a prophet subsequent to Muhammed" (Grim & Finke 2011, 187). In Saudi Arabia, people "are routinely arrested for holding religious services in their homes" (Fox 2008a, 228). In addition, the government places a variety of restrictions on Muslims of Shi'a belief. Mosques have been closed and religious practices dictated.

In Iraq, Christians have suffered "church burnings, kidnappings and beheadings of priests, bombing of Christian owned liquor stores and beauty parlors, cold-blooded murder, and harassment of Christian women for not donning veils and the black shrouds mandated by the Islamists' dress codes" (Halik 2008, 25). Iraqi policies have changed in the wake of the American intervention in 2003, but the law still provides that Islam receives preferential consideration. Other Middle Eastern Islamic nations have similar repressions of religious freedom, though some are better than others.

Islamic restrictions on religious freedom are perhaps most severe in the Middle East but are not limited to those nations. In the Comoros, for example, "non-muslims are legally permitted to worship but are not free to speak to Muslims about their faith" (Marshall 2008, 142), and such actions may be punished by a fine and imprisonment. Christians have been imprisoned for alleged evangelizing. The nation has sought to eliminate its local Krishna believers. Pakistan has become increasingly fundamentalist in its Islam and increasingly oppressive.

Bahrain is regarded as a relatively modern and moderate Islamic nation, yet it too engages in religious discrimination. It prohibits conversion from Islam or marriage to a non-Islamic partner. Morocco is also more liberal but restrictive of any conversions. Non-Muslims may worship but only after obtaining a license from the government. Libya is overwhelmingly Muslim, yet it has a reasonably respectable record of protecting religious freedom, though proselytizing Muslims is not allowed, and religious property has been confiscated. Qatar generally allows religious freedom.

Central Asian nations have also oppressed religion. In Uzbekistan, for example, the state puts restriction on proselytizing and other religious practices. Over one thousand people in the nation "were arrested and several dozen tried and sentenced for religious activities" (Marshall 2008, 420). Evangelical Christians were allegedly tortured by the state. Kazakhstan has been quite hostile to religious freedom, and Baptists were prosecuted for "unregistered religious activity," though at the time "no such offense then existed" (Marshall 2008, 233). Azerbaijan, by contrast, has focused on religious reconciliation and sought to maintain separation of church and state, though private acts of religious violence have occurred. Tajikistan appears concerned with Islamic extremists but has been generally tolerant, though some Christians have been arrested for religious practices. Practices of the Kyrgyz Republic are similar. Turkmenistan has forbidden some religious activities.

Indonesia is the largest Muslim country in the world, but it has moderately good religious freedom, though it has seen some violence and a prosecution for encouraging conversion to Christianity. There are religious tensions, though, and the Baha'i faith has been prohibited. Some religious books have been banned (Boyle & Sheen 1997). In addition, Indonesia has seen sporadic episodes of religious violence. The government has restricted religious speeches and dissemination of materials.

Islam is the official religion of Malaysia, and some government positions are reserved for Muslims. Some local governments have enacted shari'a criminal codes, enforced in religious courts. Malaysian courts have occasionally denied individuals the opportunity to change their faiths. So-called deviant Muslims may be discriminated against (Boyle & Sheen 1997). The State Department reports that the nation has banned numerous "deviant" interpretations of Islam, and has caned those who committed violations of shari'a, such as engaging in "illicit sex" (International Religious Freedom Report).

Islamic influence has also seeped south into Africa. Kenya, for example, permits the use of shari'a in certain cases but generally pursuant to private agreement and formally allows conversions. Mali is predominantly Muslim, but typically protects the religious rights of Christians and others. The State Department gives the government a good rating but notes that private entities may be abusive. Oman and Senegal are also Islamic nations that are generally protective of religious liberty. Mauritania, by contrast, can be quite oppressive, and its penal code provides the death penalty for Muslims who refuse to pray, and Mauritanians are all essentially compelled to be Islamic. Christian churches have been closed and Christian books have been confiscated by the government.

Nigeria is religiously divided between a Christian south and an Islamic north. This has produced considerable conflict and the murder of thousands in religious battles. Some regions of the nation have adopted shari'a law, which makes apostasy a crime punishable by death. These regions have also seen forced abductions of children and forced marriages and conversions. While the national government generally respects religious freedom, local governments may be repressive.

The preceding discussion focused on Muslim repression. While the oppression of minority religions may be most severe in Islamic states, it is by no means confined to them. One report found that of the 143 countries with two million or more people, 123 of them (86 percent) "have documented cases of people being physically abused or displaced from their homes because of a lack of religious freedom" (Grim & Finke 2011, 18). Thirty-six of the countries had more than one thousand individuals abused or displaced because of religion. Abuse of religious freedom remains widespread throughout the world, in nations of many religious backgrounds. Although Islamic repression is extensive and best known, many non-Islamic nations also deny fundamental elements of religious freedom.

China has a history of suppressing religion. While the days of aggressive Maoism are long gone, the Communist Party still controls the state, with official atheism. With reform of Maoism, China became somewhat more liberal toward religious believers. However, this produced a proliferation of religious activity that concerned governing bodies about possible Westernization; they responded with a tightening of restrictions on religion (Leung 2005).

After a Christian group raised money and legally purchased a church, called Shouwang, in 2010, the authorities evicted the congregants. When they attempted to pray outdoors, many were arrested. Other believers have suffered a similar fate. Mosques, as well as houses of Christian worship, have been closed by the government. One suspects that the problems of religious freedom in China are less about religion itself and more about the need for control of the population, characteristic of communism.

China allows many churches to operate, but they may have to affiliate themselves with a patriotic religious association. Some are punished for "illegal religious activities" that disrupt social stability. The country maintains a State Administration for Religious Affairs that registers and controls religious groups. Unregistered groups may not have the right to operate humanitarian programs. Even some very traditional religions are not recognized by the nation.

Some Chinese authorities have imposed restrictions on teachers' and students' engagement in religion. Even approved religions may receive directives from the government about the content of their comments (Grim & Finke 2011). Catholic groups have been pressured to demonstrate an independence from the international church in Rome. Christians have been prohibited from speaking about various topics, including abortion, the Second Coming, and creation stories (Marshall 2008).

Falun Gong is a native Chinese belief system that appears to threaten the national government. It was labeled an "evil cult" by the government. Its believers have occasionally been seized, and its materials have been taken from homes. Perhaps 250,000 followers have been committed to reeducation camps (Grim & Finke 2011). Forms of physical and psychological coercion have been used to force Falun Gong members to convert away from the belief.

China has also repressed religious freedom of Buddhists in Tibet. Monks have been arrested and subjected to beatings in prison. Protestors have disappeared. The government has asserted state control over the lives of monks and nuns, and the admission of new monks has been monitored. Gaining "a traditional religious education is extremely difficult or impossible in Tibet" (Marshall 2008, 135). The Chinese government has even assumed the authority of selecting religious leaders, such as the Panchen Lama.

The people of India appear to be especially religious in nature. India is riven by religious division, though. The country makes an effort to be respectful, with national holidays recognized for several major religions. Courts have prohibited compulsory school praying. But restrictions exist. The national penal code lists offenses to religion, including statements intended to wound the religious feelings of others. The national Supreme Court found in 1977 that the expressed constitutional right to propagate religion did not imply a right to convert another to one's religion. A number of the nation's states have religious anti-conversion laws. Missionary work has been restricted. There are intermittent spasms of violence between Hindus and Moslems.

Bangladesh is similarly fractious. A majority Islamic nation, Bangladesh has seen discrimination against religious minorities since the time of its creation. In 1979, the country declared the properties of the nation's non-Muslim minority to be "vested properties" under the law, which meant that they could be confiscated at any time. Allegedly, 60 percent of the property held by these minorities has been confiscated for a time at least (Marshall 2008, 88). Hindu women report that they have been required to wear Muslim dress. Religious minorities have had difficulty obtaining government jobs, and Hindus claim that their property has been confiscated.

Sri Lanka is largely a Buddhist state. Although its constitution promises religious freedom, its judiciary rejected a request by Catholics that sought legal incorporation for their religious order, finding that the constitution did not recognize a right to propagate any religion. In Bhutan, NGOs claim that religious "conversion is illegal, that no religious materials are permitted to enter the country other than Buddhist texts, and that Buddhist prayer is compulsory in all government schools" (Fox 2008a, 203). In Burma (Myanmar), only officially recognized Buddhist orders are allowed to operate, and government officials have banned expressions of Christianity. Thailand mandates religious education in public schools. Evangelical Christians contend that they have suffered government discrimination there.

Nepal explicitly prohibits any proselytizing for alternative religions and has sought to ban foreign missionaries. Police have reportedly sought to intimidate Buddhist celebrations and have harassed believers. Some Buddhists have been forcibly deported from the country.

Laos is unfriendly to Christians. Many have been imprisoned in recent years, and believers have been forced to sign forms abandoning their religion. Some believers have been forced to prove their faith by participating in animist rituals or drinking alcohol and blood, practices shunned by Laotian Christians. Vietnam has a variety of restrictions on religion, and certain Christian and Buddhist groups have been prohibited from distributing their religious literature. Vietnam requires that religious groups register with the government and submit to government control to maintain their legality. The nation requires government-approved training of Buddhist monks, and members of religious groups not formally recognized by the national government are arrested and harassed.

A large number of Asian nations place material limits on the rights of religions to build or repair places of worship. Some, including Burma, Cambodia, and China, restrict access to places of worship. Many have at least occasionally engaged in harassment of followers of minority religions, including Indonesia, Laos, and Malaysia. A majority of Asian nations place some restrictions on proselytizing and place controls over publications by minority religious groups. Thailand has laws prohibiting speech that insults Buddhism and has restricted missionaries and minority sects.

Vietnam has placed a number of restrictions on religious practices. Protestant congregations have experienced harassment, and their property has been attacked on occasion. Religious denominations must be officially recognized, and the government exercises some control over them. Churches may not purchase land for themselves. All religious publishing must be run though the government. Religious affiliation is noted on individuals' identity cards, and local officials have engaged in discrimination.

Other parts of Asia, such as Japan, are strongholds of religious freedom. There is broad freedom to practice nearly any religion. Religions do not need to be licensed; they may be registered as corporations to receive tax exemptions. There have been some concerns that Unification Church members have been subject to legal "deprogramming." The Japanese courts have found that strict separation of religion from state was impossible and allowed support of Shintoism. There is some discrimination against Buddhists and adherents to new religions. Taiwan similarly is quite protective of religious freedom. South Korea also has a good record, though North Korea is generally restrictive of religious practices in general.

Significant religious discrimination is fairly limited in South America. The region is historically Catholic, and some nations have required those holding high public offices to be Catholic. In Colombia, Protestant churches have complained that they must pay extra taxes and suffer some discrimination in owning or renting places of worship. Nicaragua appears respectful of religious differences, though religious communities seeking legal recognition must obtain governmental approval. Peru appears to offer slight benefits to the Catholic Church but is generally respectful of religious differences. Argentina has stricter registration requirements for non-Catholics. Evangelicals in Venezuela have been subjected to property expropriations.

A number of other South American nations restrict proselytizing. A few have arrested or harassed non-Catholics. Columbia has required children to show a Catholic baptismal certificate to enter public schools and formally recognized only Catholic marriages. Other nations, though, have shown considerable respect for religious freedom. Ecuador, for example, typically regards all religions with equal respect. In general, efforts to reduce the growth of Protestantism in the continent have not been adopted.

The Mexican state has been hostile to religion in general. Historically, religious groups could not gain legal recognition or own real estate, and foreign missionaries were prohibited from entering the country. These restrictions have been relaxed, but the state still controls religious activities in public spaces. The free speech of religious bodies remains restricted. The federal government is authorized to regulate religion, and churches cannot exist as legal entities. Government consent is required to construct new churches.

Sub-Saharan Africa, for all of its difficulties, is generally a region of considerable religious tolerance. Christians have long lived alongside Animists and others in peaceful toleration. While many of these nations show little respect for individual rights in general, they commonly allow minority religions to coexist. Namibia, for example, allows broad religious freedom, as does South Africa. Freedom is not universal in Africa, though, as Zimbabwe's government has harassed religious groups seen as subversive. The Democratic Republic of the Congo has occasionally arrested believers for political reasons. Sometimes, missionary groups must fight through complicated bureaucratic procedures in order to operate. Overall, though, the U.S. State Department and others give the nations of this region high marks for the protection of religious freedom.

Communism has considerably declined in the world, but Communist states remain and they are typically unfriendly to religious belief. China has been discussed. Cuba has arrested Catholics as threats to the government, though it has relaxed such restraints over time. Nevertheless, members of minority religious groups have been harassed and detained, and religious expression is controlled by the government, with no access to the mass media. North Korea allows three religious organizations but controls them. Christianity is considered a threat to the leadership, and churches have been locked and believers punished. The country is closed, but there are reports of religion-based killings. Russia seemingly has strived to protect religious freedom, but local institutions have sometimes been restrictive, and nontraditional denominations claim to have suffered discrimination.

The states of the former Soviet Union have seen considerable religious tension. The Central Asian states commonly discriminate against non-Muslims, whereas the historic Christian Orthodox states likewise discriminate. There have been hundreds of attacks on Protestants, Catholics, and other Christian believers (Corley 2008). The nations of the former Soviet Union put many restrictions on minority religions. Limits on public observance, the rights to build or repair places of worship and access to places of worship are common. Nearly all these states require sometimes restrictive registration of religions and prohibit minority religious proselytizing. Arrest, detention, and harassment are documented in Georgia, Belarus, Uzbekistan, and other nations of the region.

Turkmenistan has prohibited foreign missionaries and confiscated Christian literature. Armenia requires registration of religious groups and those refused registration cannot publish newspapers or broadcast programs. Belarus functionally prohibits all religious activity by groups not registered with the government. There is considerable diversity of practice, though, as Tajikistan and Kyrgyzstan place relatively few restrictions on minority religions, while Azerbaijan places many restrictions on minority religions. The

Baltic states of Lithuania, Lativa, and Estonia tend to do well at protecting religious freedom.

The Western democracies are commonly seen as places of religious freedom. The notion of religious freedom itself is linked to the Enlightenment and the countries of European civilization. But some of these countries, such as Denmark, Greece, Iceland, Liechtenstein, and Norway have official state religions. Finland maintains two state religions. While the status of such official religions may not be practically significant, the nations of Europe do engage in discrimination. In Greece, minority religions, such as Mormons and Evangelical Christians "are often arrested for proselytizing" (Fox 2008a, 117), and the Orthodox Church receives a variety of government benefits. Norway is a Lutheran country that provides mandatory Christian education in public schools. In Spain, minority religions "report difficulties in gaining permits to build places of worship" (Fox 2008a, 128). Yousif (2000) reports that Muslims have experienced problems in Britain, Germany, France, and Sweden in gaining approval to build mosques or Islamic centers.

The French approach to religion is known as *Laïcité*, which may be translated as "secular" but generally means the separation of religious society from civil society. In contrast to general religious freedom, this approach suggests at least suspicion of religion. The French judicial system, though, has required neutrality and tolerance toward religion, much like in the United States (Gunn 2004). National law prohibits religious discrimination. The protection is not complete, as evidenced by French bans on religious clothing in schools and other sites. In general, though, individuals may choose and practice their religion in France without much government interference.

Great Britain is known for religious tolerance, and its laws have made various accommodations of religious belief. In addition, it provides state funding to religious schools but was historically reluctant to allow funding of Islamic education. Norway has a state church, but its policies on religious freedom appear quite liberal. Switzerland has adopted some policies to restrict proselytization by foreign missionaries. The growth of Islamic believers has obviously promoted some internal conflict in European nations, and some have responded by restricting the rights of believers to build places of worship, and some Muslims claim to have been targeted for arrest.

The general religious freedom of Western Europe is stronger than that found in emerging nations of Eastern Europe. Romania has been dominated by the Orthodox Church, and its dominant position "has contributed to a reluctance to tolerate other religions, especially new religious movements, contributing to a culture of intolerance, including sporadic violence" (Marshall 2008, 341). The Greek constitution affirmatively prohibits proselytization, and statutes make the practice punishable. In Bulgaria, some municipal regulations have restricted the distribution of religious literature and proselytizing. In Bosnia and Herzegovina, the primary concern seems to be the weakness of administrative and judicial systems in pursuing and punishing private cases of harassment.

The United States today is quite protective of religious freedom by global standards. Proselytization is freely conducted. The nation essentially has a free religious marketplace, with new theological approaches emerging, growing, and attracting followers. Compulsory prayer in public schools was famously proscribed by the Supreme Court. While this country is free by global standards, there are some criticisms of U.S. protection of religious freedom.

Historically, the American record of religious freedom is not all positive. For a long time, Native American religious practices were unprotected, including "outright prohibitions on tribal religious rituals, dances, dress, hairstyle, language, and access to religious sites" (Liviatan 2011, 74). The persecution of the Mormons in the nineteenth century is particularly dramatic, as they were driven out of regions throughout the country and saw members murdered before finally being accepted in Utah. The country exhibited "considerable hostility to religious groups" that were outside Judeo-Christian customs (Way & Burt 1983). Although much of the violence against Mormons was private, the federal government prosecuted Mormons for polygamy, imposed test oaths denying them voting rights, and ultimately confiscated their property. The Supreme Court upheld these actions (Laycock 1993).

The Mormon experience occurred notwithstanding the constitutional First Amendment, which is not much tribute to its inherent power to protect religion. It was not until the latter twentieth century that the Supreme Court began vigorously enforcing religious freedom. And this Supreme Court action may well have needed the First Amendment as a basis, suggesting it could have value. The recent Court has not been entirely favorable to religious freedom, and several hotly contested cases have gone the other way.

Considerable criticism greeted the Supreme Court's opinion in *Employment Division, Department of Human Resources of Oregon v. Smith* (1990). Individuals were discharged from their jobs because they used peyote for sacramental purposes, and they were denied unemployment compensation because use of peyote violated the law. The Court held that as long as a law was neutral in its application, its interference with an individual's practice of religion did not exempt that individual from compliance. The case was heavily criticized and considered something of a low point in free exercise jurisprudence in the United States. The principle, though, is not terribly surprising, and it seems unlikely that any nation would invoke religious freedom to allow a practice such as human sacrifice. One sees this in application in prohibitions on genital mutilation of young girls, even if such a practice is perceived as being religiously commanded. The state cannot be expected to allow absolute freedom of religious practice, and a general deference is presumably the best practice. But the dimensions of that deference are quite unclear, as is the entity that should ultimately decide on the proper degree of deference. Thus, religious freedom in the United States is not so broad as some might wish.

The extent of repression of minority religions varies greatly throughout the world. In some regions, especially the Middle East, considerable persecution remains, and individuals may be killed over their religious beliefs. Some Asian nations contain comparable repressive measures. In more developed regions, such repression is marginal, if not absent. African nations, though not particularly developed, also are often good at protecting religious freedom. A variety of nations, such as those of South America, take a reasonably strong position in the global protection of religious freedom.

Religious Laws

Beyond the affirmative oppression of minority religions is the question of governments adopting religious laws. Some of these may be explicitly religious, such as the imposition of a compulsory Sabbath day. Other actions are less directly religious but are primarily promoted out of religious impulses. Restrictions on alcohol distribution or consumption and reproductive freedom are examples of the latter.

When an Islamic nation adopts shari'a as the foundation of its legal system, it plainly is adopting religious laws as statutes based on religious beliefs. The importance of religious laws is quite plain in Saudi Arabia. The Committee to Promote Virtue and Prevent Vice maintains enforcers to ensure that businesses are closed to permit compulsory prayers, prevent close contact between unmarried males and females, and ensure that females have appropriate Islamic coverings.

Other nations have comparable restrictions. Shari'a prohibits a variety of activities such as gambling and some live music and dancing, and restricts the foods that may be eaten. It regulates the conduct of business in various ways. Afghanistan banned cable television for religious reasons (Marshall 2008). Adultery is illegal and may be severely punished, even if it is the product of rape.

Shari'a religious legislation often engaged in discrimination based on gender. Women are not given equal treatment and "are disadvantaged in inheritance, divorce, child custody, and certain criminal matters, such as domestic violence and rape" (Marshall 2008, 85). Pakistan makes punishable the use of any words or images that might "defile the sacred name" of personages related to Muhammad (Boyle & Sheen 1997, 230). In Nigeria in 2002, a woman was sentenced to death for adultery, though the case was eventually abandoned.

Asian nations have adopted a variety of religious laws, including dietary laws, limitations on alcohol, and religious restrictions on marriage and inheritance. Brunei, for example, prohibits alcohol and requires Halal practices for the slaughter of meat. These nations commonly impose prohibitions on abortion. A majority of the region's countries have dietary laws, restrictions on alcohol, religious restrictions on marriage and inheritance, blasphemy laws, constraints on religious dress, and other religious laws.

For the goal of religious harmony, Singapore has adopted legislation against causing inter-religious enmity or carrying out political objectives under the guise of religious belief. In practice, though, this can be quite repressive. The minister responsible for implementing the law can place a restraining order on any religious authority engaged in politics or "subversive" activities. Various Asian nations have local governments that "legislate the state's dominant religion" (Fox 2008a, 216).

Religious laws are common in states regarded as less religious. Some have laws against blasphemy, including the United Kingdom. In Costa Rica, the Roman Catholic Church has exercised its influence to censor material it deemed detrimental to the Church. France has a law prohibiting the wearing of religious symbols in schools, which inhibits the freedom of some. Laws restricting public dress are found in many nations, including Belgium, France, Germany, Canada, and Switzerland.

African nations tend to have relatively few religious laws. Nations more influenced by Islam do have laws similar to those of Middle Eastern countries, such as restrictions on public dress, and a few countries do have blasphemy laws. But many nations have some laws that incorporate religious principles.

The United States has a high degree of protection from religious laws. Between the establishment clause and the promise of religious freedom, the government of this nation is perhaps less involved in religion than any other nation of the world. The courts of the United States have enforced the so-called separation of church and state to prevent compulsory school prayers and forms of aid to religion. Still, elements of religion remain unrestricted in the United States. The currency, the pledge of allegiance, and other commonplace things refer to God, if not a particular faith.

Religious Regulation

Many nations have government agencies that are charged with monitoring religion, in the interests of the state. Grim and Finke (2006) report that nine out of ten countries ask religions to register with the state. Such registration requirements are common, but they give the state an opportunity for involvement in religious practice. Over one hundred nations have government offices charged with supervising religious groups (Grim & Finke 2006). Registration requirements are common in Western Europe and Asia. In a substantial minority of countries, the registration requirements proved clearly discriminatory in nature (Grim & Finke 2011).

This regulation is not intrinsically anti-freedom, except insofar as it inevitably imposes some additional costs on religions in conforming to the agencies' demands, including demands for information. The requirements of such regimes may be "routine and innocuous" (Podoprigora 2004, 426). Refusal to register need not mean that the religion cannot continue to function in the nation, but a religion that does not register typically gives up some benefits.

Moreover, the regulatory process may be used to discriminate against the religious or make their lives difficult. The rules provide discretion to government officials who may abuse their authority. Podoprigora (2004) reports that the United Kingdom has arbitrarily denied rights to certain religions. Lack of registration may trigger restrictions on proselytization. Liviatan (2011, 63) contends that the formal system of recognizing religions has "evolved into a de facto multi-tiered discriminatory apparatus, enabling the classification of religious movements into different categories with different rights." The laws generally give broad discretionary authority to the regulators. One study found that 20 percent of religion bureaus acted coercively toward one or more religious groups (Grim & Finke 2011). Registration may be denied to or revoked from groups disfavored by the state, for whatever reason. In Bulgaria, the state sought to dictate who would serve as the Chief Mufti of the nation's Muslim community. Some contend that "...the greatest assault upon the sovereignty of religious institutions derives from state-imposed regulations rendering the very existence, or at least the effective functioning, of such institutions dependent upon their registration with political authorities" (Van der Vyver 2004, 92).

Direct regulation of religion is not so common in Middle Eastern nations, probably because they control non-Islamic religions via religious laws and oppression. Syria, a more religiously diverse nation, does require recognition of competing religions, and the government requires permits for all their meetings, save worship itself. Some of the nations do regulate Islamic beliefs, though.

Asian nations also have regulation of religion. Thailand registers religious groups and requires that they not be politically active, though the law does not appear to be enforced vigorously. Many other Asian nations have comparable registration requirements and discriminate against small religions or even large ones sometimes. Singapore has refused to register the Jehovah's Witnesses. In Indonesia, the registration system discriminates against those who do not belong to one of the six religious groups, and their believers may find it difficult to officially register births or marriages.

A number of African nations require religions to register, though they may be liberal in their application of the requirement. In Zambia, Liberia, Mozambique, and Equatorial Guinea, for example, there are no reports of religions being refused such registration. In Sudan, by contrast, the government has denied registration to various Christian groups. Chad is more generous but has banned a Sufi group from operating in the country. Guinea's registration process is reportedly quite slow and may take years.

Most South American nations require religions to register with the state. The requirements may be more or less restrictive. In Columbia, there are many laws that regulate non-Catholic religious entities. Paraguay has a registration requirement, but it is largely unenforced. Others have similar circumstances.

European regulation of religion is mainly concerned with controlling cults. The line between a religion and a cult may be a hard one to draw, but it is reasonable that governments be concerned about at least the extreme cults that may induce mass suicide among their followers. Cults purportedly engage in "brainwashing" of believers. Unfortunately, the regulation of cults may well go beyond these extremes, and religions also arguably engage in a form of brainwashing.

Much of the European controversy involves Scientology. Nations such as France and Germany have been very skeptical of Scientology. In Germany, Scientology is considered a dangerous sect and in some regions, Scientologists are barred from renting public spaces. Private sector discrimination against Scientologists is widespread (Boyle & Sheen 1997). Other religions that have suffered from the registration requirements include Jehovah's Witnesses, the Unification Church, and Mormons.

In France, religious groups must apply to a local prefecture to be recognized as an association of worship in order to receive tax-exempt status. The government has certain criteria in this evaluation but retains considerable discretion in whether or not to approve a group. Consequently, "the regulation of religion soon reflected the zeal of local officials and the pressure of local groups" (Grim & Finke 2006, 36).

European regulation of cults has reached numerous organizations that Americans at least consider obvious religions. Jehovah's Witnesses and various evangelical organizations have been labeled as cults by France. Consequently, they may be subject to as much as a 60 percent tax on funds they receive.

The German government provides some religions with "public law corporation status," which offers various preferences. Like France, Germany initially refused to recognize Jehovah's Witnesses as a religion but after protracted litigation, the government recognized that they should be entitled to religious privileges. The nation prohibits public employees from wearing Islamic dress, though it allows this to private citizens.

Italy has a three-tier hierarchy for religions. The top tier, which provides the maximum of rights, had extended to only six religions. Major religions, including Hindus and Moslems, are not recognized at this level but only in the second tier. This tier gets less government recognition in the form of subsidies. Still other religions in the third tier get less respect, and this includes Scientology and the Church of Christian Science.

Austria divides faiths into legally recognized religious societies, confessional communities, and mere associations, based on the history of the practice and the number of followers claimed. The legally recognized religious societies have more rights, whereas others may be denied the right to engage in various activities, are ineligible for certain subsidies, and are prohibited from teaching their religion in public schools, along with other restrictions (Marshall 2008). Portugal divides religions into four categories, with different legal rights, and funds the Catholic Church from state revenues.

The European Court of Human Rights has found a simple registration requirement to be acceptable. However, the application of the requirement, it notes, may be unacceptable and illegal. The court found that Greece had used the registration requirement to impose prohibitive conditions on practice for certain non-Orthodox religions.

Eastern Europe has seen registration requirements used to restrict religions found to be undesirable (Van der Vyver 2004). In Belarus, registration has been used to marginalize some non-Orthodox religions. Georgia has a hierarchy of religions, and while minorities are often respected, children receive Orthodox instruction in public schools. Slovakia has a legal hierarchy of religions that discriminates against groups including Mormons, Nazarenes, Kirshas, and Scientologists. These groups may practice their religions, but they lack the rights of public worship services. The registration system in Kazakhstan is used as a tool for state control of religion. Missionaries may be prohibited and groups may be banned from operating outside the town of their registration. Uzbekistan requires formal religious regulation, and many religions "have been denied legal status on arbitrary grounds" (Marshall 2008, 422).

The United States is largely free of religious regulation. A new faith need do little more than hang out a shingle to try to attract followers and obtain the benefits of being a religion, including the tax deductibility of contributions. Scientologists and Jehovah's Witnesses, among other groups, are free to practice.

Simply requiring the registration of religious groups plainly imposes some burden on religion, but not necessarily a great one. The requirement may be abusively applied, though, and Lindholm et al. (1998, 92) suggest that the registration requirement may be "the greatest assault upon sovereignty of religious institutions" today. This seems a bit extreme in light of the minority oppression previously discussed, but the registration requirement is potentially a significant restraint on religious freedom.

Government Favoritism of Religion

Rather than attempting to restrict or regulate minority religions, a government might instead simply choose to provide special benefits to a favored religion. This favoritism is precisely what the U.S. establishment clause is meant to prohibit. Equal treatment of all belief systems might be considered a component of religious freedom.

Government favoritism might take many forms. The declaration of a given religion as the state's religion is certainly a form of favoritism, at least psychologically. Numerous nations have state religions. While this phenomenon is typically associated with the Middle East, multiple Western democracies also have state churches, including Malta, Denmark, Finland, Iceland, Greece, and Norway. Some Western nations, including Norway and the United Kingdom, have religious requirements for officeholders. In Malaysia, it is government policy to "infuse Islamic values" into its citizens (Fox 2008a, 198). Religious requirements for public office are common in the Middle East.

The typical form of government support for religion is financial. Numerous governments subsidize some religions. Such funding is common among Middle Eastern countries, which also have mandatory religious education. Religious funding in Africa is much less common, though a number of countries do provide finances for religious education. Nigeria provides some financing for other religious projects. Swaziland allows only Christian broadcasts on state television.

Clergy receive some state funding in many developed countries, including Denmark, Finland, Germany, Norway, Portugal, and Spain. The Belgian government provides subsidies to those religions that are publicly recognized, including salaries and pensions and repair of religious buildings. Russia has entered into agreements with the Russian Orthodox Church that give it privileges in education, law enforcement, and other matters. In other countries, including the United States, religious organizations get tax exemptions, but these are not unique to religion and are available to other charities.

Education of children is another source of favoritism. Under the German constitution, religious education in state schools is a duty for most states. Religious instruction in Greece is required, though parents may opt out, in theory at least. Costa Rica requires religious education in Roman Catholic Christianity by law, though parents may seek an exemption. Sweden makes religious education compulsory. Nearly all the states of the former Soviet Union fund religious education, as do most Asian nations. Islam is a required subject in the schools of Brunei. The Ivory Coast subsidizes Christian education.

The Catholic Church has a preferred status throughout South America. In Peru, for example, all schools include religious education, which is typically available only in Catholicism. Teachers must be approved by a Catholic bishop. Jamaica also provides religious education, but it also specifies that students cannot be forced to take classes in a religion other than their own. In Mexico, though, religious instruction is prohibited.

In some cases, the favoritism is even more dramatic. Pakistan has a shari'a court, which has the power to judge national laws or other government actions and review decisions for conformity with Islamic law.

In the United States, such favoritism is greatly restricted by the application of the constitutional establishment clause. In *Everson v. Board of Education* (1947), the Supreme Court first made clear that the state could not grant substantial assistance to religious schools. The Court has subsequently written that the establishment clause "absolutely prohibits government-financed or government sponsored indoctrination into the beliefs of a particular religious faith" (*Epperson v. Arkansas* 1968, 103–104).

The net effects of such favoritism are uncertain. It might seem like subsidizing one religion would give it an unfair advantage. But such favoritism necessarily entangles the government to some degree with the favored religion, and government involvement may not truly be to the belief's benefit. The subsidies could make the religion less efficient and competitive in a religious marketplace. Moreover, some individuals might resist a religion precisely because it was the favored one.

The limits of favoritism might be seen by analogy to education. In the United States there are universities, such as the University of North Carolina, that are supported by the state government. There are also private universities, such as Duke, that receive no automatic direct governmental support (though they may compete for grants from the government). Yet few would claim that the favoritism makes the University of North Carolina a plainly better school than Duke. Indeed, the top universities in the nation, from Harvard to Stanford, are typically private schools. The government subsidy to public schools does not seem to have harmed their private academic competitors.

Conclusion

Despite the international legal recognition of religion as a protected freedom, as well as internal national guarantees of religious freedom, such freedom is commonly compromised throughout today's world. It is not uncommon for believers to face discrimination due to their religion or to be required to surmount various hurdles in order to practice their faith. The degree of antireligious discrimination varies widely throughout the nations of the world.

There are some regions of the world where a choice of religious belief may mean death to an individual. Fortunately, this extreme repression is not so great as it has been in the past, though it still significantly exists in some nations. However, it remains relatively common that religious believers may be restricted in their practices and even punished for actions taken pursuant to their religious beliefs. Some religions receive favoritism, while others suffer disadvantages at the hands of the state. The precise international extent of deprivation of religious freedom, though, requires a closer analysis than can be provided by anecdotal evidence.

This book will attempt to capture the relative degree of religious discrimination internationally and analyze it quantitatively. The quantitative aspect of the analysis permits a direct comparison among countries and a search for the factors, such as constitutional protections, that help ensure religious freedom. Of course, reducing religious freedom to a numerical measure is quite difficult. The next chapter will discuss the measures I use. While none of them are perfect metrics for religious freedom, they can come close to providing a valid measure for many aspects of such freedom.

3

Measuring Religious Freedom

The previous chapter catalogued the various types of regulation of religious freedom in today's world. Restrictions on the freedom were varied, including death in some cases, and prohibition of religious choice. Other restrictions, such as registration, have a much lesser impact on religious freedom but can compromise choice for some. In order to conduct an analysis of the role of constitutions, I need to cumulate a nation's restrictions on religious freedom into some overall quantitative rating for that country.

Measuring human rights quantitatively is a notoriously difficult task. There is no common measure, such as money. Rights violations come in many types, and it is unclear how to cumulate them (Landman & Carvalho 2010). Moreover, the extent of any particular rights violation across the world's nations is hard to measure. Nations may not self-report rights violations, and those reports that do exist may not be trustworthy. Surveys have various limits for cross-country comparisons. The most commonly used tool is expert assessment, though such a measure clearly depends upon the reliability of the experts. Even the expert scales that exist have a great weakness in categorizing nations into very few categories, with little differentiation made among many of the countries assessed. Coding on such a truncated scale loses much valuable variation, as there is considerable difference in practices among the best and worst nations for human rights (Landman & Carvalho 2010). There is no perfect measure for quantifying human rights.

Yet quantification is important for making conclusions. Ample qualitative research has identified a particular time that a right was, or was not, violated in a particular country. Perhaps the constitution protected it or failed to protect it. Such information can be valuable but does not tell us very much about how to protect rights. If a constitution failed to provide protection, perhaps the situation would have been worse without the constitutional right. Perhaps the situation was unique to the circumstances of the country studied and could not be generalized. Just as we don't decide the efficacy of a drug based upon individual anecdotes, neither should we draw conclusions about constitutions or other devices to protect human rights.

Religious freedom is probably the field for which the best data on rights protection are available. Instead of a three-point scale describing the right, religion has fine-grained measures that draw smaller distinctions among the nations. Moreover, there are multiple independent measures. The quality of the data considerably facilitates my research, but it does not resolve all questions, such as the comparative significance of different types of government actions.

There is no clear and undisputed overall measure for a nation's religious freedom. Different forms of restrictions would have to be weighed and compared against one another for significance. But there is no clear basis for making such decisions. Suppose a nation requires its businesses to close on a holy day. How can this be compared with a law prohibiting proselytization? The impact is certainly less, but how much less? There is also surely question of the degree to which certain government actions (e.g., the prohibition of abortion rights) are indeed religious in nature.

Despite the difficulties, conducting a rigorous analysis to identify the determinants and consequences of religious freedom requires some reduction of the measure to numbers that can be analyzed through statistical methods. Quantifying religious freedom is quite a daunting task. Historically, Freedom House has provided a fine source for researching various issues of freedom. The data for some variables goes back numerous years, but the coding is fairly crude; cases are scored on a seven-point scale, which leaves little room for nuance or differentiation. Other measures have been created, but they tend to consider the effect on only a single religion or cover a very limited number of countries.

Also, the basis of the Freedom House measure was vague. In the beginning, the scale was almost entirely opaque. It was hard to pinpoint which features caused a nation to receive a particular numeric score. The situation has improved and scoring is now based on a checklist of questions, though the questions are surely an incomplete measure of the breadth of rights. The general civil liberties score has no questions specific to religion. Moreover, when Freedom House "uses a mix of sources to arrive at a 'mean' account, there is very little transparency offered as to the precise mix of sources, their number, and the ways in which pieces of information ultimately are used to yield a country score for any given year" (Landman & Carvalho 2010, 89). Means for quantifying most forms of rights are still quite primitive.

Fortunately, researchers more recently have undertaken great efforts to provide just this quantification necessary for my analysis. Indeed, the international quantitative measures for religious freedom are much better than for any other measure of freedom. The following section reviews the measures that I use.

RAS Measures

Jonathan Fox of Bar-Ilan University in Israel has created the Religion and State (RAS) project to measure religious freedom throughout the globe. This project contains a finely detailed analysis of religious freedom in different countries. The RAS categorizes countries broadly by their approach to religion (hostile, separationist, supportive, etc.), but my focus is on the measure for actual government practices. The RAS breaks down the restrictive practices into several categories.

The first category is labeled "restriction on minority religious practices." This is the clearest form of repression and analogous to the minority oppression described in the preceding chapter. The factors considered are:

Restrictions on public observance of religious services or holidays
Restrictions on building and maintaining places of worship
Restrictions on access to places of worship
Forced observance of religious laws
Restrictions on formal religious organizations
Restrictions on private religious education
Arrest or severe official harassment of the religious
Restrictions on the ability to obtain materials for religious ceremonies
Restrictions on the ability to disseminate religious literature
Restrictions on observance of religious laws for marriage, burial, etc.
Restrictions on ordination of and access to clergy
Restrictions on conversion to minority religions
Forced conversions
Restrictions on proselytizing
Requirements of registration of minority religions
Restrictions on observance of religious law

For each of these practices and for each country, the RAS gave a score of:

0 – not significantly restricted
1 – slightly restricted for some minorities
2 – slightly restricted for most minorities or sharply restricted for some minorities
3 – prohibited or sharply restricted for most or all minorities

The country is then given a score that is the sum of the numerical assessment for each of the sixteen different measures.

Each government practice is equally weighted and added to produce a cumulative score. The practices are, of course, not equal in significance. Arrests and forced conversions are surely more restrictive than registration requirements. Fox lacked any objective basis for weighting them, so he left them all equal (Fox 2008a).

The second RAS category is religious regulation. The categories assessed in this category are:

Restrictions on religious political parties
Arrest or severe official harassment of the religious
Restrictions on religious organizations other than political parties
Restrictions on the formal observance of religious practices
Restrictions on public religious speech
Restriction on access to places of worship
Restrictions on the ability to disseminate religious literature
Arrests for religious activities
Restrictions on religious public gatherings
Restrictions on the public display of religious symbols, dress, or the like
Other religious restrictions

For each of these practices and for each country, the RAS gave a score of:

0 – no restrictions
1 – slight restrictions, rare and on a small scale
2 – significant restrictions occasionally and on a moderate scale
3 – the activity is illegal or the government often engages in this activity on a large scale

The overall score for the category is calculated by adding up the scores with equal weighting, as with the restriction on minority religious practices scale.

The third category of RAS is for religious legislation. This category covers a broad area ranging from imposing religious practices on society at large to the involvement of government in religious practices. The specific matters coded for this scale are:

Dietary laws
Restrictions on the sale of alcoholic beverages
Personal status defined by clergy
Laws of inheritance defined by religion
Restrictions on conversions away from the majority religion

Restrictions on interfaith marriages
Restrictions on public dress
Blasphemy laws
Censorship of publications for being antireligious
Mandatory closing of businesses for religious days
Other restrictions on activities during religious holidays
Standard religious education in public schools, if optional
Mandatory religious education in public schools
Government funding of religious education
Government funding of religious charities
Collecting taxes on behalf of religious organizations
Official government positions, salaries, or funding for clergy
Other forms of funding for religious organizations
Government approval requirement for clergy or religious speech
Official clerical appointments made by the government
Existence of an official government department for religious affairs
Government officials given a position in the state church
Religious officials given a position in government
Religious requirements for government officials to hold office
Existence of religious courts with jurisdiction over some legal matters
Legislative seats awarded along religious lines
Prohibitive restrictions on abortion
Religious symbols on the national flag
Religion listed on state identity cards
Requirement that religious organizations register with the government
A government body that monitors minority religions or sects
Religious restrictions on women
Other mandatory religious practices or prohibitions

Each of these is coded as a dummy variable, reflecting whether or not the nation has the practice in question. Again, all the measures are not of equal importance, but the creator of the scale noted that colleagues did not agree on which were the most important (Fox 2008a), so there was no weighting of the factors.

The RAS also provides a composite score incorporating all its measures of religious freedom. This required some rescaling of the underlying measures, and the cumulation of different factors is to some degree "mixing apples and oranges" (Fox 2008a, 54). In addition to the scores just discussed, the RAS includes coding for the degree to which states are hostile to particular religions or favor certain religions. However, it still provides a rough guide to government involvement in religion, which can be supplemented by the underlying scores. My research uses the scores from 2002, but they tend to be quite stable over time.

The distribution in Figure 3.1 is roughly normal, with a long right tail. The left tail is censored at zero, or it might show a similar distribution.

The RAS score is my primary scale for this analysis. It is not necessarily the best measure; that can be disputed and different metrics may be better for different purposes. However, the RAS measure is the most objective of the available measures. In addition, the RAS scale is a measure of the content of a nation's law. Because this book focuses on the law of freedom of religion, it is an appropriate measure.

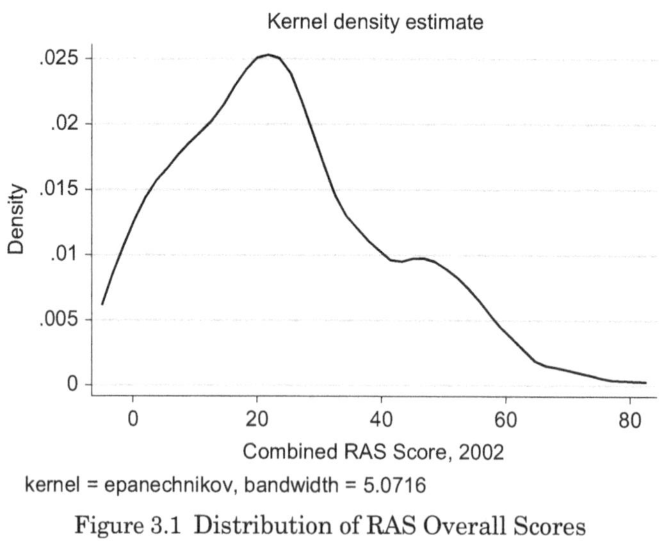

Figure 3.1 Distribution of RAS Overall Scores

Nevertheless, the RAS scale has clear imperfections. While its list of government interference in religion is a good one, it cannot be comprehensive because some governments may employ restrictions for which there is no coding. The RAS does not consider every conceivable method of restricting religious freedom. It focuses on the mere existence of national laws; it also includes some measure of the enforcement of those laws.

The RAS scale makes no attempt to measure the oppressive effect of not enforcing the law. Suppose a mob, perhaps tacitly encouraged by the government, murders members of a religious minority. After this occurs, the government looks the other way and makes no attempt to arrest or prosecute the murderers. This is a case in which government inaction represses religious freedom.

Such instances are not measured by RAS. Of course, such inaction is largely outside the scope of constitutional law. Freedom of religion is a negative right, not to be taken by the government itself. It does not protect a person from the action of private parties, and the constitutional right typically does not require the government to come to one's defense against private parties. Perhaps it is irrelevant to an analysis of constitutional law, but it is certainly relevant to the state of religious freedom in a nation. Indeed, one might fear that a prohibition on governmental restriction of religious freedom might only channel repression into private avenues that the government conveniently overlooks.

Although imperfect, the RAS scale offers great benefit in measuring the relative state of religious freedom throughout the world. The RAS measures have been used on various research projects to date and have produced credible results. This is probably the best single measure of religious freedom.

ARDA Measures

Another set of measures that overlaps the RAS scores was produced by the Association of Religion Data Archives (ARDA) based on U.S. State Department international religious freedom reports, much like the RAS data (Grim & Finke 2006). Each United States embassy annually prepares a report on its host country, according to specific guidelines, and that report is reviewed by officers with expertise. While qualitative in nature, the reports contain certain specific information for each country that could be coded quantitatively.

While the comparative State Department analyses may be compromised by a relative lack of information for some countries, they are generally regarded as very reliable and the most comprehensive information available on religious freedom (Grim & Finke 2006). The reports are quite harsh even on U.S. allies and do not appear to be politically biased. The source is considered to be the most extensive and reliable one available (Grim & Wike 2010). Marshall (2009) suggests that the source is generally exemplary, but identifies some limitations. The State Department reports were given quantitative coding with an instrument of more than two hundred items, investigating the nation's treatment of religion. As a result, ARDA provides three sets of fine-grained scores of interest.

The ARDA approach is to take the information from the State Department reports, code them into categories, and then use a statistical technique known as a factor analysis. This identifies a single latent variable underlying the data. Although widely used and sophisticated, the difficulty with the approach is that the measure cannot be directly observed, so one can guess but not be certain exactly what the measure captures.

The first measure is government favoritism of religion (GFI). This measure considered factors such as unbalanced governmental funding of different religions, the degree to which policy favors a given religion, the inequitable funding of religious matters, and government funding of religious schools, clergy, and other activities. Analysis of the data found that favoritism was quite distinct from regulation (Grim & Finke 2006).

The second measure is government regulation of religion (GRI). The types of issues that this factor considers are the prohibition of missionary work, restrictions on proselytizing or preaching, interference with worship, and general matters such as whether government policy contributes to freedom of religion or does not respect freedom of religion. A single measure was created that captures the concept in a single dimension, with its reliability validated (Grim & Finke 2006).

The GRI score has as a component whether the constitution provides for religious freedom. It is clearly problematic to test whether contributions produce religious freedom, when the variable being assessed includes religious freedom. The measure of constitutional protection is not the same, and constitutional protection is only one part of GFI, but the association would still give reason to question this association.

The third ARDA measure is social regulation of religion (SRI). Unlike all the measures discussed previously, SRI does not involve government action. Instead, it assesses a company's culture and the degree to which its social groups and religions place limits on religious freedom. Such social restriction "can be a more powerful force than government restrictions, as in the case in countries like Iraq, Afghanistan, India, and Pakistan, where conversion to another religion can lead to ostracism or physical violence" (Marshall 2008, 497). This is the first set of quantitative information on this issue.

The SRI scale considers measures such as negative attitudes toward nontraditional religions, negative social attitudes toward conversions to such religions, negative attitudes toward proselytizing, actions taken by existing religions to drive out newcomers, and other factors. Although the social regulation overlapped with government regulation, statistical analysis indicated that they appeared to reflect different concepts (Grim & Finke 2006).

Some countries are high on both GRI and SRI, and others have low scores for both. For a few countries, though, the two are quite disparate. China and Vietnam are examples of nations with high government regulation and much lower social regulation. Other countries, generally in Africa and Europe, have much higher scores for social regulation than government regulation.

The goal of my study is to assess the effect of constitutions on religious freedom. Logically, one would expect a much more profound effect on GFI and GRI than on SRI. The constitutions of the world apply to government action and do not control private, social action (though supplementing statutes may do so). A constitution may influence a nation's culture, however. Indeed, the constitution for a nation such as the United States has become something of a secular religion. Americans might be said to "worship" the freedoms provided by the Bill of Rights. As I will show, James Madison believed that constitutional provisions could inculcate values in a population. If so, a constitution may affect measured SRI as well. The SRI measure may capture the degree to which government protects parties against private attacks on religious freedom.

The SRI scores may capture the national culture, in the form of exclusionist religious culture. Rather than using the government, the people use private means to suppress minority religions. Of course, one might expect such culture to show up in governmental policies as well. The SRI does not just measure the culture, though, because a nation might have a private culture of repression that the government restrains. Thus, government actions could protect believers or places of worship from attacks.

Another related scale is an overall measure of religious freedom, called the Restrictions on Religious Freedom (RRF) index. RRF coded the State Department reports on 243 items that included the legal regulation of religious freedom and the socio-religious hegemonic practices of religions within the nation, including factors such as private prejudice toward believers in particular religions. The legal regulation measure included the presence of constitutional guarantees, though these were only a small part of the measure. Overall scores were given for each nation through use of factor analysis. This measure has the value of being fine-grained, differentiating among nearly all nations, and having very broad national coverage. It has the disadvantage of including the constitution as a factor measured and including extralegal discrimination against religion, which constitutions might not be expected to reach.

The ARDA scores are a little more opaque than the RAS ratings but contribute an important source of additional information. The breakdown between regulation and favoritism is helpful, though surely favoritism can be a sort of regulation, and the social measure (SRI) is also interesting. A comparison of the SRI scores with world survey data suggest their accuracy (Grim & Wike 2010). Although no quantitative measure could perfectly capture the somewhat amorphous concept of religious freedom, the RAS and ARDA scales appear to be roughly reliable overall.

Comparing RAS and ARDA Scores

The two sets of data should provide complementary evidence. Both have good coverage, but they include different nations and, for example, the RAS has better coverage of African countries. One would expect them to be similar, because both rely centrally on the same source (State Department discussions), but they seek to measure somewhat different things from the data in this source. In this section, I look more closely at the two sets of scores and compare them.

Consider the nations with the most religious freedom and least religious freedom for each of the scales. Below I list the top and bottom three nations for each metric.

RAS Minority Restriction

Best – numerous nations (including Nicaragua, Ghana, New Zealand)
Worst – Saudi Arabia, Iran, Sudan

RAS Religious Regulation

Best – numerous nations (including Hungary, South Africa, Brazil)
Worst – Cuba, Uzbekistan, North Korea

RAS Religious Laws

Best – United States, Namibia, Japan
Worst – Saudi Arabia, Jordan, Iran

RAS Overall

Best – United States, Congo, Lesotho
Worst – Saudi Arabia, Iran, Maldives

ARDA Government Regulation

Best – numerous nations (including Ukraine, South Africa, Brazil)
Worst – Saudi Arabia, Mauritania, Belarus

ARDA Government Favoritism

Best – numerous nations (including Guatemala, Botswana, Philippines)
Worst – numerous nations (including Saudi Arabia, Mauritania, Romania)

ARDA Social Regulation

Best – numerous nations (including Norway, Peru, United States)
Worst – Iran, Saudi Arabia, Iraq

Restrictions on Religious Freedom

Best – numerous nations (including South Korea, Barbados, Guinea-Bissau)
Worst – Saudi Arabia, Afghanistan, Azerbaijan

The results generally have facial validity. The worst nations are typically in the Middle East, except for RAS regulation, for which the worst nations are the communist nations. Occasional scores look curious. Denmark, for example, is very nearly the worse nation for the ARDA government favoritism score, worse than countries considered theocracies.

One problem with some of the scales is identical scores for numerous nations; there may be twenty or more nations with perfect scores, which does not allow differentiation among countries, typically at the top end. This affects all the scores other than RAS religious laws and RAS overall.

The various scales can be compared in a correlation matrix, which shows the percentage of correlation between any two sets of different scales. A perfect correlation would be 1.00. A total lack of correlation would be 0.00. Table 3.1 reports the results of this matrix.

The correlations among many of the variables are relatively high, though they are sufficiently different to show that they are measuring different aspects of religious liberty. The correlations tend to be lower

Table 3.1 *Correlation Matrix of Religious Freedom Measures*

	RAS Minority	RAS Regulation	RAS Laws	RAS Overall	ARDA GRI	ARDA GFI	ARDA SRI	RFF
RAS Minority	1.00							
RAS Regulation	0.50	1.00						
RAS Laws	0.60	0.31	1.00					
RAS Overall	0.80	0.56	0.81	1.00				
ARDA GRI	0.65	0.62	0.47	0.64	1.00			
ARDA GFI	0.36	0.13	0.34	0.55	0.43	1.00		
ARDA SRI	0.56	0.40	0.42	0.64	0.63	0.44	1.00	
RFF	0.63	0.45	0.58	0.70	0.61	0.34	0.68	1.00

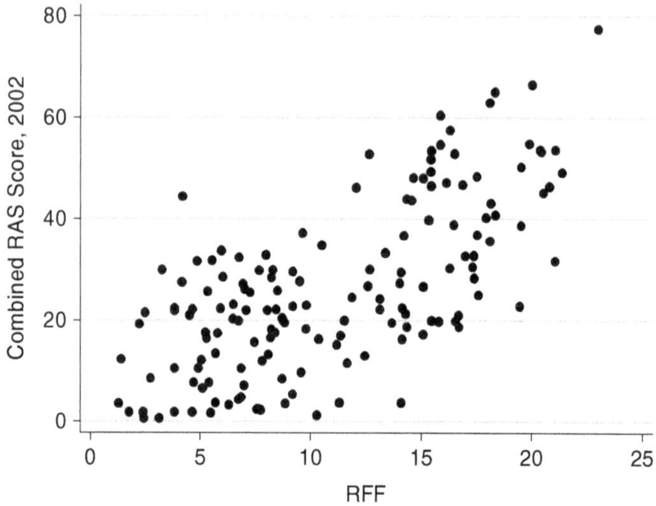

Figure 3.2 Comparison of RAS Overall Score with RFF Score

for the ARDA GFI index, whereas the ARDA GRI index has more in common with the RAS scores.

To illustrate the association of the variables with relatively high correlations, Figure 3.2 shows a scatter plot of national scores on the RAS overall measure and the RFF overall measure of religious freedom. If the two were perfectly correlated, the figure would show a straight line of data points beginning in the lower left and stretching diagonally to the upper right.

There is a plain pattern from the lower left to the upper right, which reflects the association between the two measures. However, there is considerable spread and disagreement about a number of nations. For example, RFF gives Uzbekistan a very good score for religious freedom, whereas the RAS overall scale gives it a poor score. Conversely, Liberia receives a very high freedom score from the RAS overall measure but only a middling rating on the RFF. There is general agreement, though, as shown in the correlation matrix, and both measures concur that Saudi Arabia is plainly the worst.

The RAS overall and RFF scores are the overall measures for all forms of religious freedom. Their differences may come from different measurement tools, but they also appear to be measuring somewhat different things. The RAS overall measure considers only government action and does so quite specifically, while the RFF measure also considers social restrictions of religious freedom.

Pew Survey Data

All the preceding data were taken from calculations from official reports from the early years of the century, 2002 or 2003. Recently, the Pew Foundation has performed an analysis of international global restrictions on religion. The Pew Forum examined State Department reports, as well as other sources, including the U.N. Special Rapporteur on Freedom of Religion or Belief, the Council of the European Union, Human Rights Watch, Amnesty International, and others. The Pew Forum used multiple coders to check for reliability.

The Pew researchers focused on two categories: government restrictions of religious freedom and social hostilities. The former assesses government repressive practices, whereas the latter considered religious discrimination by private individuals or groups. The former is the category most likely to be influenced by a national constitution, though the two are clearly correlated. An overall score was created for each, based on the assessments in numerous underlying questions.

The overall score for government restriction had a significant component of constitutional content, but the Pew researchers considerately made available to me the evaluations for each of the subcategories that went into the general indexes, so I could segregate the questions about constitutional content from those about actual protection of religious freedom in different nations.

As noted, several of the questions went to the specific content of constitutional protections, including:

1. Does the constitution, or law that functions in the place of a constitution (basic law), specifically provide for "freedom of religion" or include language used in Article 18 of the United Nations Universal Declaration of Human Rights?

2. Does the constitution or basic law include stipulations that appear to qualify or substantially contradict the concept of "religious freedom"?
3. Does the country's constitution or basic law recognize a favored religion or religions?

Although phrased as yes/no questions, the responses provide more subtle distinctions. For the first question, the response could be that national laws and policies provide for religious freedom, that the laws and policies provide for religious freedom generally but not in some instances, that there were limited national protections for religious freedom but not general respect, or that national laws and policies did not provide for religious freedom. Each is given a quantitative coding on a scale of 0 (the most freedom) to 1 (the least freedom).

Other questions answered in the Pew analysis went to the state of religious freedom in practice in each of the nations. Some of these questions had relatively little differentiation among nations, save for a few oppressive outliers, but others are useful for empirical analysis. They include:

1. Does any level of government interfere with worship or other religious practices?
2. Is proselytizing limited by any level of government?
3. Was there harassment or intimidation of religious groups by any level of government?
4. Did any level of government use force toward religious groups that resulted in individuals being killed, physically abused, imprisoned, detained, or displaced from their homes, or having their personal or religious properties damaged or destroyed?
5. Does the government have an established organization to regulate or manage religious affairs?
6. Do some religious groups receive government support or favors, such as funding, official recognition, or special access?
7. Do all religious groups receive the same level of government access and privileges?

Some of these were coded as yes/no questions, but many had gradations, reflecting the relative degree to which the government engaged in the practices about which the question was asked. I will make use of some of these, especially when they measure factors absent from the RAS measure.

Perhaps the best overall measure from the Pew analysis is the question: "Taken together, how do the constitution/basic law and other national laws and policies affect religious freedom?" The answers were on a four point-scale:

- 0 – National laws and policies provide for religious freedom, and the national government respects religious freedom in practice.
- .33 – National laws and policies provide for religious freedom, and the government generally respects religious freedom in practice; but there are some instances (e.g., in certain localities) where religious freedom is not respected in practice.
- .67 – There are limited national legal protections for religious freedom, but the national government does not generally respect religious freedom in practice.
- 1 – National laws and policies do not provide for religious freedom, and the national government does not respect religious freedom in practice.

This scale appears to capture well the overall state of religious freedom in a nation, though the limited scaling of answers permits only limited differentiation among countries. Note that as with the RAS scale, higher numbers mean less religious freedom.

The recent Pew research is partially a product of Brian Grim, who had previously been involved in the ARDA measures. The Pew data have some limitations for my purposes. The categories generally have only three to five different scores available. This means that numerous nations are given identical scores on each of the measures, though their practices are surely not identical, allowing less differentiation. Nevertheless, they provide a valuable supplemental check on any findings.

One would expect some correlation between the Pew scale and the RAS and other measures of religious freedom. One wouldn't expect identity because they measure somewhat different things and cover a different time period. Because the Pew numbers follow just a few years after the others, though, one should expect

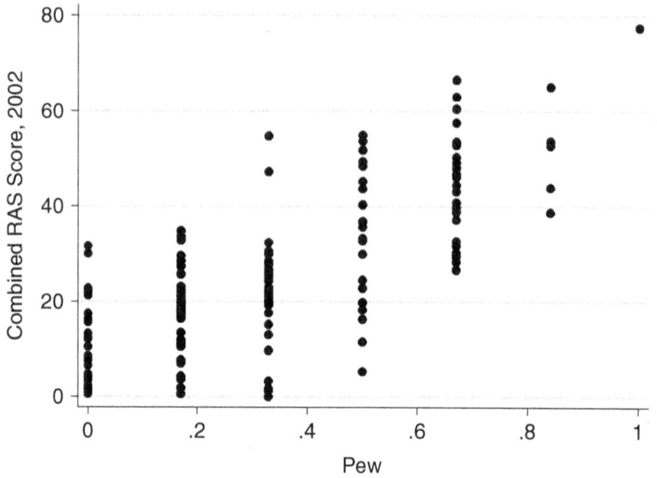

Figure 3.3 Comparison of RAS Overall Score with Pew Score

commonality. To check the association, I produced a scatter plot (Figure 3.2) for the RAS overall scores with the Pew measure for protection of religious freedom.

The Pew measure has less differentiation, hence the vertical lines in Figure 3.3. Overall, though, the association appears to be a high one, greater than that for the RAS score and the RFF score.

The strength of the RAS score for my purposes is its focus on the content of legislation, but its potential weakness is its failure to measure whether that legislation has actual practical effect. The correlation with the Pew score on measures of perceived religious freedom adds confidence that the RAS measure also captures national practice. Moreover, the Pew scores measure some important concepts not counted by RAS or ARDA.

Conclusion

There is no unambiguously correct single way to measure religious freedom. Such freedom can be compromised in various different ways, and there is no objective way to give a weight to one form of restriction as opposed to another. The indices that do exist provide considerable insight into practice around the world.

My primary measure will be the RAS scale. This is a test of the effect of constitutions, and the RAS is more of a direct measurement of the law, where constitutions would be expected to have effect. Constitutions might well influence the legal culture, as James Madison expected, but this is not their designed role. The RAS scale also appears to have broader coverage of restrictions and contains data on particular restrictions so that they may be examined in more detail. Another major advantage of the RAS is its finer differentiation, as it does not group many nations as equivalent. The RAS's focus on the law has limits, though, because even a perfect measure of the law may not reflect religious freedom.

The ARDA scale provides individual measures, using factor analysis, which is a sophisticated means of identifying a common dimension of nations. While this is useful, the precise meaning of that common dimension is a little opaque, and it is possible that it is driven by restrictions of religious freedom that we would consider less severe. The overall scale also eliminates the possibility of looking closer at the particular aspects of religious freedom influenced by the factors studied. The Pew data, by contrast, deal with many particular aspects of religious freedom. The strong positive correlation among the scores gives some confidence in their mutual reliability and the commonality of their ability to capture de facto religious freedom in the nations of the world.

There are differences, though, and the three major scales use somewhat different resources and capture different aspects of religious freedom. Not only do they differ in focus on the law as opposed to social practice, they also consider different matters as issues of religious freedom. The RAS scale is my primary variable of interest, but considering all of them enables me to assess which factors, legal or social, are most robust in influencing religious freedom, however measured. If some of the variables influence one of the measures but not others, or have reverse effects on different measures, that too can inform the understanding of how constitutions and other factors influence religious freedom in societies.

4

Social Factors and Religious Freedom

My analysis of the factors that may produce greater religious freedom begins here. This chapter considers the societal factors that may contribute to, or undermine, religious freedom. Surely countless factors could explain a national culture of religious freedom. These include the nature of the religion itself – some faiths may command broader allegiance and some are more restrictive of others' freedom. Other relevant societal factors include democracy, the rule of law, and per capita GDP. These associations must be considered as part of the legal analysis.

Religion

It may be that certain religions are more likely, due to their theology, to grant greater or lesser freedom to other faiths. Religion is competitive and not naturally tolerant of competing faiths. But some religions may be naturally more aggressive, while others have greater respect for personal freedom.

Some have suggested that Islamic belief may be fundamentally authoritarian and anti-freedom in general. Huntington (1996) suggests that this applies especially to religion, contending that politics and religion are intrinsically fused in the Muslim world. Fish (2002) empirically demonstrates that Islamic nations have less freedom. He suggests the countries may be authoritarian by nature, which he grounds in its practices of female subordination. Islamic countries have substantially less press freedom (Connolly-Ahearn & Golan 2007).

The association of Islamic nations with less democracy and less personal freedom may not be intrinsic to the religion. The Islamic nations of the Middle East tend to be blessed with substantial oil resources. But economists have found that this may be a "resource curse" that causes corruption and authoritarianism in government. Ross (2008) suggests that the gender discrimination associated with Middle Eastern states is more attributable to oil than to Islam.

A common intuition, at least in the West, is that Islamic believers are inherently less likely to grant freedom of religion to others. The notion of apostasy, such as a conversion away from Islamic belief, is controversial. An Egyptian intellectual was gunned down by those who accused him of apostasy. The religion's approach to apostasy has not materially changed since the religion's second century (Saeed & Saeed 2004), though the approaches taken by Islamic nations to apostasy differ. Pryor (2007, 58) reports that "Islamic doctrine places little emphasis on individual rights, especially by those Muslim sects such as the Shi'a whose leaders have stressed a theocratic approach toward government."

The Qur'an, though, is not plainly against freedom of religion, recognizing the diversity of religious traditions. It clearly states that an individual should never be forced to accept a religion against his or her will. It regards Judaism and Christianity as historically valid religions of the Islamic God. The Qur'an did not criticize these religions, but treated them with respect, though it did not take the same tolerant approach to some other religions that involved idolatry (Saeed & Saeed 2004). Moreover, the roots of other religions share Islam's belief system. Early Jewish law prescribed death as a punishment for apostasy, and medieval Christianity did likewise. The Bible says that one who blasphemes the name of the Lord shall be put to death." Yet Judaism and Christianity no longer adhere to these beliefs, or at least do not attempt to enforce them. This change may not be intrinsic to the religion but related to other societal factors at play.

Yousif (2000) argues that the prevailing concept of religious freedom is a Western one, treating belief as a purely private affair. He argues that Islamic law is an essential part of the religion. The concept of religious freedom "has room for only those who subscribe to its own particular perception of religion, that being a private personal matter." The public advocacy of "so-called religions' which make a mockery of the supremacy of God cannot be tolerated in an Islamic state, since it contradicts and threatens the basic teachings and principles of the state which are to protect the integrity of its religion" (Yousif 2000, 36). Individual freedom is only sacred "as long as it does not violate the Law of God" (Yousif 2000, 38). Some think that shari'a is simply incompatible with Western notions of religious freedom (Venter 2010). If this is the genuine Islamic perspective, one might expect that the religion would show more poorly on the measures used in this study.

One survey found that violent religious persecution "is not only more prevalent among Muslim-majority countries, but it also generally occurs at more severe levels" (Grim & Finke 2011, 169). That survey found that 46 percent of Muslim-majority countries were at the highest level of persecution measured, as compared to only 11 percent of Christian-majority countries. Perhaps this is due to the growth of fundamentalism in these nations. Pryor (2007) found that the greater the percentage of Muslims in a nation's population, the lower the level of political rights of the people.

The box plot in Figure 4.1 displays religious freedom by the nation's majority religion. The measure for religious freedom in this figure is the combined RAS score for laws infringing on such freedom. Higher scores represent more laws that restrict religious freedom.

Muslim nations are more restrictive of religious freedom and at a level that is statistically significant, at least as compared with Christian nations. Their average is about twice as many laws restricting religious freedom as in Christian nations and about a third more laws than the nations grouped as other. A breakdown of

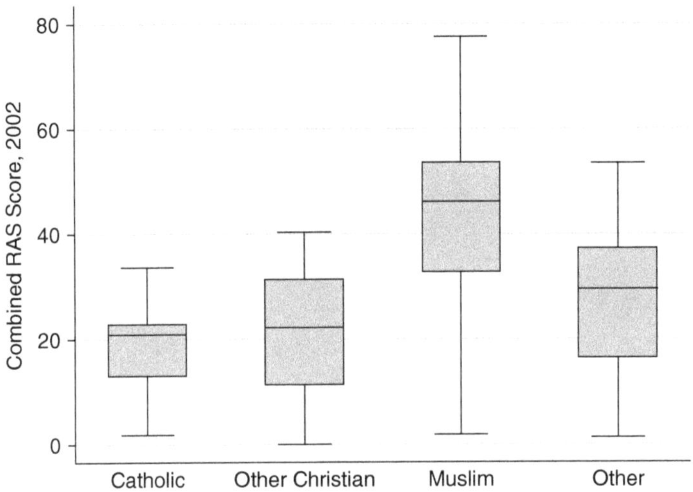

Figure 4.1 Overall Religious Freedom by Majority Religion

the "other" category shows that Animist nations tend to be quite protective of religious freedom by this measure, with lower average scores than for Christian nations. Buddhist nations, though, tend to have higher scores, not too dissimilar from those in majority Muslim countries.

The box plot simply distinguished among nations with given religious majorities. Many nations have no such majority, and the association of religion and religious freedom may be due to the overwhelming majorities of some Islamic populations. Figure 4.2 shows the same measure of religious freedom based on the national population that is Islamic, using a quadratic fit for the data.

Infringement on religious freedom obviously increases along with Muslim population. The rate increases, with higher numbers, suggesting that it is large numbers of Islamic believers that associates most strongly with infringement on religious freedom. However, there is some increase in restricted religious oppression even at low levels.

The mere fact that Muslim nations tend to give less religious freedom does not establish a causal association between this belief

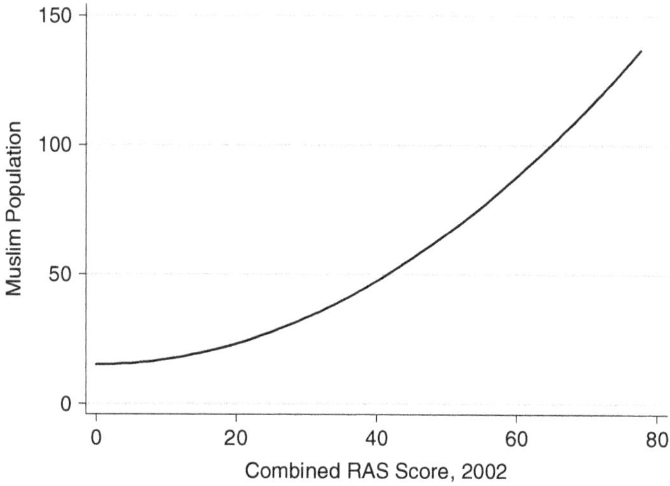

Figure 4.2 Religious Freedom by Islamic Population

and repression. In today's world, Christianity appears a tolerant religion, not provoking the repression of other faiths. But historically, Christianity is the religion that produced the Inquisition and the Crusades. So it may not be Christian faith per se that tolerates other religions but something else associated with modern day Christian believers. Similarly, the positive association between Islam and compromised religious freedom may be some factor other than religious belief.

The association may be due to other factors possessed by those nations. These countries may systematically have other qualities, such as national wealth, that cause the difference. Or perhaps they have constitutions that offer less protection. Still, the difference is sufficiently distinct that this religious grounding for freedom should be analyzed.

I certainly would not proclaim that any one religion is intrinsically more repressive than others. History indicates that religious practices vary over time. For purposes of this study, however, I would consider the Muslim population to be a factor influencing a nation's religious freedom. It will be an important variable to control in statistical analyses.

Democracy

One might expect democratic governance to have an effect on a society's religious freedom. The commonly expressed fear is one of a tyranny of a majority, in which a society with a dominant religion would vote to suppress alternative beliefs. Conversely, though, one might expect democracy to increase religious freedom. People may simply have a desire for a free society. Additionally, people might wish to extend freedom to others out of a concern that in the future their own freedom might be compromised. The effect of democracy can only be evaluated on a relative basis, and it is compared with an autocratic system, where a governing individual or group simply imposes his or her will. A fundamentalist religious autocrat might be quicker to suppress freedom, but a more benevolent one might be more willing to allow freedom than even the populace at large. If a society has a dominant religion, one might expect an autocrat to form a strategic alliance with that religion and suppress others. The views of the people surely matter in assessing the effect of democracy.

Polling shows some popular support for religious freedom. The Pew Forum asked individuals throughout the world if it was "very important" to live in a country that protected their religious freedom or the religious freedom of others. Overall, 76 percent said it was important that their religious freedom be protected, and 62 percent said it was important for the religious freedom of others be protected (Grim & Finke 2011, 42). The latter number is a healthy majority for protecting the freedoms of others, even when the person questioned was in a majority group.

One cannot be too sanguine about this polling, however. It is easy to say one is for religious freedom in the abstract, without consequences. The question was asked in the abstract and did not involve a scenario in which a religion might be considered somehow threatening. If Islamic terrorists attack America, Americans might be more inclined to reduce the freedom of Muslims. There appears to be a natural human tendency for members of a group to have prejudice against those outside the group (Jackson & Hunsberger 1999), and religions may be profoundly significant groups for at least some individuals. While polling in America reflects great respect for religious freedom, it is common for at least state and local governments to engage in religious discrimination (Grim & Finke 2011), which calls the polls into question.

The irreligious may be particularly vulnerable to democratic pressures. Toleration among different religious beliefs may not extend to those who have no beliefs. While tolerance has obviously increased in America, lessening prejudices against Jews, Catholics, and other groups, atheists are still viewed with great suspicion. While more than ninety percent of Americans would vote for an African American, a Catholic, or a Jew for president, a majority say they would not vote for an atheist (Edgell, Gerteis, & Hartmann 2006). A Canadian survey found greater religiosity was associated with more animosity to nonbelievers (Jackson & Hunsberger 1999). One poll found that only 18 percent of the public at large believed that atheists could preach against God in a civic auditorium (Brest 1985).

The concern about democracy is that a majority of religious believers will use the state to discriminate against nonbelievers or other religions. Grim and Finke (2011, 57) noted that although the Puritans came to America seeking religious freedom, "they had no intentions of granting religious freedom to all." This is what is commonly called the tyranny of the majority, which the American Founders feared. Judicial enforcement of the First Amendment was designed to avert this outcome.

Ronald Dworkin (1986, 449) declared that the "United States is a more just society than it would have been had its constitutional rights been left to the conscience of majoritarian institutions," but he promptly concedes that he has no empirical support for this claim. Although the courts condemned segregation in *Brown v. Board of Education* (1954), majority institutions soon followed with much more effective action against racial segregation.

It is commonly assumed that majorities have little regard for the rights of minorities, but the theory and evidence is not so obvious. First, it is unclear that the majority benefits from restriction of freedom. How does denying a minority sect the right to worship profit a majority? It may be that the majority has a taste for homogeneity in society that could motivate such restrictions. However, the majority could well have a taste for diversity or tolerance that would prevent such restrictions. Indeed, if only a minority of the majority religion preferred such tolerance, that fact could defeat the power of the majority to impose its will on minorities, when combined with minority votes. Perhaps the greater risk is that the majority will simply be insensitive to the interest of religious minorities, when enacting legislation for other reasons. Elections are driven by the median voter, who is likely to be less intense in any preferences for oppression. And a majority must confront numerous policy issues at any time, competing for the agenda with items that would restrict the interest of minorities. Democracy offers a tool for removing abusive leaders from office (Poe & Tate 1994).

A second reason why majoritarianism need not lead to majority tyranny is the fact that majorities are commonly comprised of multiple minority groups. James Madison addressed this in Federalist No. 10, where he contended that large republics such as a nation, are less susceptible to majoritarian tyranny, because they contain a greater diversity of groups. Democracy encourages compromise that accommodates differing views and yields lessened repression (Henderson 1991).

Ackerman (1985) notes that smaller groups can be more effective politically because they tend to have more group solidarity and lower organizational costs. One would expect a minority religion to have a stronger preference intensity for pursuing its own faith than the majority does for oppressing it. This opens opportunities for minority influence. They may trade votes on matters of significance to the majority to gain benefits for their minority group. Because of stronger preference intensities, they may be expected to prevail over majority groups (Downs 1957).

Moreover, the theory of a homogenous majority is rarely the case. Most individuals are members of majorities on some matters and minorities on other questions (Cross 2000). James Madison (1961b, 162) contended that "in the society so many separate descriptions of citizens as well render an unjust combination of a majority of the whole very improbable . . . ." A majority is commonly a cumulation of minority groups, reflecting each of their interests on specific matters. Policy is formed through negotiation among these groups. Dahl (1967, 456) contended that "no single group can win national elections – only heterogenous combinations of groups can." Democratic decision making is not the "march of great majorities" but the "steady appeasement of relatively small groups" (Dahl 1967, 146). Elected officials commonly appeal to minority voter interests.

Future uncertainty should also contribute to protection of minority interests. We may not know our own future status and we certainly don't know the future political setting. A Catholic is a member of a Christian majority in this country, but Catholics themselves are a minority. The Catholic might change his or her faith or marry a person of another faith, giving him or her an interest in minority protection. The Catholic might well fear that setting a precedent of repressing a non-Christian minority could be used against Catholics in the future. Given this uncertainty, a risk averse person might want to create structural protections for minorities, as he or she could be a member of a minority in the future. There is a widespread belief that the rights of all may depend on protecting those at the fringe, and the civil liberties of the Bill of Rights are "now thought to be good for everybody" (Riker 1982, 7). Religious liberty may be largely a product of individual faiths' uncertainty over whether they would prevail in a struggle for power (Riker 1982). The government that oppresses one faith now could turn on another faith later (Laycock 1996). Even if they were confident today about their ability to prevail, they might have doubts about the future.

Even if majoritarianism tended to restrict the individual rights of dissenters, it does not follow that democratic institutions, such as legislatures, would do so. In the United States, the majoritarianism of the elected branches is compromised by numerous features, including the state-based representation of the Senate itself, its filibuster, committee systems, and other factors. Empirical research suggests that the actions of the legislature reflected public opinion only about two-thirds of the time or less (Page & Shapiro 1983). The legislative branches may be roughly majoritarian, but they regularly disagree. The House and Senate commonly divide over policy, and either or both may disagree with the president, though each entity is considered to be a majoritarian one.

Indeed, the record of U.S. majoritarian institutions with respect to rights is generally a good one. For much of our history, the Bill of Rights did not apply to state governments. During this time, it was majoritarian institutions that disestablished religions in several states and protected freedom of worship (Dinan 1998). Women went to the Supreme Court to gain suffrage but were rebuffed. They prevailed at the ballot box. There is thus reason to think that majoritarianism may promote freedom.

In civil rights, we have seen majoritarian institutions at the state level engaged in discrimination. Federal courts eventually fought for civil rights, but federal elected institutions did likewise. Congress and the president have consistently pursued the expansion of civil rights, and their efforts sometimes have been resisted by the judiciary. Spann (1993, 3) claims that "historically, minority interests have fared better before the representative branches of government than before the Supreme Court." Civil rights laws have been passed prohibiting discrimination in many spheres of society, and affirmative action has been extended to minorities.

Poe, Tate, and Keith (1999) suggest that democratic governments will be less repressive in part because they have less opportunity, given that the structure of such governments makes "extensive use of repression more difficult to arrange." In addition, they suggest that democratic governments will be less willing to repress because they offer outlets of release through which conflict can be more peacefully channeled.

Empirical research has generally confirmed that democracy is protective of individual human rights (Bueno de Mesquita et al. 2005). Keith (2002), in her study of constitutional provisions, found a positive effect for democracy. Poe and Tate (1994) likewise found that democracy was a profound protector of human rights, as did Armstrong (2009). None of this research has considered religious freedom, however.

The association of democracy with freedom of religion can be tested by comparing the nations of the world. I have discussed the measures for religious freedom, and such a test also requires a measure for the relative democracy of nations. The concept of democracy is not so easy to measure as is the raw size of different religious

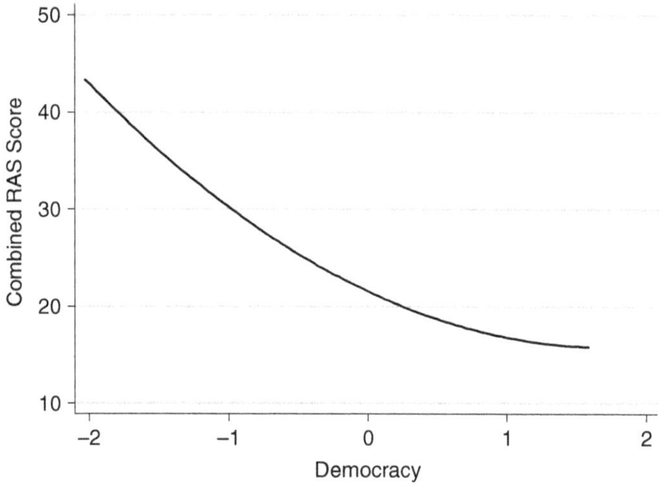

Figure 4.3 Democracy and Religious Freedom

populations. There are relative scales for democracy, though, and I use the one that is probably most common in research, that of the World Bank (Kaufman, Kraay, & Mastruzzi 2004). This index combines other indices and uses conventional measures of the accountability of public officials, but it also includes measures of individual rights as matters of democracy.

The association between democracy and religious freedom can be casually examined through a simple association. Using the World Bank's measure for democracy, the Figure 4.3 depicts the association of democracy with the overall religious freedom measure.

The effect of democracy on religious freedom appears to be strong and consistent. Nations with low levels of democratic governance have high numbers of laws restricting religious freedom. Nations with high levels of democracy tend to have fewer than half as many such laws. The association is a steady one, though it appears less dramatic at higher levels of democracy.

Fox (2008a), using a different measure, found that democracies prevented the highest levels of restriction of religious freedom. My results suggest that the benefits of democracy may go beyond that, with greater levels of democracy steadily increasing religious freedom. Braithwaite & Bramsen (2011) found a strong relationship between democracy and the separation of church and state. They suggested that such separation might promote democracy, rather than vice versa. Such directionality is always a concern, but it seems more likely that democracy is the explanatory variable.

Driessen (2010) claims that the type of state action on religion matters with respect to democracy. Friendliness to religion, he suggests is consistent with democracy, when hostility is not. Using the GRI and GFI scales discussed in Chapter 3, he finds that government favoritism to religion is commonly associated with higher levels of democracy among nations, while government regulation of religion is the opposite.

Democracy will produce different results for religious freedom. Switzerland in 1980 rejected a popular referendum that would have provided for separation of church and state (Garlicki 2001). But in general democracy appears to promote such freedom. This basic data appears to dispel the basic tyranny of the majority concern. Majorities do not use democracy to suppress religious freedom, instead they use their authority to enhance it. As with any correlation, directionality is a concern. Instead of democracy producing religious freedom, perhaps religious freedom promotes greater democracy. The possibility is worth consideration, but findings of the next chapter will dispel this concern.

Rule of Law

The rule of law is exalted in modern society. It seems intrinsically good, as it suggests that people are treated equally before the law. Of course, the notion of rule of law is rather ill-defined. Some regard the rule of law as simply "all good things." For some, the rule of law implies a certain content of the law, embracing liberal democracy. The rule of law implies a certain moral perspective in this view. Religious freedom might be considered an intrinsic requirement of this view of the rule of law. Of course, the fundamental problem with this approach is that there is nothing approaching a consensus on what the required moral content of such a rule of law is. Therefore, it is impossible to measure.

The better vision of the rule of law, sometime called the "thin" version, is procedural. This notion derives from Fuller (1969), who suggested that the rule of law requires certain attributes such as generality, publicity, conformability, and other factors involving the operationalization of legal content, without reference to the morality of that content. The rule of law directs that the law should be applied and enforced effectively, regardless of how unjust that substantive law might seem to be (Macedo 1994). Rawls (1979, 211) suggests that a system "based on the denial of human rights, on extensive poverty, on racial segregation, sexual inequalities and religious persecution may, in principle, conform to the requirements of the rule of law better than any of the legal systems of the more enlightened Western democracies." The Nazi death camps were legal in the Germany of the time and not contrary to the rule of law. Indeed, the rule of law might be most appealing to a repressive authoritarian, who would want to use the law to control any actions of his or her citizens that were not desired.

To some degree, the rule of law, especially of constitutional law, is seen to combat the threat of majoritarian tyranny. The evidence just provided on democracy and religious freedom might seem to dispel fears of such tyranny, but the examples from Chapter 2 show how religious majorities have indeed oppressed minority beliefs in many states. One fundamental aspect of the law is equality. Legal rules apply the same to all, whether in or out of government (or a particular religion). The rule of law is contrary to the arbitrary decision-making characteristic of authoritarian rulers. When the constitution commands religious freedom, surely its enforcement through the rule of law should enhance such freedom.

The effect of the rule of law on religious freedom is quite uncertain, though, at least under procedural definitions of the concept. It suggests that the laws of the nation are enforced throughout a society, regardless of what they are. If constitutions protect religious freedom, one might expect that the rule of law enforcing those constitutions would likewise be protective. However, a nation's laws might affirmatively restrict religious freedom. If a country legally prohibited religious conversion, for example, its enforcement according to the rule of law would limit religious freedom. The rule of law may simply be a proxy for state control of a society, and this may be contrary to the protection of religious freedom.

Henderson (1990) observes that law is a major tool of social and political power that may be readily captured for authoritarian ends. Indeed, law may "always be authoritarian ... because a major premise of law is that people will accept and obey it" (Henderson 1990, 383). By its nature, law is a form of social control, which may be used for good or ill. Horwitz (1977) reviews how the rule of law in historic England was used to suppress the poor. This was surely the view of Marx, who saw the rule of law as oppressive. The Fugitive Slave Act in the United States was the law, but its enforcement was not considered a good thing. It is not difficult to identify laws, enforced per the rule of law, with immoral consequences.

One imagines that fascist states of the past had a strong rule of law. Nazi Germany had various laws restricting Jews, and they were apparently enforced with vigor. Whether the Nazis actually conformed to the rule of law is contested, but one can certainly imagine an authoritarian government that adopted repressive laws legally and then enforced them as behaving consistently with the rule of law but undermining individual freedom. It is generally believed that the formalist lawyers of Vichy France enforced repressive Nazi laws, according to the dictates of the rule of law (Weisberg 1992). The effect of the rule of law on freedom of religion is thus uncertain.

The practical effect of the rule of law has seen extensive empirical research, analyzing its effect on economic growth and various other factors. Similarly, religion and religious freedom have been extensively studied, using quantitative methods. The effect of rule of law on religious freedom, though, has seen little empirical analysis.

The effect of the rule of law presumably depends on the content of the law. If the law restricts religious freedom, a stronger rule of law will be more restrictive. Indeed, rule of law means that legislation will be better enforced, which could encourage nations to pass more restrictive legislation, confident that it will be implemented. If the law provides for freedom, though, the rule of law might encourage more freedom. Perhaps the equality implied by rule of law also should further freedom. The theoretical association of rule of law and religious freedom is indeterminate.

To test the association between religious freedom and the rule of law requires a quantitative measure for the rule of law, which seems more difficult to capture than even democracy. The World Bank has developed a scale for national rule of law, which I use (Kaufman, Kraay, & Mastruzzi 2004).

Because the rule of law is so vaguely defined, any scale will be debatable. The World Bank measure has been criticized for not closely relating to the theory of the rule of law, and the aggregation method makes it somewhat unclear exactly what is driving the scale. There may be no better measure, though. The aggregation helps reduce biases of individual sources, and the surveys used by other single measures may be biased by media coverage, atypical experiences, and different views of the meaning of the rule of law. The World Bank measure combines assessments of the courts, including judicial independence and fairness of judicial process with measures relating to crime and police enforcement.

Figure 4.4 displays the association between the World Bank rule of law measure and the RAS scale for overall religious freedom.

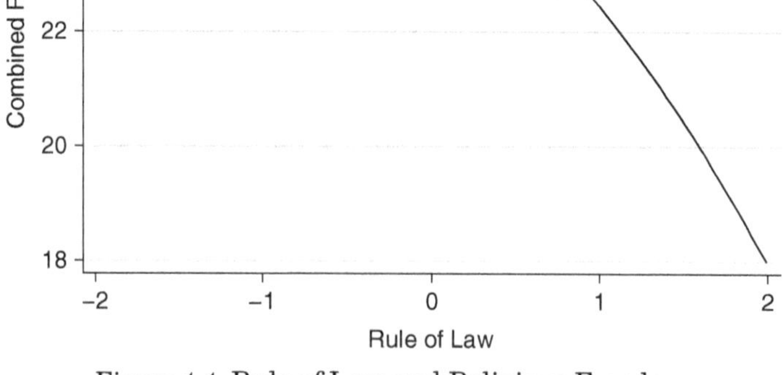

Figure 4.4 Rule of Law and Religious Freedom

Stronger rule of law in a nation has little effect on the religious freedom measure until it reaches about the median level for rule of law, after which a stronger rule of law is associated with much greater religious freedom. In general, the rule of law seems to have quite a positive effect on religious freedom, at least for nations with above average rule of law ratings.

National Income

Richer countries may tend to have more (or less) religious freedom. Wealthier nations tend to have a variety of different government practices than do poorer ones. Indeed, research has found that richer nations tend to be freer in general than poorer countries. One might think that greater wealth might cause people to shift their concern to nonmaterial matters, such as individual freedom. Henderson (1991) suggests that additionally national income could make the citizenry more satisfied, lessening the need for various repressive measures. Wealthier nations may be more stable and give the government less need to repress its people; in fact, poorer countries are more likely to take political prisoners or engage in torture (Mitchell & McCormick 1988, Henderson 1991). It is not clear, though, that wealth causes greater freedom; it may be that greater freedom causes nations to become richer.

The most studied aspect of wealth and religion is a concept known as secularization (McCleary & Barro 2006). This theory suggests that as personal income grows, religion becomes less important to people. This theory began with a considerable pedigree, being put forth by thinkers ranging from Comte to Weber to Marx. Not so long ago, some even predicted the extinction of religious belief, in light of its diminishing significance in Europe (Gorski & Altinordu 2008). But this history is also revealing of the weakness of the theory – the demise of religion has been predicted since the 1700s, but it remains with us.

It may be that economic growth simply provides individuals with more outlets other than church. Some economic theory suggests that as people grow richer, the opportunity costs of investing in religious practice are greater. People may spend considerable time on religious belief, both inside and outside their place of worship. The time spent on religion might be more profitably invested in money-making enterprises. Alternatively, greater wealth may also enable individuals to choose a variety of other, more expensive activities, in lieu of religious practice. As science does more, we might rely on religion less. Secularization may be due to an increased number of nonreligious activities competing with the religious. This view considers religion as an economic marketplace endeavor, just like any other business.

While the secularization hypothesis was based primarily on simple observation of broad trends, some research supports this hypothesis. A study of declining church attendance in Scotland found that economics could explain some of this and noted that religion seemed more popular during recessions (Smith 1993). Broader studies of belief in Western European nations have confirmed the process (Verweij, Ester, & Nauta 1997). Throughout the world, postindustrial societies put less emphasis on religion than do industrial societies, which in turn emphasize religion less than agrarian societies (Norris & Inglehart 2004). Bruce (2002) argues that secularization occurs, though not that it is universal and inevitable. Countervailing factors may ward off secularization in some circumstances, but he argues that the underlying trend remains in that direction.

The welfare state provides one explanation for the secularization hypothesis. As nations become richer, states tend to offer more benefits to the disadvantaged. This can supplant the role of the churches in offering charity and security to their members. Historically, religious groups have often played a major role in providing for the welfare of their community. State provision is an alternative.

One study empirically tested whether the level of religious participation in society varied inversely with the per capita level of social welfare provided by the state and found that it did (Gill & Lundsgaarde 2004). This does not suggest that people are religious simply to obtain the material benefits of charity (or to altruistically serve others through religion), but it suggests that this is one factor that is associated with religious belief. The authors indicate that greater welfare spending may produce a smaller but more theoretically focused church. The decline in Western European church attendance accompanied the growth of national income and the increased welfare state.

While the considerable religious belief of Americans has been cited to contravene the secularization hypothesis, one can see aspects of religious economics in American religious practices. Churches certainly engage in marketing for followers, including advertising. Mainstream religions in the nation have declined, and some growing religions have offered a more "user friendly" approach to church attendance. Church facilities have also evolved. Some churches have Starbucks to provide attendees with coffee, and contemporary music is increasingly introduced into services. Congregations have adapted with shorter services and alternative services more convenient to members. Some have big screen televisions and show video clips. Such actions reduce the cost of belief and might therefore be expected to stimulate demand. Moreover, the marketing of religion may not be a great success. A study found that Americans gave as much to the Church in the 1980s as they had in decades before, but Bruce (2002) noted that they spent much more on other items, and the percentage given to religion had declined materially.

Religions plainly engage in competition for followers, most obviously evidenced by proselytization. This requires strategic business judgment, just as in any other competitive enterprise (Miller 2002). Although religions to some degree sell the original, they innovate to stay vibrant. Televangelism is religion promoting itself in the market. Religions promote brands, just like any other enterprise. A majority of the clergy recognize the importance of marketing (McDaniel 1989).

In rational choice religious economics, there are producers (such as churches) that strive to maximize their members or resources, or some other determinant of their success. They attain their goals by attracting religious consumers. The reasons why a person might choose to consume a religion are manifold, ranging from eternal life to a comforting community in which to raise a family, among many others. It is this theory that argues that religious pluralism, in a competitive market, encourages greater belief, as discussed in Chapter 1.

Some have criticized the secularization hypothesis, contending that religious belief is not properly considered an economic activity. Bruce (1993) argues that even the testable hypotheses of the economic theory do not provide evidence because the results could be explained via other reasons. He notes that people generally do not diversify their religious portfolio, hedging their bets by belonging to multiple faiths, though this might seem rational. Nor do people typically calculate the cost–benefit of religious belief, though some argue they consider belief more in economic terms than the alternatives (Iannaccone 1995, 82). Arguably, religion should not be considered in pure economic terms.

Others embrace the economic analysis of religion but contend that the secularization hypothesis gets the theory wrong. They take a supply-side approach to the religious market, suggesting that religion will evolve and grow so long as the government permits it to do so. (Iannaccone 1991). It is state involvement in religious affairs that produces secularization. True separation should encourage religiosity.

Many claim that world history has disproved the secularism hypothesis. Religious belief in America appears to be much greater than at the time of the nation's founding (Swatos & Christiano 1999). Religion has persevered as the world has grown richer. Belief has not disappeared and appears quite strong in today's world. Islamic fundamentalism has spread in the Middle East, and Christian fundamentalism has grown in the United States. Christianity "has been growing exponentially in the so-called developing world" (Hirschl 2010, 1). Orthodox churches have surged after the fall of communism.

Modernity may have resurrected the importance of religious belief in some regions. Modernization tends to undermine tradition, which has created a backlash in favor of religion (Fox 2004). The growth of democratic politics empowers believers to press their views as government policies. Perhaps modern communications and other developments help empower religion. Religious influence remains strong in many parts of the world, notwithstanding the secularization hypothesis.

Yet the professed secularization certainly can be seen in Western Europe, where the decline of religion has paralleled its growth. Similar patterns can be seen in Australia, New Zealand, Japan, and

Canada, among other nations (Norris & Inglehart 2004). However, "[n]ew religious groups are emerging far more quickly than secularization theorists would predict," and established faiths "continually demonstrate the ability to win converts in many parts of the world" (Gill 2001, 117–118).

Lambert (1999) takes a moderate view, consistent with the supply-side hypothesis. He suggests that wealth and secularization is a fact, but that religions can adapt to this by offering new services and presenting themselves differently. He theorizes that the circumstances make world affirming approaches and self-spirituality more important than in traditional religion. Pluralism enables all these groups to grow and adapt to modern needs and desires.

Cross-country research has found relatively little relationship between national income and religiosity, after controlling for other relevant factors, such as education and urbanization. However, this research suggests that greater income may affect the type of religion provided, if not the amount. Barro & McCleary (2003a) found that greater religious belief in heaven and hell was associated with greater economic growth, while greater monthly church attendance was associated with weaker economic growth. While their analysis suggested that the religious variables were affecting growth (rather than vice versa), they also found that religiosity responded to economic variables. The effect on belief need not be identical to effects on attendance. Their subsequent research (Barro & McCleary 2006) found a negative association between per capita GDP and religiosity, consistent with the claims of secularization.

Secularization theories have focused on the extent of religious belief in a society, rather than on the degree of religious freedom the society allows. If secularization were true, one might expect it to also produce changes in the religious freedom granted to the populace. A society in which religion is less important might be expected to have a lesser incentive to oppress religion. The repression of religion commonly found in Islamic nations would seem unlikely if the people did not care so much about religious belief. Religion, like any activity seen as relatively unimportant, would be tolerated. This would be consistent with findings that secularization is associated not just with individual beliefs but also with weakened religious hierarchies

(Chaves 1994). If so, one would expect greater wealth to be associated with greater religious freedom.

The directionality of secularization on religious freedom is not so obvious, however. If religion is less significant, it may become easier for the state to repress. When religious belief conflicts with some other social value (perhaps gender rights), the lessened importance of religious belief makes it less likely to prevail, at least in a democracy. Consequently, such secularized societies would be more likely to restrict religion, because religion would be less able to fight back against attempts to regulate its practices.

Yet another possibility is that increased economic growth, and some form of secularization, could reshape religion, rather than increasing or reducing it. To the extent that some of the value of religious belief comes from community friendships and social support, individuals may substitute away from it to find other secular activities that offer this. Religion uniquely provides other things, though, including other worldly rewards that do not have readily available secular substitutes. The so-called secularization process could therefore have a negative feedback on religious intensity, in which religion focuses more on the theological goods and less on the social ones. This in turn could make some religious groups more intense and possibly more interested in limiting other religious groups. The lessened religious belief by others of the society could magnify the intensity of the believers' efforts. Ultimately, the effect of economic development on religious freedom is theoretically indeterminate.

In general, greater wealth is associated with greater individual freedom. Richer nations, such as those of Western Europe, typically have more individual freedom than poorer ones, such as those in Africa. This association does not mean that wealth produces greater freedom, though. The causation may run the opposite direction; greater freedom produces greater wealth. Research suggests that political liberties tend to produce economic freedom, which in turn causes greater economic growth (Dawson 2003). One might expect to find a positive association here because freedom of religion caused greater economic growth. This was the hypothesis of Poe, Tate, and Keith (1999), who suggested that greater material scarcity might be expected to increase the need for repression.

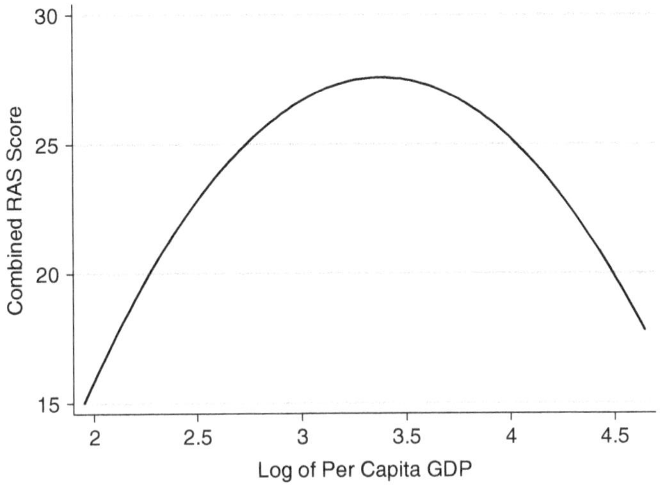

Figure 4.5 Per Capita GDP and Religious Freedom

The data enable some test of the effect of economic wealth on freedom of religion. Just as democracy and Islamic populations can be compared with scales for religious freedom, so may wealth. I simply compare the national level of per capita GDP with the national RAS scores for religious freedom.

Figure 4.5 shows the association between the log of the nation's per capita GDP and the overall religious freedom score.

Intriguingly, for much of the scale, greater per capita GDP is associated with more religious repression, but at a certain level of wealth, the direction reverses, and greater per capita GDP is associated with greater religious freedom. The highest levels of religious freedom, on this scale, are found among the very poorest and the very richest nations, with more religious repression among other nations. Perhaps this shows a secularization effect at higher levels of national GDP, though the high level of freedom among the poorest nations is intriguing. Perhaps this is a sort of reverse secularization – these countries are too poor to worry about controlling religion; they must focus on material things. Of course, it is also possible that some other variables explain the pattern seen on the effect of per capita GDP.

Combined Analysis

These preliminary results suggest that certain societal factors are associated with greater or lesser religious freedom in the nations of the world. Democracy appears to promote religious freedom. The people have grown to the point where they believe all faiths are worthy of respect, even those not their own. In today's world, a greater Islamic population appears to lead to a tendency to restrict religious freedom. The effects of the rule of law and national wealth are not so clear, though, on a theoretical level.

Consider the surprising findings on per capita GDP. Perhaps Islamic population drives restriction on religious freedom and perhaps the poorest nations are not Islamic. The apparent protection associated with poverty may simply be a reflection of the fact that they have little Islamic population. Many of the poorest nations of the world are in sub-Saharan Africa. These nations also tend to be protective of religious freedom. This may be *because* they are poor or it may simply be happenstance. The association may be spurious.

The same is true of apparently positive findings. Democracy is highly associated with a stronger rule of law and with higher per capita GDP. At high levels, all three variables are associated with higher measures of religious freedom. Because the three are found in common, though, the effect may be attributable to just one of the factors, with the others tagging along.

There are basic statistical techniques, such as multiple regression, which can analyze the effect of one factor in light of the effect of other factors. Because my measure is a count variable of laws, the poisson regression method is proper. The variables in this preliminary study are the percentage of the population that is Muslim, the nation's scores for democracy and rule of law from the World Bank (Kaufman, Kraay, & Mastruzzi 2004), and the log of the nation's per capita GDP.

Table 4.1 reports the results of such a regression of these variables and whether they had a positive or negative effect on the RAS overall measure of religious freedom and its measure for minority oppression. When the association is a statistically significant one (at the 0.10 level), the direction of the effect is bolded.

Table 4.1 *Multiple Regression of Social Factors and RAS Religious Freedom*

	Overall Religious Freedom	Minority Oppression
Islamic Population	Negative	Negative
Democracy	Positive	Positive
Rule of Law	Negative	Negative
Per Capita GDP	Negative	Negative

All of the results are statistically significant, and the results for democracy have an unusually high level of statistical significance. Higher Islamic population is associated with less religious freedom. Intriguingly, nations with a stronger rule of law and a higher per capita GDP also have less religious freedom.

The findings to be drawn from this are not entirely clear. Figure 4.4 showed that the rule of law appeared to be strongly associated with more religious freedom, but the multiple regression showed the opposite effect. This is due to the multiple regression procedure, which controls for other variables. Rule of law is highly correlated with democracy, and the results show that for any given level of democracy, rule of law is negative. The same association may be true for per capita GDP and, as Figure 4.5 suggests, the effect of income on religious freedom may vary by the nation's average income level. The primary conclusion that can be drawn is that democracy promotes religious freedom. The association with democracy was much more significant than that for other variables, both in terms of statistical probability and of substantive significance. The results for the RAS variables for regulation and religious laws are similar, but for these measures the Islamic population numbers and per capita GDP do not have statistical significance for regulation.

To check the preceding results for the RAS religious freedom scores, I conduct the same analysis for two alternative metrics. The multiple regression with these variables is run on the national overall RFF measures and the GRI scale of government regulation of religious freedom, with results reported in Table 4.2.

Table 4.2 *Multiple Regression of Social Factors and Alternative Measures of Religious Freedom*

	RFF	GRI
Islamic Population	Negative	Negative
Democracy	Positive	Positive
Rule of Law	Positive	Negative
Per Capita GDP	Negative	Positive

These results are consistent with the RAS overall scores for democracy, with both finding a statistically significant positive effect. Islamic population is consistently negative, but not statistically significant for the GRI scaling. For rule of law, there is a consistent negative score for GRI but a positive (though not statistically significant score) for RFF. For per capita GDP, the results are opposite. Differences in the results may simply mean that one measurement tool is better than another. But any differences are plausibly explained by the fact that they are measuring somewhat different things. For example, the differences between RFF and GRI could well be explained by the fact that the former scale includes state support of religions, while the latter does not.

The results for SRI are also interesting. On this scale, Islamic population is negative with statistical significance, while democracy and per capita GDP are positive with statistical significance. SRI is a measure of private, nongovernmental restriction of religious freedom. The results are especially intriguing for democracy. The association may suggest that democratic governance restricts private limits on religious freedom. On the other hand, it may be that SRI causes less democracy. If so, the apparent positive effect of democracy may be a spurious one. The positive effect of democracy may simply result from the fact that democracies tend to exist in nations with less social pressure to restrict religious freedom and that this pressure, rather than the democracy itself, explains the religious freedom results associated with democratic governance.

Finally, I consider the association of the societal factors with the Pew scale for religious freedom (Table 4.3).

Table 4.3 *Multiple Regression of Social Factors and Pew Measure*

	GRI
Islamic Population	Negative
Democracy	Positive
Rule of Law	Negative
Per Capita GDP	Negative

All results were statistically significant. These results conform to those for the RAS and other scales. Democracy is strongly positive in producing religious freedom, whereas the other variables are negative.

All the associations just reported do not consider the role of the nation's constitutional legal system (except insofar as it is affected by the variables). Because it is constitutions that typically promise to guarantee religious liberty, they might be expected to have an effect and one that influences the role of the other variables. The following chapters will examine the effect of constitutional provisions and combine them with these effects.

Conclusion

Religious freedom is not purely a matter of law, and various characteristics of a society may influence its protection. The social determinants of religious freedom are in some cases surprising. The association of Islam with higher levels of restricted religious freedom is probably unsurprising to any casual observer of the contemporary world. The positive effect of democracy is a material one, suggesting that fears of majoritarian tyranny may be overblown. Rule of law seems to have negative effects on religious freedom, and the procedural nature of this variable, including police enforcement, suggests that the rule of law may be used to restrict such freedom. The typically negative effects of per capita GDP are intriguing, and the explanation is not an obvious one.

The reports in this chapter are simple univariate analyses, however. As such, they don't consider the role of other factors in the nation. Rule of law, democracy, and per capita GDP tend to be highly correlated. Consequently, the results for one factor in isolation might be simply capturing the effect of another variable with which it is highly correlated. This effect is illustrated by the multiple regression results reported in the tables. Nor are any substantive legal factors considered. This book sets out to test the effect of legal factors on religious freedom. If constitutions do matter, their role must also be considered. The different social factors may operate differently, under different constitutional settings. The effect of the constitutional provisions will be examined closely in Chapter 6.

5 Constitutions and Religious Freedom

The Constitution is venerated by Americans. Kammen (1986) observes that since the nineteenth century, Americans have worshipped the Constitution. For some, the U.S. Constitution is like a secular religion. One would expect such strong feelings of devotion to have some effect. Just as religion affects the behavior of believers, so should a beloved constitution.

The true value of constitutions is uncertain, however. Constitutions are not magical enforcers of their dictates; rather, they depend on the cooperation of those they are adopted to constrain. James Madison referred to rights expressed in the Bill of Rights as mere "parchment barriers" (Madison 1961a, 146). He suggested that experience proved that a bill of rights was ineffective at the time it was most needed. He claimed that history showed repeated violations of parchment barriers at the hands of overbearing majorities.

Learned Hand (1960) declared that Americans rested their hopes for liberty "too much upon constitutions," when rights truly depended on the "hearts of men and women" throughout the society. Judge Frank Easterbrook (1992, 71) claims that the importance of law is overstated and that freedom is not attributable to "constitutional language" but instead to "civic culture." He claims that no evidence indicates that differences in state constitutional language have had any effect on practice. For the federal Constitution, he argues that its language has regressed to the mean, with "precise or sweeping language" being "watered down" and with vague language used as a "receptacle for modern views" (Easterbrook 1992, 78). Corwin (1936) claimed that the constitution was not a cause but a consequence of personal freedom. Among social scientists, there is an "assumption that the law is meaningless," and that any "regime that is willing to murder, torture, or arbitrarily detain its citizens will have little compunction against violating words on a piece of paper" (Apodaca 2004, 292). Constitutionally expressed rights are considered to be "worthless scraps of paper" (Keith 2002, 113).

Despite all the doubts, faith in constitutions remains. The people certainly are believers. Wright (1997, 381) said that "of course" a bill of rights "matters – and it matters immensely." While he accepts the importance of a spirit of liberty, Wright suggests that such a spirit sometimes nods and requires a bill of rights for protection. Constitutions provide clear standards against which a nation can be judged and articulate norms that may have an effect on the conscience of the public or even the rulers (Keith 2002).

Riker (1982) believes that the constitution and its institutions (democratic and judicial) are vital to the preservation of the liberal state, respecting freedoms. But he also concedes that every time he has convinced himself that he had "found an instance in which constitutional forms do make a difference for liberty, my discovery comes apart in my hands" (Riker 1976, 13).

One certainly can observe instances of unenforced bills of rights in the nations of the world. The Stalinist constitution of the U.S.S.R. was generous in extending freedoms to the people but was essentially ignored in practice (Hendley 1996). Epp (1998, 13) claims that among "the many new bills of rights created since 1945, some are shams, and even those that are not are quite flexible in practice."

The constitution is the law, of course, but laws may be unenforced, and legal language must be interpreted and applied to specific controversies. A majority, or whoever is in power, might simply ignore constitutional provisions. While the U.S. Constitution is widely regarded as governing, its principles have been applied very differently over time, with major decisions being reversed by later Supreme Courts. Likewise, in Pakistan, the judiciary under an unchanged constitution shifted from the aggressive protection of religious minorities to the abdication of any such protection (Mahmud 1995). A casual reader of the news is surely aware that there is a gap between constitutional guarantees and national practice.

Even within the United States, the Bill of Rights has not been consistently enforced in any particular way. Easterbrook (1992, 72) observes that there is "enough plasticity in the Bill of Rights – and enough forgetfulness about our constitutional history – that the Constitution has been remade in contemporary image several times." Yet Easterbrook (1992, 79) also declares that "[o]nly a fool would deny that decisions under the Bill of Rights have affected many persons' lives, that some decisions created substantial change, and that our nation's focus on 'rights' (and legalism in general) influences our culture deeply." The effect of such protections is contested. While we should not presume that constitutional rights ensure freedom, neither should we dismiss the possibility. Nations continue to create written constitutions, so they apparently see some functional value to the practice.

A constitution may be simply aspirational, setting out the nation's ideals, with little expectation they would be put into practice (just as the religious may devote themselves to the ideals of their belief system, even as they commonly fall short in practice). Alternatively, a constitution might be adopted for symbolic purposes, to raise a nation's stature or respect in the world community or perhaps to attract foreign capital (Law 2010). The value of rights recognition is highly uncertain. Madison (1789) stated that the inclusion of the Bill of Rights would not be "altogether useless," which is scarcely high praise. The remainder of this chapter considers the theories and evidence on the potential value of specific bill-of-rights protections generally, with a focus on freedom of religion.

It is surely safe to say that a constitution is not a perfect guarantee of rights. Historically, and today, various nations have had paper protections that were not respected in practice. In other cases, such as Australia, human rights are well protected without any rights provisions in a constitution (Ginsburg 2010). But this comparison is too binary. The important issue is whether constitutional guarantees of rights offer some net protection at the margin. Australia, without any bill of rights, may illustrate this. The Australian high court has rejected claims of religious conscientious objectors, permitted government funding of religious schools, and permitted a prohibition on the ability of Aboriginal children from exercising tribal religions (Babie & Rochow 2010). The presence of constitutional bill-of-rights protections might have produced different outcomes in these cases. The following discussion explains why constitutions may matter at the margin.

Why Might Constitutions Matter?

If constitutions are so insignificant, one might wonder why so enormously much time and effort is put into their drafting and enforcement. Nations devote great importance to the drafting of a new constitution or the amending of an existing one. This surely provides some persuasive evidence that they matter somewhat. The degree to which constitutions matter and the way in which they matter, though, are contested.

It is somewhat easier to see how constitutions' structural provisions would matter, though, than those of a bill of rights. Structural provisions are to some degree self-enforcing. A senate can protect its own rights, as may a president. An individual right, by contrast, has no structural protector. An authoritarian may "find it much easier to persecute dissidents than to abolish a rival government institution, such as the legislature, that is likely to possess greater ability to fend for itself than a handful of malcontents" (Law 2010, 383). This is confirmed somewhat in Elkins, Ginsburg, and Melton (2009). They found that constitutional assignments of parliamentary power conformed to actual parliamentary power, while the same did not appear to be the case for rights, using Freedom House measures. The analysis was quite rough though and did not match particular rights with performance.

Hardin (1999) argues that constitutions perform a coordinating function, creating rules for the political game to avoid the inefficient instability of constantly rearguing such rules. In the process, they create an equilibrium with the power of inertia behind it. Because moving such an equilibrium may be costly, it tends to prevail in the absence of any powerful countervailing influence. Constitutions thus create a more stable social order.

Suppose some group sought to overturn the constitutional equilibrium. They would have to consider whether the benefits of their overturn were greater than the costs associated with loss of stability. Inevitably there would be transaction costs associated with the change and risks, including unanticipated consequences, which are common. And they would have to recognize that the loss of stability would make their overturn much more fragile and unstable itself. Even if they reached these conclusions, they would have to convince a majority of actors as well. One might expect that a better strategy would be for the group to work within the structure to achieve as much of their ends as possible, while preserving the basic stability of the system. This effect is enhanced by the fact that the dominant political power has, by definition, assumed power within the system.

Game theory provides support for this thesis. Any governmental arrangement will be a repeated play game over time. As is customary, a measure of cooperation is beneficial for all players of the game. Cooperation, though, commonly depends on building some reputation for trust (Levinson 2011). A willingness to comply with overarching rules, such as those of a constitution, can be valuable to a party's ability to build such a reputation and play the game effectively. Democrats, when in power, would respect the rights of Republicans in order to help avoid the risk of repression when they are out of power. The same rationale might apply to competing religious groups.

The reasons why constitutions might be respected is simply that people recognize they are better off operating under an agreement than with none (Ginsburg 2010). The lack of such an agreement could produce endless conflict, even over relatively minor issues. The text is useful for facilitating coordination around the constitutional equilibrium, almost without regard to the nature of its content.

A strategic party would sacrifice some immediate policy success to achieve greater future success. Samaha (2008, 656) describes as a case when "a penalty for early withdrawal helps the depositor save for a big-ticket item at the end of the year." The self-interested calculation of political actors can produce adherence to constitutional commands (Levinson 2011). Levinson (2011) notes that the American anti-Federalists quickly accepted a constitution they vehemently opposed because they realized that this state of the law was preferable to rebellion and potential anarchy.

There is no guarantee that the equilibrium of a society will be the one set down in a constitution. Some nations have had constitutions of rights that plainly do not reflect their societal equilibria. However, the constitutionalization of principles applies some impetus for this equilibrium in accordance with those principles. A written constitution can help coordinate actors around an equilibrium by enhancing the "focalness" of coordinating agreements (Carey 2000). If a government action is plainly unconstitutional, it will have to defend that action against popular constitutionalists and probably legal actions. Such a defense might fail and, even if it succeeds, will be costly. To the extent that the constitution is popular, governmental action contrary to that constitution would be unpopular. Any government desiring popularity would be less likely to take such action.

If constitutions are a coordinating device, how would one decide on the content of such constitutions? Those who create constitutions operate in varied circumstances, with varied interests and motives. Oftentimes, they would want to create a coordination that encouraged religious freedom. In addition to whatever ideological freedom-loving motives they might have, the recognition of such freedom could help avoid civil strife, a potential future uprising by believers, and could encourage international trade and cooperation with nations of all different religions.

Constitutions, and bills of rights in particular, may be seen as such a form of national precommitment device. This is often described by analogy to Ulysses' decision to lash himself to the mast so that he could hear the song of the Sirens without being bewitched by it (Elster 1979). While this theory is typically applied to institutional arrangements, such as separation of powers and an independent judiciary, it may also apply to bills of rights (Holmes 1995). Precommitment may be used as a device to reduce the effect of temporary majoritarian passions. Precommitment can be used to prevent a society, like Ulysses, from becoming a slave to its passing passions.

The theory is that future utility is improved by an entrenching precommitment, rather than leaving matters to contemporary choice (Ferejohn & Sager 2003). If religious freedom is in society's interest, for reasons such as those discussed in Chapter 1, precommitment may be a wise strategy. Without precommitment, some future ruler (majoritarian or otherwise) might eliminate such freedom and impose a religion on the people, in a momentary burst of passion.

Even if someone would consider that momentary burst of passion a legitimate majoritarian governance device, it will inevitably influence beliefs thereafter. Religious oppression could remain well after it stopped being the majoritarian preference. We are committed to periodic democratic elections. If a burst of partisan passion cancelled elections, the easing of that passion might not immediately bring them back. Government officials may stack the deck for policies with structures that are more durable than the coalition supporting them (De Figueiredo 2002).

The precommitment could prevent this effect. There are no realistic precommitment devices that absolutely ensure the commitment will be followed (even burned bridges may be rebuilt). The value of the device is in adding costs to diverging from the precommitment, making divergence less likely. Thus, marriage is a precommitment that goes beyond cohabitation because divorce implies various legal costs that go beyond simply moving out. A precommitment to constitutional commands provides "economic growth and prosperity, military organization and mobilization, and the accumulation of the massive amounts of knowledge necessary to manage a large society" (Levinson 2011, 710).

One certainly sees this effect in contract law. Both parties may benefit from trading with one another. Yet they will not do so if they are unsure that they can rely upon the promises of the other party. By entering a binding commitment to fulfill its promises, each party can gain the benefit of the deal. For this to work, of course, there must be a way to make a binding commitment. With contracts, this is essentially served by the court system, which enforces contract terms. Whether the courts can effectively fill this role for a bill of rights is one of the things I am testing.

The broad veneration of America's Constitution provides psychological reinforcement for the strategy of precommitment. It makes it more difficult to ignore a relatively clear constitutional command. Levinson (2011, 704) observes that the "contractarian view of constitutional commitment has been central to Americans' constitutional self-understanding since the Founding." Of course, constitutional terms have changed in meaning over time, but perhaps this change is much slower than it otherwise would be.

No precommitment, constitutional or otherwise, provides a guarantee. In the United States context, Ackerman (1995) suggests that the nation has undergone constitutional moments when the earlier understanding of the commitment was upended and a new order established, without formally amending the Constitution. The New Deal is a primary example of this effect. At the judicial level, prior precedents interpreting the Constitution are sometimes reversed, obviously changing the nature of the constitutional precommitment. The salient fact, though, may be the rarity of such events. Although the constitution is centuries old, its precommitment remains largely unchanged.

Indeed some precommitment in and of itself, regardless of the content of the precommitment, may be a sound strategy. It demonstrates that a government is willing and able to commit to the promises it makes. This may be a necessary pragmatic strategy for the attraction of foreign capital, immigrants, or ordinary citizens, who will take action on a belief that the government will fulfill its promises. One might expect such precommitment to be especially valuable to authoritarians, who otherwise could be prone to sudden, arbitrary actions. Assuring outsiders that such arbitrary actions will not be taken could better induce their cooperation with the national government. Constitutional rights may serve as valuable signals to the international community that a government is willing to be bound by law (Farber 2002). This may attract their resources.

The Ulysses analogy and precommitment theory has been criticized by Waldron (2005) and others on theoretical grounds, but it may also be challenged pragmatically. Whether a bill of rights is such a true precommitment is uncertain. One classic precommitment device is burning the bridges one crosses, but it is unclear that a constitution can have such a powerful effect in practice. It is unclear whether and to what degree constitutions are truly a binding precommitment device. However, it should not simply be assumed that they are not. A constitution could serve as a sort of external commitment that makes it more likely to be fulfilled (Ferejohn & Sager 2003).

While constitutions may be seen as external commitments, this is not entirely true. A constitution is mere parchment that may be ignored. Arguably only the internal commitment of the governing entity applies to the constitution (Ferejohn & Sager 2003). Structures may be created, though, to make internal disregard of the precommitment harder. Constitutions include prerequisites to government actions and checks on those government actions. These enforcing mechanisms might include democratic governance or judicial review, as discussed now.

James Madison on the Bill of Rights

At the time of the original constitutional convention, James Madison disapproved of adding a bill of rights to the text. He had various arguments, such as the adequacy of government limits imposed by constitutionally enumerated powers and the fear that listing some particular rights could effectively demean others. He also believed that national democratic governance could protect rights. Madison was not entirely sanguine about relying on democracy, though. He also wrote that while a "dependence on the people is, no doubt, the primary control on the government; but experience has taught mankind the necessity of auxiliary precautions" (Madison 1961a, 160). However, he also feared that democracy would trample any constitutional protections written into a bill of rights.

Madison eventually reversed his position and actually fathered the American Bill of Rights on the belief that constitutional expressions of individual rights could have a positive effect by educating and influencing popular opinion to protect rights (Leibiger 1993). Madison contended that the constitutional declaration of rights could "acquire by degrees the character of fundamental maxims of free government, and as they become incorporated with the national sentiment, counteract the impulses of interest and passion" (Finkelman 1990, 332). Bills of rights would be "admonitions to the people, teaching them to subdue dangerous impulses of passion and interest" (Sheehan 2005, 46). They could serve as a standard for testing the validity of government actions.

In today's world, the American Bill of Rights is often seen as antidemocratic, but Madison believed that it operated in tandem with democracy and public opinion to protect rights. He thought the Bill of Rights could strengthen majoritarian governance by limiting the behavior of government officials (Levinson 2011). This appeared to be Madison's primary theory about the value of a bill of rights. Constitutions are commonly seen as restrictions on democratic governance, but Madison seems to have seen the Constitution as an inspiration to such governance.

Madison also saw some promise in judicial enforcement of a bill of rights. He understood that judicial review might enforce the rights against majoritarian encroachments. In Madison's speech to the first U.S. Congress, he suggested that judges "will consider themselves in a peculiar manner the guardians of those rights; they will be an impenetrable bulwark against every assumption of power in the legislative or executive; they will be naturally led to resist every encroachment upon rights expressly stipulated for in the declaration of rights" (Leibiger 1993, 463). He elsewhere suggested that a bill of rights would "naturally" lead courts to "resist every encroachment on rights" by the other branches of government (Bodenhamer 2012, 61). Thomas Jefferson likewise viewed the courts as defenders of the Bill of Rights (Goldwin 1997). Although Alexander Hamilton was perhaps the foremost proponent of judicial protection of individual rights, it was a general theme among the founders (Smith 2009).

Madison's two theories of possible significance of a constitutional bill of rights remain the leading theories. American history gives reason for some skepticism over both theories. The Bill of Rights of this country has not changed over time. Democratic processes have periodically produced various and serious infringements on individual liberty, such as the Alien and Sedition Acts at the very beginning of our republic, but the judiciary historically did little to overturn these actions. In Madison's day, the courts did little to protect individual rights.

In more recent years, both the democracy and the judiciary have shown distinctly more concern for protecting individual rights. As the law remained the same, this suggests a social transformation. But perhaps this social transformation was inspired by the Bill of Rights, or empowered by the Bill of Rights. There is some indication that public opinion adjusts to align with the constitutional opinions of the Supreme Court (Persily 2008), which suggests that the second judicial enforcement theory provides a basis for the former democratic enforcement theory. Sometimes called the legitimation theory, it suggests that the people trust the courts' decisions. The remainder of this chapter will analyze the theory underlying the potentially protective effect of a bill of rights.

Democracy and the Bill of Rights

Madison's first theory was that the Bill of Rights would establish civil liberties as part of American popular culture, defended by the people themselves. The preceding chapter demonstrated that democracy was very protective of women's rights, but this association was not linked to constitutional protections. The theory is that a bill of rights would "powerfully shape popular culture" to create a culture of liberty (Epp 1998, 13). It might "serve as a socializing tool that conditions the expectations of the public, promoting the development of a rights consciousness among the mass public" (Keith 2010, 370). The Bill of Rights thus would promote democratic protections of individual rights. In general, though, the definition and protection of rights is largely assigned to the judicial branch.

Indeed, constitutionalization is said to take matters out of the hands of the public. It empowers an unelected judiciary to override the actions of the elected branches. The controversial actions of the courts are often those invalidating democratically adopted laws because they contravene the Constitution.

Some legal academics in recent years have been strongly pushing a concept of "popular constitutionalism" that calls upon the public to play a greater role in interpreting and enforcing the constitution. The theory has arguably taken the academy by storm in recent years. Kramer (2004) contends that judicial review should be abandoned in favor of the people's interpretation. Although the mechanics of its operation are a little obscure, he argues that the people should be able to overturn a Supreme Court decision. He trusts the people to make decisions, not a judiciary representing the elites. Kramer laments how the people have supinely accepted the determinations of the Court on constitutionality.

Kramer's popular constitutionalism has seen considerable criticism. The precise means of its operationalization is unclear. Exactly who speaks for the people, who are so diverse they are unlikely to speak with a single voice? In various ways, courts are better suited to resolve constitutional disputes than are the people (Sager 2005). The extraordinary popular ignorance about the Constitution noted earlier cannot be ascribed to judicial supremacy but simply other priorities of individuals. In many cases, one would imagine popular constitutionalism to be equivalent to no constitutionalism because the people are simply unaware of the constitutional violation (such as by a police officer in an individual prosecution). The system would simply produce general deference to whatever a government official chooses to do.

In the context of freedom of religion, it seems clear that popular constitutionalism would have permitted compulsory school prayer, given the polling and the backlash against the Court's decision. Powe (2005) suggests that Kramer's popular constitutionalism is blinkered, so that he only sees it when he agrees with the cause. One suspects he would not have written this book in the Warren Court era. In the context of religious freedom, challenged actions are taken by the elected branches. Assuming that those branches are roughly reflective of the popular will, then popular constitutionalism would provide no constitutional protection over and above ordinary democratic procedures. While Kramer is correct that the elected branches often protect liberties, the combination of the elected branches and the courts may protect relatively more liberties.

Tushnet (1999) makes a similar argument to that of Kramer and seeks to answer the latter argument. Tushnet questions whether judges are any better than the people at constitutional interpretation and prefers more democratic interpretation. Moreover, he suggests that the Court's judicial supremacy in America affirmatively undermines democratic constitutional interpretation. The judiciary looking over the shoulder of Congress creates a "judicial overhang" in which the representatives do not make their own assessments of constitutionality but defer to whatever the courts say. Congressional concern for the Constitution may rank "relatively low in most politicians' calculations today" precisely because of judicial review (Tushnet 1999, 66). There is some anecdotal support for this effect; Senator Specter once backed restrictions on habeas corpus he considered unconstitutional on the ground that the court would "clean it up" (Kleinerman 2009). In nations where parliament has authority to decide rights questions, the evidence suggests that they take the responsibility seriously (Hiebert 2005).

Tushnet suggests that the judicial desire to exercise power will cause it to unduly limit congressional action. In my current context, religious freedom, this presumably would yield a judiciary that offered more freedom, limiting congressional restrictions (though the necessity of those restrictions is not considered). Tushnet thinks that the American people can provide sufficient protection of civil liberties on their own, without judicial enforcement. He concedes the people may occasionally get it wrong (e.g., flag-burning prohibitions) but only for infrequent, insignificant cases. The truth of this may be questioned, though.

The argument for the judicial overhang may be a bit naïve. There is no obvious incentive for members of Congress to put great weight on the constitutionality of their actions regardless of judicial review. Politicians certainly have their ideological commitments. Moreover, they plainly put great weight on gaining reelection. Whittington (2009, 228) suggests that political actors "are too readily seduced into straying from the straight constitutional path when it serves their immediate electoral or policy needs." Perhaps some legislators are sufficiently noble to put the Constitution above their self-interest, but to rely on a majority to be so noble seems something of a leap of faith.

Note that this theory also suggests that majorities are not so committed to the freedoms in and of themselves. If the elected branches cared about the rights as policy matters, they would be indifferent to the constitutional decisions but would advance the rights, simply as policy matters. Legislatures have frequently acted to promote rights, regardless of the Constitution. The civil rights legislation of the 1960s was passed, not because the Constitution compelled it, but because the legislature wished it. Legislatures recognized individual rights to firearms ownership well before the Court did. Tushnet's theory, though, suggests that one key is a democratic commitment to the Constitution itself, not the content of the rights contained therein. This arguably echoes Madison's position that the Constitution would be a source of democratic respect for individual rights.

New Zealand is often held out as an example of how parliamentary supremacy on rights questions is the best model, without overriding judicial review. Yet the New Zealand experience may not be so positive as often claimed. The lack of judicial review has arguably produced less protection of criminal rights, at least in "hard cases" (Kelly 2011). Waldron (2005), a great defender of parliamentary supremacy, has attacked the New Zealand legislature's attention to rights, absent judicial review.

The degree to which the Constitution does inspire the populace per Madison, though, is quite uncertain, and the theory may be a naïve one. Legislators, and people more generally, may often act in their self-interest without respect to the constitutional rights of others. There is evidence to this effect from polling conducted over the years in the United States.

The classic analysis is McClosky & Brill (1983), who assessed American popular opinion on numerous questions of civil liberties. They found that overwhelming majorities of the population favored freedom of worship. The results on the right of atheists to make fun of God were more mixed. Forty-eight percent of the mass public, a plurality, recognized that this right was legally protected, but only 26 percent, a distinct minority, thought that it should be legally protected. This does not suggest that the Bill of Rights inspires democratic tolerance, as a considerable percentage don't recognize that the Bill of Rights requires it and, of those who do, a substantial number disagree with the Bill of Rights protection. McClosky and Brill also found that elites tended to be much more tolerant.

More recent polling of Americans does not suggest that the Bill of Rights has an overpowering effect on beliefs of citizens. Their understanding of the Bill of Rights may be challenged. A 1991 poll conducted by the American Bar Association found that only 33 percent of Americans knew that the Bill of Rights was found in the first ten amendments to the Constitution. Twenty-two percent thought it was an act passed by Congress, and 10 percent said they did not know. A majority of Americans thought it was a measure to insure equality for citizens, while only a small minority knew it was to prevent abuses by the federal government.

The ABA poll was not an outlier. A 2006 poll conducted by the McCormick Tribune Freedom Museum found that only about 25 percent of Americans could name more than one of the fundamental freedoms recognized by the First Amendment; a higher percentage thought that it gave women the right to vote. A First Amendment Center poll in 2002 found that only about 20 percent of Americans knew that freedom of religion was a right guaranteed by the First Amendment. A 2011 poll of registered voters in Illinois found that 30 percent could not name any of the rights guaranteed by the First Amendment, and 40 percent could name only one of the rights. Only 20 percent knew the content of the Tenth Amendment, and 45 percent thought a right to education was part of the First Amendment. A March 2011 *Newsweek* poll found that 44 percent of Americans were unable to define the Bill of Rights. Devins (2007, 1340) claims: "How much does the public know about the Constitution? Next to nothing." Kammen (1986) describes popular ignorance of the Constitution and how it has existed for hundreds of years.

In September 2003, Gallup conducted a poll on various constitutional religious issues. In the poll, 78 percent of Americans favored nondenominational prayer at public school ceremonies; 64 percent of the people favored providing federal funds for social programs run by Christian organizations. But only 41 percent of those polled favored providing federal funds for social programs run by Islamic organizations.

Farnsworth (2007) questions whether the people truly have constitutional views, claiming that they don't care much about politics, much less constitutional reasoning. When individuals do think about politics, they care about their policy preferences, not the content of the Constitution. This should be clear to any informed person listening to discourse on the Constitution on television news channels. The notion of popular constitutionalism seems terribly naïve and not truly constitutional. While popular constitutionalism could have some appeal on some issues, it is a prescription for the denial of individual rights by majorities. Tushnet (1999) largely concedes this point, arguing that the notion of rights in the Constitution is overly individualistic in approach.

If Americans are so unaware of the Bill of Rights, it is difficult to maintain that it inspires democratic protection of rights. Perhaps it has seeped into the collective unconscious's understanding. In the First Amendment Center Poll, 83 percent said it was essential that government provide the right to practice the religion of one's choice, 69 percent believed it was essential to protect the right to practice no religion, and only a small fraction of the populace thought it was not important. But the same poll found that Americans were not fully supportive of the First Amendment. Indeed, 47 percent of Americans said that the First Amendment went "too far" in the rights that it guarantees. The results suggest a strong democratic preference for religious and other freedoms but do not suggest that the preference is the direct product of the Bill of Rights. Maybe the Bill of Rights plays a role at the subconscious level, but there is not supportive evidence.

Nor is it clear that greater education or awareness of Bill of Rights protections would enhance respect for individual rights. Green et al. (2011) conducted an experiment using high school students with different curriculums, one designed (with the help of the Bill of Rights Institute) to promote awareness of constitutional rights. Students who had the special curriculum effectively increased their knowledge about the contents of the Bill of Rights and civil liberties. However, these more knowledgeable students showed no enhanced support for the protection of civil liberties, even though the experiment had ample power to detect even small effects.

Yet another difficulty with popular constitutionalism is democratic preference itself. It is not at all clear that the populace wants the power to interpret the Constitution. The people seem quite happy with judicial supremacy. The judiciary traditionally polls better than the other branches of government, who presumably would be the implementers of popular constitutionalism (Friedman 2009). Perhaps the people know their limitations and choose to delegate interpretive authority. In this event, judicial supremacy *would be* popular constitutionalism.

But even if one rejects the ultimate notion of popular constitutionalism, taking authority from the judiciary, Madison's theory could have weight. The presence of constitutional rights could inspire the people and make it less likely they would choose to violate such rights. Our general worshipfulness toward the Constitution makes this plausible, though popular ignorance about the Constitution makes the claim of uncertain validity.

Judicial Enforcement

If the Bill of Rights does not inspire popular defense of its rights, such as freedom of religion, perhaps the courts may be counted on to ensure such protection. Darrow and Alston (1999, 488) note that a judiciary may be seen as critical for ensuring that paper rights are enforced. Buchanan (1988) sees the judiciary as a neutral third party that can hold the elected branches to constitutional commitments. The very existence of a bill of rights may transfer power to the judiciary (Beatty 2001), and a judiciary interested in power would therefore be interested in furthering the Bill of Rights enforcement. Judicialization and constitutionalization are often considered symbiotic, with constitutions providing for the expansion of judicial power (Law 2010).

Nations have increasingly adopted constitutions, and those constitutions have included an ever increasing number of personal rights (Law 2010). This has produced a "judicialization" of politics (Hirschl 2006). The constitution and rights in particular give the courts an entrée into the nation's resolution of certain important political issues. This in turn gives political interest groups an incentive to mobilize legally, to attempt to capture in court what they may have lost in the legislature, and this effect further empowers the judiciary. Especially when democratically elected politicians are unable to agree or unwilling to take a stand, the field is left to the judiciary. Rights constitutionalization gives the judiciary the necessary hook to take a more aggressive role in national policy making. Dotan's (2005) comparative study concluded that bills of rights have spillover effects, increasing the use of litigation to create social reforms. In the Scandinavian countries, judges have been central to ensuring the constitutionality of laws (Husa 2000).

Judicial protection of constitutional rights is dependent upon much more than the rights themselves. Judges hear only the cases brought before them; they do not seek out rights violations. If a party lacks the knowledge or resources to pursue an action, it goes unremedied. In addition, judicial procedures may interfere with the vindication of rights.

One requirement of American law is standing, which holds that only individuals injured by a violation may sue. When plaintiffs objected to the national day of prayer as unconstitutional, the Seventh Circuit dismissed the case, without addressing constitutionality, because it found that the plaintiffs had suffered no legal injury from the practice (*Freedom from Religion Foundation, Inc. v. Obama* 2011). Standing is particularly a problem with the establishment clause, and the Court has carved out a very narrow exception allowing taxpayers the ability to challenge congressional actions. For many violations of religious freedom, this is not a problem. Rosenberg (1991, 12) notes that doctrines like standing and other technical doctrines undermine judicial enforcement and that "the legal process tends to dissipate significant social reform by making appropriate remedies unlikely."

While procedures may occasionally interfere with judicial enforcement of constitutional rights, the judiciary faces two more foundational questions. The first is whether courts can be counted on to rule in favor of constitutional rights according to law. The second is whether, even if they do so, those decisions will be implemented in practice.

Will Courts Uphold Constitutional Rights?

The defense of the judiciary in enforcement of the Bill of Rights is that it will uphold the principles of freedom expressed, even when popular majorities and the elected branches seek to infringe upon them. In this sense, the judiciary may be said to be countermajoritarian. This countermajoritarianism is often a basis for criticizing the judiciary as an unelected and antidemocratic elite, governing without legitimacy. Critics suggest that the lack of democratic legitimacy means that the courts inappropriately assume policy-making authority in areas such as abortion rights.

But this purported countermajoritarianism is also the basis for claims that the courts will protect the Bill of Rights against popular passions. We are not merely a democracy, or there would be no need to constitutionalize individual rights. The rights were to protect against infringements on freedom by the tyranny of the majority. Surely democracy will not counter majoritarian tyranny.

The reliability of judicial countermajoritarianism as a protection for individual rights, though, is quite uncertain. There is no reason, besides perhaps a sense of duty, why a judge would enforce the Bill of Rights. Some question whether such duty is sufficiently motivating. There is little evidence that judges are uniquely qualified or good at supporting the Constitution (Cross 2000).

In the imaginary optimum, a principled court would stand up for basic freedoms, above all political considerations. This vision may be naïve in two respects, however. First, some argue that the judges do not truly interpret and apply the law as written, but instead read their own political preferences into policy through their decisions. If so, the judges would only advance the Bill of Rights when it aligned with their ideology and could undermine the Bill of Rights when it did not. Second, some question whether the judiciary is truly countermajoritarian. Judges are people, of course, and may be moved by the same popular passions as the majority. Moreover, the elected branches have some authority over the courts, ranging from impeachment to providing them funds, and they could therefore undermine the independent judgment of the judiciary.

The first criticism, that judges are essentially ideologues and not law interpreters, is the "attitudinal" theory of judicial decision making, associated with Segal & Spaeth (1993). Americans commonly complain of willful political decisions by the justices of the Supreme Court, and the authors provided empirical documentation. In the vast majority of cases, the votes of the justices fell along predictable ideological lines. Any observer of the Court knows that Justice Douglas reliably voted for the more liberal result in cases he heard, while Justice Thomas commonly votes for the conservative result.

This view was propounded long ago by the legal realists. Since that time, a great deal of empirical analysis conducted by political scientists is supportive of this attitudinal view of judicial decision making. Judges, especially the justices of the Supreme Court, commonly render decisions predictably and in accord with ideological stereotypes. Some political scientists have maintained that judicial opinions are entirely ideological and in no way based on the law. The justices first identify their preferred conclusion and then use legal materials to justify it, in this view. In American history, liberal justices have been more vigorous in striking down government actions under both the free exercise clause and the establishment clause of the Constitution.

For judicial enforcement of a constitution to affirmatively advance the rights expressed in the constitution, some legal aspect of the constitution must drive judicial opinions. If judges are deciding according to their ideology, and not the terms of a constitution, it is quite difficult to maintain that the constitution is being enforced by the judges. The attitudinal model is therefore a profound challenge to the theory that constitutions matter. Hiebert (2005, 237) suggests that the defenders of judicial rights enforcement "have never fully overcome the challenges" posed by legal realism.

Attitudinalism has focused on judges making ideological decisions, which will have different approaches to matters of religious freedom. It is also possible that judges will have their decisions affected by their personal religious beliefs. Just as they may be inclined to vote their ideology, judges might be more likely to vote in support of their personal religion, as opposed to other faiths. If a national judiciary were representatives of a dominant religion, they might show less respect for the freedom of minority religions.

Songer and Tabrizi (1999) found that the religious affiliation of judges made a difference in their votes. Evangelical Christians were more conservative on cases involving issues such as the death penalty and obscenity. Cross (2007) found that judges' religions showed very little effect on votes, independent of ideology, at the circuit court level. Neither of these studies focused on religious freedom cases, however.

Sorauf (1976) examined sixty seven religious freedom cases decided between 1951 and 1971. He found that the judges' religion seemed to be strongly associated with outcomes. Yarnold (2000) examined a much broader sample of cases involving religious liberty between 1970 and 1990. She found some differences, but they were not statistically significant, and the fact that the plaintiff was the same religion as the judge showed no effect. Sisk (2004) found that religion showed a powerful effect in these cases. Jewish judges and those from nonmainstream Christian denominations were significantly more likely to support plaintiffs in free exercise cases, and Jewish judges were especially pro-plaintiff in establishment clause cases. Other evidence suggests that judicial preferences in religious freedom cases varies over time (Fox & Tabory 2008).

There is considerable evidence that ideological attitudinalism is an important determinant of judicial decisions, at least at the Supreme Court level. There is some evidence that a judge's religious background influences his or her position on freedom of religion cases. The judiciary's protection of constitutional rights may thus vary, depending on the composition of the deciding court.

However, the case for the attitudinal model of judicial decision making is not so strong as often portrayed. If judges were truly attitudinal, one would observe results in a random sample, but the cases decided by the Supreme Court are far from a random selection of disputes. The apparent attitudinal decision making is thus entirely consistent with legal decision making. The Court may shun cases that are relatively clearly governed by law and accept for review only those that are most legally indeterminate. The law could therefore drive the content of decisions, even when they appeared attitudinal.

In addition, the voting at even the Supreme Court level is not so political. A substantial number of Court opinions are unanimous, notwithstanding the very divergent attitudinal opinions of the justices. The analysis of Segal and Spaeth (1993) leaves a large number of decisions of individual justices unexplained. Edelman, Klein, and Lindquist (2008) found that a large number of the justices' votes failed to fall along ideological lines, as expected. A majority of cases saw some differentiation contrary to typical ideological voting. Conservative justices sometimes render liberal opinions, and vice versa. While this fact does not entirely refute the attitudinalism hypothesis, it demonstrates that the voting of the justices is more complex than simply fulfilling their ideological preferences. Another study found that the justices were influenced by facts about the courts that they were reviewing (Lindquist & Klein 2006). When legal standards are included as a variable, they may have much greater power than the attitudinal model (Cross & Nelson 2001).

Kritzer and Richards (2005) have adopted a more refined approach to studying Supreme Court opinions. Their analysis considered "jurisprudential regimes," legal standards created by one opinion exercising control over the outcomes of subsequent cases. They have found that such regimes are powerful determinants of the votes of justices. This study is important in that it recognizes the case selection effect. Once the judiciary has established a legal rule, they simply don't take additional cases on that question and accept cases that allow it to define the boundaries of that rule. Other research has found that strong precedents have an effect on the justices' decisions (Hansford & Spriggs 2006). While the ideological preferences of the justices have an effect, the law remains a powerful determinant of Supreme Court opinions.

Moreover, even pure attitudinalism does not defeat the enforcement of religious freedom. Sometimes, the Court's ideologies will align with the protection of such freedoms. When this occurs, the Court will enforce the rights, even contrary to majoritarian preferences. These decisions will set precedents with which the Court will have to grapple even when preferences are contrary and increase freedom at least to some degree.

In addition, the studies of attitudinalism have focused unduly on the Supreme Court. While that court makes the final rules, it doesn't make so many of them. Attitudinalism at the Supreme Court level is much stronger than in lower courts. The Supreme Court is the highest court, whose decisions should be followed, but it also has control over the cases that it hears and resolves very few controversies. American law is largely the product of circuit court decisions (Cross 2007), because their decisions are final in the overwhelming majority of cases.

Dotan (2005) considered the meaning of a bill of rights in Israel and Canada. He found that the precise content of the right was not dispositive, as judicial ideology was more important. He writes that "[b]ills of rights do not oblige courts to do anything" but that they do "empower courts to do the things they want to do" (Dotan 2005, 340). However, this latter effect is significant, and the content of rights does have an important influence on judicial practices.

It is asserted that if "objectively constrained constitutional interpretation exists, we have yet to see it, which cases substantial doubt on whether we are ever likely to see it" (Peretti 1999, 51). The unattainability of pure objectivity, though, does not eliminate the possibility of some benefit. The ideological nature of judicial decision making does not necessarily undermine judicial constitutional rights protection. It implies that at some times, with some ideologies, the courts may not protect rights. At other times, though, when a different ideology prevails at the Court, it may aggressively protect individual rights.

Attitudinal voting by Supreme Court justices need not limit protections of the Bill of Rights; it may strengthen them. The liberal justices of the Warren Court, voting attitudinally, produced many of the strongest decisions supporting freedom of religion in America. Attitudinal decision making could well further religious freedom. Attitudinal voting does suggest that constitutional protections are not an automatic guarantee. A court that is ideologically disinterested in religious freedom might do little to enforce the constitutional protection. But even with attitudinal voting, the Supreme Court may provide some, if not entirely consistent, protection for individual freedoms. Consequently, ideological voting does not undermine the possibility that judicial review will enhance the protection of religious freedom.

Another criticism is that judges, when not ideological, are simply too deferential to the other branches of government or popular opinion and hence will fail to rule based on express constitutional rights. Dahl (1957) famously proclaimed that the Court was never long out of line with majority opinion, suggesting that its major purpose was to legitimize the dominant national political alliance. O'Brien (1996, 364) observes that a "number of political scientists theorize and draw on various kinds of data to support the hypothesis that the Court usually registers public opinion and legitimates policies of the prevailing national alliance, rather than playing the role of a countermajoritarian institution over the long haul." Research suggests that "Supreme Court decisions, historically, have seldom strayed far from what was politically acceptable" (Rosenberg 1991, 13). Some research (Mishler & Sheehan 1993) suggests that the Court's decisions followed the public mood, albeit with some time lag (perhaps due to attitudinal decision making).

The Court may not be countermajoritarian for various reasons. For one, the justices are citizens, subject to the same experiences and media as other citizens, and they might be expected to react similarly. They are appointed by members of the elected political branches. Justices may care about how they are perceived by the public (Baum 2006). This may be pragmatic in part. Judges may well be aware that their powers of judicial review are dependent on maintaining the respect of the public. Several justices "have been quite candid in acknowledging the Court's dependence on popular support" (Friedman 2009, 371). Rosen (2006) contends that the judiciary is our "most democratic branch" as it commonly defers to public opinion on major issues.

Friedman's recent magisterial work argues that the Supreme Court is consistently majoritarian in its orientation. He engages in a sweeping history of judicial decisions and finds that "Supreme Court decisions tend to converge with the considered judgment of the American people" (Friedman 2009, 14). When *Lochner* era justices fell out of step with popular opinion, their antiregulatory rulings did not last. Friedman argues that the so-called judicial activism of the Warren Court was actually aligned with public opinion in many instances. He concedes that the school prayer opinion was an unpopular one but suggests that the justices may simply have misread public opinion of the time. He concedes that First Amendment matters are where the justices are most likely to depart from popular opinion.

Friedman's book soon saw criticism. For example, Driver (2010) and others argued that Friedman too often conflated the views of newspapers and journalists as the views of the American people. Finding that opinions correlated with the views of newspaper editors was not the same as finding a correlation with the overall popular will. A number of countermajoritarian opinions of the Warren Court were emphasized. On criminal rights questions, the Court has driven public opinion, rather than vice versa (Driver 2010).

The meaning of the alignment of judges with public opinion is unclear; perhaps it is just that the law itself tends to be aligned with public opinion, and the judges are merely enforcing that law. But it could well be that the judiciary is attentive to public opinion, to protect its place in government. Research also shows that when public support for the Court declines, the public will support congressional moves to restrict judicial authority (Clark 2011).

There are a variety of measures by which the Congress may punish the court for rulings they dislike. The Constitution provides for the power of impeachment of judges. This authority, of course, is very rarely used and never, in recent times, due to mere unpopular opinions. This rarity, though, may simply be a sign of anticipated reaction (Peretti 1999). Perhaps the judiciary is deterred from making the sort of rulings that could produce an impeachment move. Alexander Hamilton suggested that the mere power of impeachment would tend to keep the judiciary in line. When Judge Harold Baer issued an opinion suppressing evidence and vigorously criticizing police practices, impeachment threats arose, and Baer subsequently reconsidered and vacated his opinion. The prospect of impeachment may make the judiciary more majoritarian.

Short of impeachment, Congress may strip jurisdiction from the courts to decide certain categories of cases. The Constitution authorizes this power, and Congress has intermittently used it to prevent judges from rendering decisions in certain categories of cases (Clark 2011). Such "court-curbing" harms the judiciary by taking away its ability to make decisions, and it may also be a threat to its institutional legitimacy. The Court's power fundamentally rests on its popular legitimacy (Levinson 2011). As with impeachment, the mere threat of such jurisdiction stripping action may deter judicial decisions.

In the 1950s, the Court made several decisions respecting the rights of suspected communists. The decisions created a substantial public backlash, given the temper of the time. Congress proposed legislation that included limits on the jurisdiction of the Court in certain cases. The Court responded by retreating and limiting the scope of its earlier decisions, permitting greater government prosecution of subversive activity, which reduced attacks on the Court (Cross & Nelson 2001).

A broad study of court-curbing threats from 1789 to 1959 found that in five of the seven identified episodes, the Court retreated in response to congressional pressure (Nagel 1965). A more recent and rigorous study found that after an increase in court-curbing proposals in Congress, the Court typically responded with decisions showing greater support for the government (Handberg & Hill 1980). Clark (2011) finds a similar effect of court-curbing threats on judicial decisions. While this effect is often overlooked, such proposals "have been a common congressional response to judicial decisions with which it disagrees" (Peretti 1999, 140).

Impeachment and jurisdiction stripping are dramatic events, and the Court is sheltered somewhat by the difficulty of congressional action and the presence of competing priorities for congressional attention. However, a potentially more powerful congressional influence over the courts lies in its budgetary control. Congress can provide or deny resources to the judiciary. Congress is constitutionally prohibited from reducing formal judicial pay levels, but it can decline to increase them, even to keep up with inflation. Congress may also deny resources for support staff, equipment, or courthouse facilities needed by the judges.

Such resources can be important to the judiciary. The chief justice commonly goes before Congress to plead for more money, and other justices commonly have accompanied him. The judiciary generally "worries about federal judges' salaries, their cost of living increases, pensions, travel budgets, sharing courtrooms (as compared to having a courtroom of one's own), building and maintenance, staff and employment policies, and the nature of federal judges' assignments (Resnik 2000). Judges may also seek additional judgeships and other relief from growing caseload pressures. The judiciary has become something like a bureaucratic agency, rather than a co-equal branch, in such budgetary questions (Resnik 2000).

Toma (1996) studied the effect of the budget on the Supreme Court's decisions. She hypothesized that budgetary favors were linked to politically acceptable decisions from the Court, and she found that the greater the ideological distance between a term's decisions and the congressional average of the relevant oversight committees, the less money was appropriated for the Court's budget. She also found that the Court appeared to respond to these signals and modify its decisions accordingly. While the association was a very imperfect one, it did satisfy requirements for statistical significance. For any economist, this budget manipulation should seem an obvious effect. But it is not absolute. Toma (1996, 37) quotes a member of Congress saying that Congress wants "a judiciary that is independent but not too independent." The Court has some space to contravene congressional preferences.

Although I have focused on the most available American experience, the effect is not limited to this country. Rarely does the judiciary of any country possess purse or sword, and it is typically reliant on cooperation from other branches. So Spain curtailed the power of its constitutional court in 1985 and other nations, such as Cyprus and Austria, have done away with them (Vanberg 2000).

Yet another concern of the Court may involve the implementation of its decisions. Lacking sword or purse, the Court needs help putting its outcomes into practice. The operationalization of decisions commonly depends on the other branches of government cooperating (Vanberg 2006). If the other branches of the government refuse to implement a judicial decision, "there is little courts can do" (Rosenberg 1991, 19). Because courts gain little from decisions that are ignored, and may lose considerable legitimacy as a result, one would expect courts to limit their decisions to those that will not be ignored. To some degree, this is circular. The greater the legitimacy of the Court, the more that the public will demand implementation of even unpopular decisions, but more unpopular decisions may undermine the legitimacy of the Court, meaning that the justices have to play something of a balancing game. They need not defer to the public on every issue, but they have to do so often enough to protect their legitimacy with the public.

The judicial deference to majoritarian institutions is sometimes plain from the face of the judicial opinion. For many issues, courts will apply a deferential, mere rationality test when a statute is challenged. Of course, for many individual freedoms under the Bill of Rights, such a deferential standard is technically inapplicable. But this does not mean that the Court cannot be deferential to the legislature, even when using a seemingly stricter standard. Researchers have noted that the Supreme Court disproportionately agrees with positions taken by the president's Solicitor General (McGuire 1998). The Court sometimes requests a brief from the government to assess its position on a case.

There is growing empirical research on the Court's responsiveness to the preferences of other government branches. Some studies have found that the Court did not appear to respond to congressional preferences, but Harvey and Friedman (2006) found that this was due to a selection effect. The Court is not required to hear cases at any given time. The authors concluded that the Court simply would decline to accept a challenge to a federal statute at a time when striking down such a law would be highly unpopular with the contemporaneous Congress. Even among decided cases, Segal, Westerland, and Lindquist (2010) found that the Court was less likely to strike down a statute as unconstitutional when the decision was likely to be unpopular with the sitting Congress. Zorn (2006) found that a dramatic shift in the ideology of Congress was accompanied by a similar shift in the Court and its willingness to invalidate statutes.

Cross and Nelson (2001) examined the likelihood of judicial deference to decisions of other federal institutions. They found that considering institutional deference helped predict justice decisions better than the pure attitudinal model. This effect varied by justice, with some, such as Justice Douglas, showing no effect of institutional deference, while others, such as Justice White, showed considerable deference.

While there is now considerable evidence suggesting that the Supreme Court is concerned with at least congressional desires, the implications of these findings should not be exaggerated. A statistically significant association is not necessarily a substantively significant one, and a degree of deference is far from complete deference. The Court may still be somewhat countermajoritarian, within constraints. Cross and Nelson (2001) found that the deference to legal rules of decisions was *greater* than the deference expressed to institutions, suggesting that the law mattered considerably to the Court, regardless of congressional position.

Research demonstrates that, for whatever reason, Supreme Court decisions tend to associate with popular opinion. One study found that the "modern Court appears neither markedly more nor less consistent with the polls than are other policy makers" (Marshall 1989, 80). The Court's opinions aligned with the opinion of the public about two-thirds of the time, when polling data was available. An updated analysis found continued association with public opinion in the Rehnquist Court era (Marshall 2008). Decisions in accord with popular opinion are also more likely to persist over time (Peretti 1999).

Judges, like popular majorities, may be caught up in the passions of the times. A law school aphorism is that judges fail to protect individual rights in times of crisis, when they are most likely to suffer infringement. Courts are said to "love liberty most when it is under pressure least" (Wright 1997, 387). Courts recognize the importance of popular opinion to their legitimacy.

Yet even if courts cannot be counted upon in time of crisis, they may still offer value. If a court stands up for rights in times of crisis only sometimes, that is still better than leaving the matter to classically majoritarian institutions alone. An occasional check is better than no check at all. And the uncertain possibility that the Court might stand up for rights is likely to make the other branches less aggressive, in order to improve their chances of withstanding the judicial review. And courts may find it easier to stand on principle in times of crisis for rights that were explicitly declared in a bill of rights (Wright 1997).

Justice Souter in the opinion in *Planned Parenthood v. Casey* (1992, 866) openly stated that the Court makes "principled decisions under circumstances in which their principled character is sufficiently plausible to be accepted by the Nation." Case analyses have shown that throughout the Court's history, public opinion has influenced its decisions in some cases. However, given the common fractionalization of the public and the political branches, the Court retains considerable room to move on policy matters (Peretti 1999).

The Supreme Court is not a purely legal, countermajoritarian institution, applying the Constitution regardless of public opinion. Public opinion exercises some pull on the Court, but it does not control the Court. One can find plenty of instances, including cases on religious freedom, in which the Court has disregarded public opinion.

The research does indicate that the Court has been, on average, at least somewhat more protective of rights than majority opinion, over time (Marshall & Ignani 1994). In the post–World War II period, the Court has used the Constitution to protect the rights of racial and religious minorities, persons accused of crimes, resident aliens, and other minorities (Smith 2009). The Court now seems to be performing its countermajoritarian role on behalf of disadvantaged minority groups. There is widespread agreement that activist judiciaries have increased protections for negative liberties found in constitutions.

Moreover, the Court tends to be much more popular with the people than the other branches of government (Friedman 2009). While this is surely due in part to public respect for legal decision making, it seems unlikely that an adamantly countermajoritarian institution would be so popular. It is often overlooked that the delegation of power, such as constitutional interpretation, to the courts may be an affirmative democratic choice of the people (Smith 2009). Of course, this delegation is presumably contingent on the Court not moving too far from popular policies.

The popularity of the Court may represent the strongest argument against Kramer's popular constitutionalism. It appears that true popular constitutionalism prefers deference to the Court. If the judiciary has made a grab for power, it is one that has been embraced by the citizenry. There is no reason to deny the people this choice. It is no different from entrusting scientific decisions to scientific experts, at the EPA or FDA or some other agency. Scientists, like judges, have their ideological biases, but the public may still prefer them to make decisions.

There are of course some plain instances of judicial countermajoritarianism, and the constitutional protection of flag burning comes to mind. Criminal defendants are never popular parties, yet the Court has not infrequently stood up for their rights. Moreover, the studies of majoritarianism of the judiciary have often focused on federal legislation. As Madison expected, many of the restrictions on such freedom have come from state government action. The judicial protection of freedom may often come in this arena. Even if a national majority wishes the protection of rights, a state may not. This state action may be corrected either by the national majority or the courts. History shows that the courts have played an important role here.

A clear case in the area of freedom of religion was the holding that the government could not require school prayer (*Engel v. Vitale* 1962). A large majority of the American people disagreed with this finding (McClosky & Brill 1983), yet the ruling occurred and has stood over time. One suspects that a large number of establishment clause rulings are probably unpopular with the majority of Americans. The 2003 Gallup poll found that 70 percent of Americans opposed the federal court opinion requiring a Ten Commandments monument be removed from a courthouse. In virtually every major poll taken on the subject, large majorities have favored the notion of prayer in public schools (Gash & Gonzalez 1998). The first such poll after the *Engel* opinion reported that 77 percent of Americans disagreed with the Court's outcome (Hall 2011). Yet this did not deter the Court from issuing the opinion.

Although religious freedom decisions have been unpopular, one could say that the Court has brought the public around to its position. Bans on school prayer were initially quite controversial but now are widely accepted as legitimate. Not that they are more popular; an examination of answers to questions on the 2010 General Social

Survey found that a majority of Americans still favored prayer in public schools. More than two-thirds of minorities and conservatives favored such prayer. But the Court's opinion is accepted. There no longer is much of a move to amend the Constitution to allow compulsory school prayer or impeach Supreme Court justices who prohibit it.

In cases such as this, the Court may simply have initiated a constitutional dialogue to stimulate public concern. When the public accepts the judicial decision, what initially seemed countermajoritarian may be truly more democratic, inspiring the public to reflection (Ferejohn & Pasquino 2010). The courts simply make American democracy more deliberative and thoughtful. Judicial review of rights questions has been defended as enhancing a societal dialogue (Hiebert 2005).

Some contend that the historical record "does not support the assertion that judicial review has been a force for protecting individual liberties" (Fisher 1998, 63). For much of American history, the courts were relatively unconcerned with rights. The Alien and Sedition Acts are examples from the beginning of our history. Before World War I there was a "pervasive judicial hostility to virtually all free speech claims" (Rabban 1997, 2). Only after World War II did the Supreme Court become an aggressive promoter of individual liberties.

In the context of religious freedom, there is the story of the Religious Freedom Restoration Act (RFRA). The law passed Congress in 1993 to prevent laws that burdened the free exercise of religion, largely in response to a Supreme Court decision finding it constitutional for the state to adopt neutral laws that happened to disadvantage particular religions (*Employment Division v. Smith* 1990). The Supreme Court, however, struck down the law as applied to the states, as exceeding congressional power to enforce the Fourteenth Amendment (*City of Boerne v. Flores* 1997).

RFRA is surely a dramatic case against the role of the judiciary in protecting religious freedom. It is a case where a democratic Congress sought to take steps to increase such freedom, and the judiciary invalidated those efforts (*Boerne* 1997). The legislature sought to strengthen the free exercise clause, and the Court held that this action went beyond its constitutional authority. While many agreed with the decision, many others saw it as a judicial limitation on religious freedom. The case was not decided under the First Amendment, though, so it doesn't inform us on judicial application of express constitutional recognition of religious freedom.

Judges have their own biases, and most judges are from majority religions. Some evidence of judicial discrimination against minority religions is found in Wybraniec and Finke (2001). Their study of judicial decisions from 1981 to 1997 found that mainline Protestant denominations were the most successful at winning court cases, at a rate more than twice that of Muslim plaintiffs. The authors also found that the *Smith* decision had an effect, and a particularly negative one for sects and new religions.

A more recent study of judicial decision making provides evidence that the Court protects the rights of minority religions against majoritarian restrictions. Sisk (2005) considered how different religions fared in constitutional litigation in America on free expression claims. Some have hypothesized that Christians receive favorable treatment in this largely Christian nation (Brent 1999). Sisk (2005) considered over seven hundred decisions. He found that minority religions did well in the decisions. Muslims were relatively successful whereas Catholic and Baptist plaintiffs were especially unsuccessful. The results do not eliminate the possibility of religious prejudice – perhaps the minority religions had much stronger cases. The results do demonstrate that the Bill of Rights' protections are in fact used often to protect the interests of minority groups. Ignagni (1993) reached similar results in a study of free exercise cases. Broader research has shown that the courts are receptive to the claims of underdogs, such as minority groups (Peretti 1999).

Considerable research demonstrates a measure of attitudinalism and majoritarianism in Supreme Court decisions. The research focus on the Supreme Court, though, may well exaggerate both effects. The Court selects the cases it will hear, typically taking those that are most legally indeterminate and salient. If it does not want to render a countermajoritarian decision itself, it may leave standing a lower court opinion that is countermajoritarian, protecting the right without deciding.

The Supreme Court is but the tip of the American judicial iceberg. It addresses only a small fraction of the legal disputes of the country, and the vast bulk of law is made by lower courts, often circuit courts of appeals. While the circuit courts are influenced by the ideology of judges, this attitudinal effect appears to be overwhelmed by legal considerations (Cross 2007). Some of those legal considerations are set by Supreme Court precedents, but many are not. Thus, the measure of overall judicial attitudinalism and majoritarianism may be greatly overstated for the legal system as a whole. Sisk (2005) studied lower courts and found considerable protection for minority religions.

Can the Judiciary Enforce Its Rulings?

Even if one assumes that the judiciary can be trusted to be a principled interpreter of the Bill of Rights in litigation, that alone cannot prove protective. Its rulings must be enforced and applied. Andrew Jackson famously dismissed and defied a Supreme Court opinion protecting the rights of Native Americans. When the Court issued a decision challenging President Lincoln's suspension of the writ of habeas corpus, Lincoln simply ignored the Court's ruling. Other presidents, including Jefferson and Franklin Delano Roosevelt, have done likewise.

Alexander Hamilton called the judiciary the weakest branch, lacking both the purse and the sword. This weakness could prevent it from effectively enforcing constitutional guarantees, such as freedom of religion. In today's world, the absence of an implementing bureaucracy may be more significant. Even if a countermajoritarian judiciary were to command (or veto) some government action as violative of religious freedom, the people and other governmental branches might ignore it. The Court typically relies on others to enforce its rulings.

The theory is that when the Court does disagree with the elected branches, its outcome will not be implemented (Hall 2011). Many subscribe to this theory. Baum (2003, 177) summarizes the literature as suggesting that implementation of decisions is "far from perfect" and the "Court is quite constrained in its ability to secure social change." Dahl (1957, 293) declared that "[t]he Court is almost powerless to affect the course of national policy." So even if courts could be reliably countermajoritarian internally, the external effect of their decisions may not be effectuated.

The classic study of judicial ineffectuality is Rosenberg (1991). His book focused on the effect of *Brown v. Board of Education*, rejecting the constitutionality of segregated education. He found that the decision had virtually no effect on desegregation in southern states, with segregation remaining at over 99.5 percent in public schools nine years after the opinion was issued. A similar effect was found in other spheres of society, though he acknowledges that a greater effect occurred in border states. Desegregation took hold only after Congress began to act on the question in 1964, more than ten years later. Rosenberg (1991) also considers the effect of judicial rulings on abortion rights, the environment, reapportionment, and criminal law and suggests that they produced at best uneven results. He concludes that courts "will be ineffective in producing change, given any significant resistance, because of their lack of implementation powers (Rosenberg 1991, 336). Moreover, he suggests that courts may be counterproductive as their "symbolic victories may be mistaken for substantive ones" and that they may deflect "claims from substantive political battles" that would be more effective (Rosenberg 1991, 341). His research also undermines the legitimation hypothesis, suggesting that Supreme Court decisions do not alter public attention to the problems they address.

Sweet (2010) considers the ability of the judiciary to implement its directives, with a focus on affirmative action. He found relatively little effect of the Court's opinions, for a variety of reasons. He notes that some organizations ignored the rulings, while others engaged in obfuscation and delay. Procedural doctrines, such as standing and mootness, frustrated the ability to challenge unconstitutional programs. He declares that "we have massive resistance to the Supreme Court doctrine all across the country, with hundreds of blatantly unconstitutional programs at all levels of the government" (Sweet 2010, 123).

Resistance to constitutional rulings has been studied in the area of school prayer. Birkby (1966) considered the response of Tennessee schools to the prohibition on school prayer. He questioned over one hundred school districts and found that most had responded to the ruling but had not eliminated school prayer. The modifications appeared to fall well short of what the Court commanded. It may be that a system has little incentive to comply until it is sued, and many districts simply do not have a plaintiff willing and able to sue to enforce the Supreme Court's ruling. Many public schools maintained devotional practices even after the prohibitions (Abel & Hacker 2006).

McGuire (2009) surveyed high school graduates from southern schools about devotional activities they had experienced. He found considerable noncompliance on matters such as graduation prayer and prayer at sports events. However, he found virtually total compliance with prohibitions on Bible reading and high compliance with prohibitions on organized prayer in schools. The research indicates that rulings on freedom of religion may be disregarded, but they obtain some initial compliance, and that level grows over time.

If courts cannot obtain compliance with their decisions, that fact alone considerably undermines its significance for the protection of constitutional rights. Moreover, noncompliance could well make the judiciary less willing to issue controversial rulings. It gets no gain from a ruling that is not obeyed. And noncompliance can threaten the credibility and legitimacy of the Court. The justices are likely to steer clear of decisions that are unlikely to be obeyed. They will anticipate whether their preferred outcomes will be followed and not stray too far from public opinion in the aggregate (McGuire & Stimson 2004). Marshall (2008) shows how the Court historically has agreed with public opinion a majority of the time, with occasional exceptional years to the contrary.

Other research, however, suggests that judicial decisions receive good compliance and do matter in practice. A study of sixty-five court cases dealing with education found that "basic compliance with court orders predominated overwhelmingly over instances of either intentional or unintentional noncompliance" (Rebell & Block 1982, 65). However, this study did not include the most controversial set of rulings, desegregation cases, which plainly saw noncompliance with court directives. Analysis of other opinions, such as pay equity cases, also finds that the Supreme Court's decision matters (McCann 1994).

Hall (2011) offers the most extensive survey of compliance with Supreme Court decisions. He divides opinions into the popular and unpopular and those with vertical or lateral compliance. Vertical means that compliance only requires the cooperation of lower courts, whereas lateral issues required cooperation from the people or other branches of government. He then examines and quantifies compliance levels for numerous Court opinions in the different categories.

For cases categorized as vertical, compliance was quite high. The Warren Court issued a number of very unpopular decisions in support of defendants' rights. Hall (2011) found that the unpopularity did not affect compliance. Prosecutors and police departments moved to nearly complete compliance with the dictates of the decisions. On abortion, he disagreed with Rosenberg and demonstrated that *Roe v. Wade* (1976) did have a material effect on practice.

Less influence was expected on decisions requiring more lateral cooperation. Hall (2011) noted that the desegregation opinions got poor compliance but demonstrated that the prayer-in-school opinions got much better compliance that generally regarded, though it plainly varied by region. In the Northeast, regular Bible readings declined from 68 percent of schools to 4 percent in the wake of the Court's opinions. In the South, though, conformity was much less; Hall (2011) estimated it to be around 30 percent. Even such an extremely unpopular opinion received moderately good societal compliance. Other unpopular lateral issues also received reasonable compliance.

The Court may get compliance for its rulings out of deference, or perhaps because it brings public attention and education to particular questions. Hall (2011, 160) concludes that the Court is still a "remarkably powerful institution" capable of "expanding or suppressing individual rights."

It seems clear that the Court is not so powerful as many Americans assume. Its decisions are not automatically implemented into practice. Sager (1978) has demonstrated that many of the commitments of the U.S. Constitution are underenforced by the courts. Some perfectly legitimate constitutional challenges are rejected because of institutional concerns about judicial competence or issues such as federalism. In those cases, the judiciary is useless.

However, the Constitution is not as weak as some academics have professed. True, judicial enforcement of the Bill of Rights is not a panacea. The judges may choose not to enforce the rights broadly. Even if they do, the judges' decisions may not be followed by greater society. But the lack of perfection leaves plenty of room for value. It is plausible that judicial enforcement could produce marginally more liberty. A judiciary that succeeds part of the time is better than nothing. Vanberg (2006) notes that the judiciary in America has considerable popular legitimacy. Because of this, resistance to a Supreme Court opinion may present a considerable popular backlash, and the "fear of such a backlash can be a powerful inducement to implement judicial decisions faithfully" (Vanberg 2006, 73). When the U.S. Supreme Court functionally decided the 2000 election, Democrats accepted the ruling and their loss even though their candidate had received more overall votes.

An interesting case arose in May 2011 that hints at some judicial value. The Iranian judiciary is theocratic, typically furthering the interests of the Islamic religion at the expense of religious liberty. But in the case, an Iranian court acquitted eleven Christians of charges based on their attendance at a church meeting in which they took Communion wine. The court cited the nation's constitution, which provided that Christians and members of some other faiths should be left free to perform their religious rites and ceremonies. The Iranian judiciary is one of the last places where one would expect a court to uphold religious freedom, but it did. Although the Iranian courts have not produced a national climate of religious freedom, they seem to have some positive effect at the margin of the law.

In addition, one must consider the effect of judicial review on legislative action. A legislature would prefer not to see its actions declared unconstitutional, which can embarrass the legislature and render its preferences less effective. Consequently, a legislature under the shadow of judicial review should be less likely to take unconstitutional action, in anticipation of the effect of the judicial review. Vanberg (2006) observes that this effect has been clearly identified in France and other European nations. The judiciary may not need to act to have an effect on national constitutional compliance; the threat of action alone may be enough to change policy.

As previously noted, however, this effect runs both ways. The judiciary may be reluctant to hear a case when its preferences or the law are contrary to those of other institutions (Vanberg 2006). If so, the research may understate the majoritarian influence on the Supreme Court. The result is a game something like mutual bluffing, with both sides threatening action to see if the other backs down. In such games, both sides tend to win sometimes, usually when their preferences are especially intense. If this describes political reality, one would expect a judiciary to have some effect, even if it is a quite imperfect one. Thus, the "open defiance of the Court has been the exception rather than the rule" (Levinson 2011, 731).

As also discussed, constitutions may be seen as a form of precommitment to enable stability and coordination. The very existence of a relatively independent judiciary is another form of precommitment, used as a means to help ensure that the substantive constitutional precommitment is respected. For this system to work, judicial decisions must be generally respected. Consequently, those with an interest in having a binding constitution for commitment purposes would be likewise interested in ensuring the power of judicial decisions. If judicial decisions enforcing private contracts could be readily ignored, people would be less likely to make such contracts.

Courts of course are no guarantee of protection of religious freedoms. A number of European courts have openly declared that their national constitutions do not require different religions to be treated equally (Garlicki 2001). Of course, this was merely a failure to protect minority religions, not an action making the situation worse than it was before. Courts surely will not guarantee religious freedom, as evidenced by the many restrictions seen around the globe, in violation of legal constitutional requirements. But courts may have some role, at the margin, in protecting freedom. Certainly, the experience in the United States suggests that courts have protected religious freedom intermittently.

How Courts Could Matter

The judiciary is plainly imperfect at enforcing the Bill of Rights, but so is every human institution, and it may still have real value. Justices may sometimes be ideological or majoritarian in their decisions. Their decisions may be imperfectly enforced. But these facts do not refute the possibility that the courts may play a significant positive role in the protection of individual rights, such as freedom of religion. The caveats on judicial protection, though, suggest that a variety of external circumstances may be relevant to the degree of protection that can be provided by the courts.

As noted earlier, some suggest that the Bill of Rights is the most vulnerable part of the Constitution because it lacks a self-interested, powerful governmental party to support it. The nature of the Bill of Rights and judicial operations, though, make the courts particularly suited to the enforcement of its protections. Lacking the purse and the sword, it is difficult for the judiciary to initiate a program, such as requiring redistribution of resources. What the courts do possess is a veto. They can prevent many government actions. They can acquit those the other branches would like to imprison.

While judges may block action by the government, they have a difficult time forcing such action. The courts may have preferences on macroeconomic policy or whether to conduct a foreign intervention, but they have no ability to effect these preferences. When the courts have sought to push an aggressive affirmative government program, such as school desegregation, they have been relatively ineffective without the assistance of other branches. When blocking government action, though, the courts may be quite effective, as enforcement of government rules typically must pass through the courts. Hence, the protection of negative rights is where courts are best able to take action.

Corwin (1934, 122) declared long ago that the "Court can forbid somebody else to act but cannot, usually, act itself." Barclay & Birkland (1998, 232) reviewed the record and found that courts had typically failed to bring about effective policy change but that they did have "the ability to delay or block the implementation of a policy." Courts are not effective as an engine but may be powerful as a brake.

The primary judicial power is the veto of government action. The primary means of enforcement of the Bill of Rights is to veto government action. As a result, the judiciary might be more effective in the enforcement of the Bill of Rights than in other constitutional areas. There is a multiple vetoes hypothesis (Cross 2000) that explains why the courts may add material protection to individual rights.

An individual right, such as religious freedom, is infringed by positive governmental action. For such an infringement to occur, Congress must overcome various internal constraints on action. The president must agree and sign the law (unless overcome by a supermajoritarian congressional override). And the law must pass judicial scrutiny. The judiciary therefore acts as something of a backstop protection for individual rights. Even if the judiciary protects rights in a minority of disputes, each example of such protection is an additional defense of rights, over and above that provided by the elected branches. Majoritarianism may be generally protective of individual rights and, when the elected branches fail to do so, the courts offer additional protection. The two are complementary.

This veto may be especially important for state infringements on religious freedom. Some of these state restrictions may be contrary to a national majority's preferences. Yet Congress may do nothing about them. This may result from limits on congressional power, deference to state interests, the considerable barriers to national legislative action, or competing demands for the time of the national legislature. In these circumstances, the judicial backstop may offer a valuable additional protection.

Eskridge and Ferejohn (1994) suggest that courts engage in logrolling with other branches of government to create additional rights. Judges and politicians have different interests, both intrinsically and by happenstance over time. The American system of separation of powers, they suggest, creates many opportunities for rights creation by the branch that happens to be most favorably inclined to the right. A court may create rights that the political system would not, and vice versa. The Court "asserts a rights-creating power for those issues it cares the most about, while deferring to the most intense rights creating preferences of Congress" (Eskridge & Ferejohn 1994, 1560). This is something like the backstop theory, but with the constitutional rights out of the picture. The courts may lose out if Congress has intense preferences against creation of the right, but the experience with abortion rights suggests that the opposition must be widespread as well as intense.

Goderis and Versteeg (2009) provide interesting evidence for the virtue of courts in protecting rights. They studied actions taken by governments after the 9/11 attack on the Twin Towers. Using an accepted scale for political terror and human rights abuses, they noted an increase in government repression after the attack in countries allied with the United States. They found that the country's degree of judicial review by an independent judiciary was protective and associated with fewer human rights abuses. While their measures for judicial review were necessarily crude, the combination of an independent judiciary and judicial review had some positive veto effect on human rights restrictions. They also counted the number of relevant constitutional rights in national constitutions and found that they appeared to reduce abuse, though the authors cautioned that this effect was uncertain. Majoritarian checks, in these circumstances, did not offer benefits.

Giving power to the courts should be a one-way ratchet in the direction of rights protection. Because they are the weakest branch of government and ineffective in taking affirmative action, the courts are not a real threat to take away individual rights (Hiebert 2005). To the extent they have influence on rights it will be in a protective direction.

The case for the importance of a judicial role does not rest in the virtue of the judiciary itself but is a structural one. If a repressive measure must pass two hurdles (executive and legislature), it will more likely be adopted than if it had to pass three hurdles (executive, legislature, and judiciary). The judiciary may often be ideological, or majoritarian, or simply wrong, permitting unconstitutional abuses to occur. But if it is occasionally legal and supportive of rights, its effect will be net beneficial. This is consistent with the empirical research of Keith (2010, 119). She found that the Court could not be relied on consistently to support rights against majoritarian pressure, and when it had challenged Congress it did so "overwhelmingly to protect rights." Way and Burt (1983) thus note that the traditional path for legitimation of a small religion "is through litigation of free exercise claims."

Because judges may be cautious, express constitutionalization may be necessary to encourage them to perform their role of an independent veto. Constitutionalization has generally empowered the judiciary to take on the other branches. However, the judiciary has little authority to take the initiative in protecting rights, as discussed in the next section.

Necessary Support Structure for the Judicial Role

Judicial support for individual rights is compromised by the fact that courts cannot take up issues *sua sponte*. The ability of the Court to enforce constitutional provisions also depends on other societal factors. Litigants favoring individual rights must bring appropriate cases to the courts to enforce the Constitution and possess sufficient resources and interest to pursue those cases to a favorable resolution. In cases where judicial decisions have not been implemented, it has commonly been for lack of plaintiffs willing and able to challenge actions in violation of those decisions. Keith (2010, 370) argues that the effectiveness of any judicial protections "would most likely be dependent upon the level of independence of the judiciary, the degree to which judges on the bench are rights-oriented, and the degree to which the courts are accessible to the general public."

Epp (1998) contends that a bill of rights alone offers little to the protection of human rights. Constitutions are not self-enforcing. The protection of rights depends on "widespread and sustained litigation in support of civil rights and liberties" (Epp 1998, 18). This is problematic economically. When a plaintiff prevails in an action defending human rights, he or she cannot capture most of the benefits of the decision, which go to others. Consequently, we would expect such litigation to be underproduced, as many potential plaintiffs will not bear the costs of action that primarily affects others. Yet, for whatever reason, some nations have seen vigorous private efforts to enforce rights.

For much of American history, until around the 1950s, there was little concern for protection of individual rights. At that point, however, concern blossomed, and the Supreme Court's agenda became primarily consumed with such rights issues. Groups including the ACLU and the NAACP came to the fore and won many a case for their respective agendas. Epp (1998) demonstrates, though, that this support structure for human rights has not developed in other nations.

The existence of such a support structure may in part be a matter of happenstance involving a nation's culture. Perhaps greater wealth enables greater resources and attention to be paid to development of a legal infrastructure. But whatever the reason, the development of more individuals dedicated to interpreting and applying the law will tend to make the law more societally important. Presumably, this helps ensure that the law is interpreted seriously. This is different from a rule of law effect because it deals with the interpretation of legal requirements such as constitutional guarantees and not necessarily its enforcement.

A constitution does provide an additional tool for such a rights-enforcement group and may thereby strengthen it. Certainly the ACLU's litigation strategy is centered on the Bill of Rights itself. Epp (1998) argues that judicial support for a rights agenda is not sufficient for the protection of rights, but it is necessary. A constitutional bill of rights could facilitate that necessary role. Epp (1998, 201) finds that in "systems in which there exist broad constitutional rights guarantees, popular movements seem especially capable of using contradictions between political practice and constitutional promise as a means for organizing support for their causes." Constitutionalization is also a form of judicial empowerment (Woods & Hilbink 2009), and the additional veto given the judiciary can serve to strengthen rights protections.

Epp (1996) considered the effect of the passage in 1960 of a Canadian bill of rights. He concluded that the charter by itself did not have a major effect on rights protection, except perhaps in the short term. It did not dramatically change the agenda of the nation's supreme court, nor its voting. The growth of rights protection in Canada was attributed to a cultural change and developing support structure for the enforcement of such rights.

Yet even the Canadian experience gives some reason to believe that constitutional language matters. The Canadian constitution contains a free exercise clause but not an equivalent of the American establishment clause. While free exercise decisions have generally tracked those of the U.S. Supreme Court, the Canadian courts initially upheld in school readings from the Bible and the recital of the Lord's Prayer, so long as objecting pupils could be excused (Sedler 1988), though it later reversed that position.

Existing Research on the Effect of Constitutional Protections

Some limited research has been done on the effect of constitutional provisions, such as bills of rights, on the operation of a society. The helpfulness of the research has been limited by the general lack of good measures for human rights protection. The very earliest research found that constitutional guarantees were unhelpful or even counterproductive (Law 2010), but they had poor tests and did not try to associate particular rights with particularized levels of repressions of those rights.

The first major study with a good design (Davenport 1996) examined constitutional provisions on fundamental rights and protection in society. Yet the sample was limited for even this study, and the author found positive effects for only three of the fourteen constitutional provisions that he examined. In some cases, nations with constitutional rights had poor performance in practice.

Cross (1999) considered the effect of a specific constitutional protection against unreasonable search and seizure on the search-and-seizure practice of a nation. The study found little effect of the constitutional protection in and of itself, but that judicial independence could protect individuals even in the absence of a constitutional provision. It appeared that judicial independence was more valuable than an expressed right. The measure for the dependent variable of protection against search and seizure came from Humana and was subjective and extremely crude in drawing distinctions among nations, however. It easily could have missed some protective effect for the right.

Law and Versteeg (2011) found that numerous nations have sham constitutions. These involve cases of promising rights and not enforcing them. The lack of control variables, though, limits the value of this research. These cases also showed that some nations without constitutional protections were good at protecting certain rights, which testifies to the fact that constitutional provisions are not absolutely necessary.

Keith, Poe, and Tate (2009) have analyzed the effect of provisions for specific individual freedoms, an independent judiciary, and the possibility of states of emergency on rights abuses, measured as "state terror." This was measured by a set of indicators that considered political imprisonment, torture, and other extreme violations of liberty. Constitutions were coded according to whether they contained ten particular recognized freedoms, ranging from freedom of speech and religion to defendants' rights. The authors found relatively little effect from the constitutional protections, though the provisions for a fair trial did have a statistically significant positive effect (Keith, Poe & Tate 2009, 632). The combination of rights had a substantively material effect, though individual rights did not. The specific rights, though, were not really matched with the protections they promised. The full implications of the research were unclear.

The detailed international data on levels of religious freedom offer a much better opportunity for empirical testing than did the prior data. Fox (2011) has conducted such an evaluation, using his RAS data. He evaluated constitutional provisions on various dimensions, such as the existence of an establishment clause, the presence of a constitutional state religion, and other clauses affecting matters such as the participation of religious groups in politics. Fox (2011) found that the presence of constitutional prohibitions did not eliminate religious legislation. He did find a significant effect for some constitutional provisions. States with an official constitutional religion plainly had more legislation restricting religion. However a formal declaration of separation of church and state had little effect, compared with constitutions that had no such reference.

Fox (2011) also conducted a multivariate regression. As I found in the prior chapter, majority Muslim nations had less religious freedom with statistical significance. Also as I found, greater per capita GDP was associated with less religion, again with statistical significance. Fox used a different measure of democracy and found a much weaker association than I did. Democracy was associated with higher levels of religious freedom, but typically not with statistical significance. With all these controls, some constitutional variables did provide additional protection for religious freedom. The absolute substantive effect of such provisions. though, was small as compared with the societal variables. He did not find that the specific wording of constitutional provisions mattered much for such protection.

To date, the empirical evidence on constitutions and rights is at best inconclusive and suggests that formal protections offer little value. But there is little research that has been conducted on the question. Moreover, the vast bulk of the research is compromised by the very limited quantitative scaling of rights available, as discussed in Chapter 3, which seriously undermines finding marginal effects. In addition, little has been done with interaction effects (such as Madison's theories of how bills of rights could matter), which could explain how rights might be effective in some, if not all, circumstances. The existing research, therefore, can give us little confidence that we understand whether bills of rights are effective in offering some protection to individual rights.

Conclusion

The existing theory and evidence on the effect of constitutional bills of rights remains uncertain. By themselves, such rights promises do not guarantee the actual protection of the guaranteed rights, but they may contribute to such protection. Perhaps a bill of rights inspires the public in a libertarian manner, though the available evidence does not appear to support this. Perhaps the legal status of the protection induces the courts to shelter the named rights. This view may be somewhat naïve because courts tend to decide many cases ideologically and be relatively majoritarian in orientation. But Kapiszewski (2011), in her study of Brazil, shows how these features are balanced with the law and ultimately contribute to greater enforcement of legal requirements.

The degree of real world protection offered by a bill of rights remains indeterminate and requires empirical testing. It is important to understand both whether such constitutionalization of rights matters and why it matters. If the important function of a bill of rights is found through its influence on people's opinions, that makes a case for greater popular constitutionalism. If, by contrast, the effect is found in judicial enforcement, that makes a contrary case and suggests that facilitating judicial enforcement is the best strategy for promoting individual rights, such as freedom of religion.

In the next chapter, I will explore whether constitutions matter and the circumstances that may influence whether they matter. I will test whether constitutional protections matter, given the other social determinants that I have identified. Moreover, I will examine whether certain circumstances are associated with the importance of constitutional provisions. This enables me to check Madison's hypotheses. Do constitutions inspire the public to provide more protection? Does the judiciary offer protections by applying constitutional provisions to prohibit restrictions on religious freedom?

6

The Constitutional Protection of Religious Freedom

This chapter embarks upon the study of whether constitutional guarantees are indeed protective of religious freedom. I begin with a series of multiple regression analyses that incorporate the existence of constitutional protections of religious freedom with my general societal determinants, in order to ascertain whether the constitutional provision makes any difference. I also consider the different circumstances for which constitutional provisions may, or may not, make a practical difference.

There is some anecdotal evidence that constitutional protections advance religious freedom. In Peru, "religious rights ... have increased as a result of a series of new constitutions" (Correa 1998, 307). The adoption of a new Columbian constitution in 1991, with additional protection for religious freedom, produced a series of decisions protecting such freedom (Hoyos 1999). The reader is probably aware of decisions of the U.S. Supreme Court that have advanced religious freedom. Canada's adoption of a Charter of Rights and Freedoms has been criticized for promoting the overly aggressive judicial defense of individual rights.

Such anecdotal evidence is subjective, though, and typically does not consider other possible explanations for religious rights.

Moreover, it cannot assess the net overall international effect. In some nations, a constitutional right may be ineffective or even counterproductive symbolic action. And the anecdotes may be biased or erroneous.

Despite the common praise for the American First Amendment, Hanburger (2003, 21) contends that the establishment clause of the U.S. Bill of Rights "is repeatedly violated every day by numerous Americans" and that the "violations are wantonly ignored by the Supreme Court." As noted in the previous chapter, it is unrealistic to expect a judiciary to enforce a constitutional provision completely or perfectly. Perhaps, though, judicial or democratic enforcement of a constitution has a net effect on the margin, even a substantial one.

A more rigorous quantitative test of the effect of constitutional provisions on freedom is necessary and provided in this chapter. Chapter 3 addressed the quantification of religious rights in a nation. The following section discusses the measurement of global constitutions and then proceeds to use those measurements to evaluate the effect of constitutional rights guarantees on the protection of religious freedom.

The Content of Constitutions

Most of the world's constitutions contain some expression of some aspect of religious freedom. The United States and a number of other nations have rather minimalist expressions, with a few words guaranteeing freedom of religion or freedom of conscience. Other countries have lengthy and detailed free exercise clauses that reference particular types of practice. All the clauses have some differences. Any rigorous analysis first requires the quantitative characterization of these constitutional provisions.

A number of national constitutions condition the freedom of religion, a concept widely known as proportionality. Hiebert (2005) suggests that this is inevitably central to all rights issues – the question is not whether the right is restricted, it is whether the right is *unduly* restricted. The conditions mean that religious freedom is not absolute but must be qualified by other national concerns. The International Covenant on Civil and Political Rights contains such express qualifiers, allowing restrictions on freedom to serve purposes such as public safety, order, health, morals, or the rights and freedoms of others. The Azerbaijani constitution recognizes freedom of religion but specifies that this freedom "should not violate public order and morals." The Bulgarian constitution declares that religious freedom "shall not be practiced to the detriment of national security, public order, public health and morals, or of the rights and freedoms of others." The Venezuelan constitution allows religious freedom "provided it is not contrary to the public order or to good customs." The European Convention on Human Rights allowed for the restriction of religion when "prescribed by law and necessary in a democratic society in the interests of public safety, for the protection of public order, health or morals, or for the protection of the rights and freedoms of others."

One might think that such proportionality exceptions are major limitations on religious freedom, allowing the camel's head into the tent, as it were. There are no clear objective or uniform criteria for performing the balancing of the right against the contrary interests (Gunn 2005). The weighting of the issues is surely a subjective one, grounded in the judges' biases or perhaps the majoritarian sentiment of the nation. This is particularly a concern insofar as "the morals or values of *ordre public* which governments seek to protect are in fact based on one particular religion" (Nowak & Vospernik 1998, 172). Fox (2011, 61) suggests that the balancing process means that "individual clauses taken in isolation are not necessarily reliable indicators of government policies" and that national security clauses are commonly used to override other constitutional guarantees.

Such proportionality requirements are not intrinsically objectionable, however. Rights generally are qualified to some degree, even absent constitutional proportionality language. In the United States, for example, the Constitution commands that there be "no law" restricting freedom of speech, but the Supreme Court has recognized various exceptions to this, such as prohibitions on fighting words and needed no proportionality language to do so. In the context of religious freedom, the decision in *Employment Division v. Smith*

(1990) held that religious freedom could be restricted in the interest of antidrug legislation. The effect of express proportionality language in a constitution is therefore uncertain. Some sense of proportionality is arguably inherent even in the liberal individual human rights tradition (Liviatan 2011). Gunn (2005, 469) contends that "all legal systems presume that states legitimately may limit the exercise of protected rights under certain circumstances."

Some proportionality is probably necessary or inevitable. A state would not permit human sacrifice as part of a religion in today's world. More relevant, states may prohibit female genital mutilation, even if called for by religion. A Dutch court compelled a farmer to participate in the national health service to protect the public health. In the United States, religious belief does not exempt one from compliance with drug laws. Proportionality plainly may be abused, especially for any "public morals" exception. But it is unclear that constitutional proportionality requirements necessarily undermine religious freedom.

A smaller number of nations have provisions comparable to the American establishment clause. These provisions are plainly intended to prevent the government from preferring one religion over another. They may be interpreted more broadly to prevent the government from preferring religion generally, regardless of faith.

Establishment clauses have various forms of expression in the world's constitutions. The Albanian constitution appears to go beyond that of the United States and declares that the "state is neutral in questions of belief and conscience." The Georgian constitution makes tribute to the role of the Orthodox Church but proceeds to command "the independence of the church from the state." Argentina declares that the federal government "supports the Roman Catholic Apostolic religion" but entitles all individuals to "profess freely their religion." The relative significance of the different wording is uncertain, but all reflect a relative commitment to an establishment clause–like protection (or not).

The opposite of an establishment clause would be the express establishment of a state religion. Several nations provide that "Islam is the religion of the state." Norway recognizes the Evangelical-Lutheran religion as "the official religion of the state." Numerous other nations also expressly recognize state religions.

Other constitutions contain vague expressions of religiosity that are difficult to categorize. The Fijian constitution thus declares that "worship and reverence of God are the source of good government leadership." Such provisions are not clearly establishments of state religions, though they might be so interpreted. Arjomand (2003) suggests that such provisions may be used to counteract the protection of religious freedom via the constitution or even perhaps through democratic measures.

To statistically analyze the effects of constitutional provisions, some coding is required. The individual language of national constitutions must be grouped into defined categories. This might be done through different approaches, and I rely on an accepted resource as discussed in the next section.

Coding Constitutions

Because constitutional provisions vary so widely in their wording, it is difficult to create quantitative coding for their protections. Giving a number to such constitutional provisions, necessary for rigorous quantitative testing, is a difficult task. The precise wording of each national constitution's protection is never the same, so they must somehow be grouped. The relative specificity of language might seem a good test, as more specific constitutions may be more precisely enforced by the judiciary or the other branches of government, although it is conversely possible that a vague constitution could empower its enforcement by other branches, giving them more space to effect their preferences. Specificity is quite difficult to measure, though. In addition, such specificity may not deal with the important matters of religious freedom and may operate in different directions, with some nations using specific constitutional language to strengthen religious freedom and others using specific language to limit such freedom.

Alternatively, they might be grouped based on the number of words used in a constitution. The U.S. Constitution, including First Amendment protection of religious freedom, is quite parsimonious, using few words. Other constitutions are much lengthier or more garrulous. The world's longest constitution has twenty times the words of its shortest (Voigt 2009). Bhutan's constitution is less than two hundred words, whereas others have swelled to tens of thousands of words (Ginsburg 2010).

The length of a constitution may have an effect on its specificity and the strength of its enforcement. Cooter and Ginsburg (2003) show that the length of a constitution has an effect on the nature of the statutes passed by its legislature. Although it is possible to capture the length of a constitution, it is difficult to capture its protections of religious freedom, as in some cases it is unclear whether a particular provision involves freedom of religion. For some constitutions, there is no single religious freedom clause, but relevant provisions are found at different places in the text.

Using more words may simply, indeed commonly, address only trivial matters or be redundant. Moreover, additional language may have opposite effects. One constitution may use more words to expressly rule out certain governmental action, while another might use more words to specifically authorize the same action. Consequently, constitutional garrulity may be a poor test for constitutional protections of religious freedom.

In some cases, the implications of particular language is sufficiently obscure that it may advance or defeat religious freedom. Such coding is therefore quite discretionary in nature. Fortunately, there is a broad international constitutional product that has coded the content of many constitutions, including religious freedom. Tom Ginsburg and Zach Elkins have comprehensively coded the constitutions of nearly all nations throughout history (Elkins, Ginsburg, & Melton 2009). The coding covers all aspects of the constitutions, including expressions of rights to religious freedom.

One of the constitutional characteristics coded was "Does the constitution contain provisions concerning a national or official religion or a national or official church?" In the coding, this question admitted of several answers. The primary codes were

- Yes, national religion specified
- National religion specifically forbidden
- Not specified

The coders had several other categories, but they might include one single nation. Thus, a nation's constitution explicitly left the question for the other branches, but this is also the implication of the "not specified" category with numerous examples.

Note that this considers only constitutional state religions. A nation might establish such a religion legislatively. But there are a myriad of forms of favoritism, and it can actually be difficult to establish whether a nation has a formal state religion (Barro & McCleary 2006). My research is concerned with the effect of constitutions, so I only consider the constitutional provisions regarding a state religion.

The meaning of a national religion certainly varies among nations. While both Argentina and Saudi Arabia formally have state religions, the provision has vastly different implications on state policy toward religion in the two countries (Fox 2011). In some cases, a state religion may be just that – the force behind government action. In other cases, it may be a symbolic, even nostalgic, nod to national history, with little practical meaning. Whereas a state religion might seem to be a major qualification on religious freedom, this need not necessarily be so.

The constitutional coding also addressed the elements of the American First Amendment by asking "Does the constitution provide for religious freedom?" and "Does the constitution contain an explicit degree of separation of church and state?" Each of these questions was simply answered yes or no in the coding, though occasionally it was difficult to provide an answer. The project also coded for other constitutional characteristics, but some had no differentiation (essentially all nations were the same).

This coding of constitutional content is surely a daunting and somewhat imprecise task. Some constitutions are quite straightforward about creating a national religion. Greece's constitution provides that the "prevailing religion" is Eastern Orthodox but does not formally establish it as the state church. The Fijian constitution declares that "worship and reverence of God are the source of good government and leadership." The implications of such a provision are quite unclear. This may be meaningless language, but Arjomand (2003) suggests that such declarations may represent extra-legal values that could empower social forces to challenge secular legality. Breaking down all the different language choices into simple binary coding is complex and surely imperfect. But this coding is the best available and at least roughly accurate.

The coding that I use is quite narrow in scope, assessing simply the existence or nonexistence of a broad right of religious freedom. It does not consider qualifying language that may apply to such rights. Other possibly relevant matters are also omitted. But it provides a sound basic resource for at least the beginning of research in this area. This scale, of course, is an imperfect metric, and additional research may delve into other questions of constitutional content, such as relative specificity or garrulity in providing such rights. This book itself will consider more measures in the next chapter.

Constitutional Religions and Religious Freedom

This section goes to the degree to which constitutional guarantees of religious freedom actually protect such freedom in national practice. To do so, I use my measures coding the content of national constitutions as variables that may determine each nation's actual practice of religious freedom, based on the scales that I set out in Chapter 3. Because other factors will also influence religious freedom, I use the powerful social determinants identified in Chapter 4 as control variables for my analyses.

Before proceeding with these studies, I add an additional variable to help measure the judicial protection of legal freedom. The rule of law variable could be considered a measure of judicial enforcement, but it may be a poor one because it also incorporates the actions of the police or other enforcers of laws that restrict religious freedom, as I discussed in Chapter 4. Consequently, I also use a variable for "legal infrastructure."

Nardulli, Peyton, and Bajjalieh (2010) set out a measure for the mechanisms of a formalized legal discourse and legal education. The quantitative number they assign to legal infrastructure is based on all the legal publications from a country and their date of origin, supplemented by the number and duration of legal education

Table 6.1 *Official Religion and Religious Freedom*

	Overall RAS	RFF	Pew
National Religion	Positive	Negative	Positive
Forbidden National Religion	Positive	Positive	Positive
Nonconstitutional Law	Positive	Positive	Positive
Islamic Population	Negative	Negative	Negative
Log Per Capita GDP	Negative	Negative	Negative
Rule of Law	Negative	Positive	Negative
Legal Infrastructure	Positive	Negative	Negative
Democracy	Positive	Positive	Positive

programs, to which a factor analysis was applied. It is not exactly clear what is being captured by this metric, but it plausibly measures the seriousness of a nation, in terms of legality, at an intellectual level.

The first analysis considers the constitution's treatment of national religion as a factor assessing religious freedom. Enough nations fell into three categories to enable testing. In my sample, about 21 percent of the countries had a constitutional national religion, in 23 percent of countries a national religion was forbidden, and around 55 percent of the nations left the matter to nonconstitutional law. Each of these was used as an independent variable, in addition to the societal factors and legal infrastructure. The results of a multiple regression using the poisson technique are reported in Table 6.1.

All the constitutional provisions appear material for religious freedom on the RAS scale, though there is a strong negative association for the RFF scale and official state religion. A statistically significant positive association on RAS was found for forbidden national religion and leaving the question to nonconstitutional law, with the former association being slightly stronger. The societal variables remain significant as without the constitutional provision, and legal infrastructure is positive but not statistically significant for the overall RAS religious freedom score.

With respect to ARDA's RFF score, a constitutional national religion is negative with statistical significance, whereas a forbidden national religion was positive but without statistical significance, and leaving the question to nonconstitutional law was negative without statistical significance. The difference between the two measures may reflect their different measures for religious freedom, though it may be due to differences in country coverage; however, these are very slight. On the Pew overall measure for religious freedom, the results were similar to those for the RFF measure, but nothing was statistically significant. The lack of significance may be due to the Pew rating system. Nations are grouped into a few categories, and many nations receive a perfect score, so the scale lacks the differentiation of the other scales.

After assessing all the results, the constitutionalization of a state religion appears to have the expected effect of reducing religious freedom, though the consistency and magnitude of this effect is not clear. Democracy is always a positive factor, and Islamic population is always a negative factor, though they do not always reach statistical significance. The legal infrastructure variable does not clearly have an effect.

To visualize the effect of a constitutional state religion without the control variables, Figure 6.1 presents a box plot that shows the relative RAS scores for the countries with no state religion

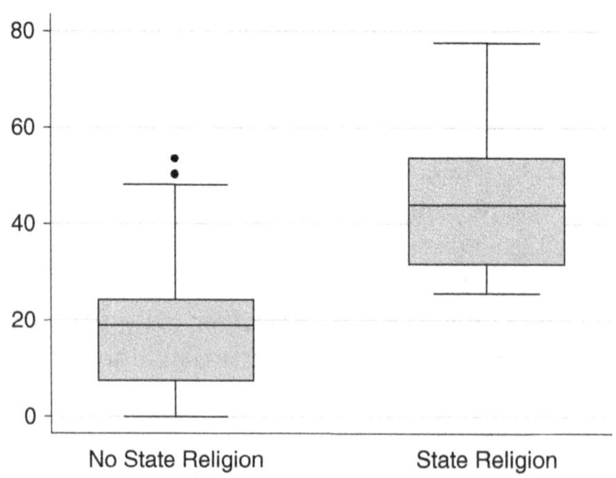

Figure 6.1 Official State Religion and RAS Scores

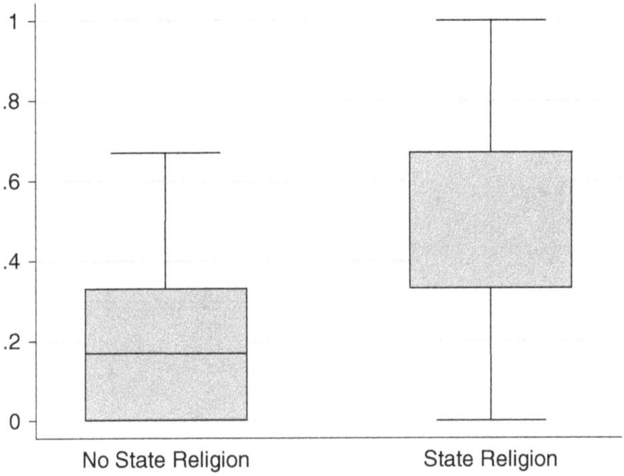

Figure 6.2 Official State Religion and Pew Scores

(forbidden or left to democratic governance) and the same scores for countries with an official state religion.

The effect of having a national religion in the constitution are pronounced. The very best RAS score for countries with a state religion was worse than the average score for a country without any formal state religion. The average restriction on religious freedom was twice as bad in nations with official state religions.

An official state religion had a negative effect on the Pew scores but not at the level of statistical significance. Figure 6.2 displays the same box plot for countries with an official state religion, using the overall Pew measures.

The difference here is not so dramatic as for the RAS scores, but still a clear one. Much of the difference is associated with Costa Rica and Argentina, nations with a state religion but perfect scores on the Pew measure of religious freedom.

It seems clear that nations with a formal constitutional state religion have somewhat less religious freedom. Forbidding a state religion may have some positive effect, as opposed to making no specification, but this effect is not an especially large one. Unsurprisingly, the presence of a state religion tends to reduce religious freedom. The affirmative prohibition on a state religion, though, has an uncertain effect.

Table 6.2 *Free Exercise and Religious Freedom*

	Overall RAS	RFF	Pew
Free Exercise	Positive	Positive	Positive
Islamic Population	Negative	Negative	Negative
Log Per Capita GDP	Negative	Negative	Negative
Rule of Law	Negative	Positive	Negative
Legal Infrastructure	Positive	Negative	Negative
Democracy	Positive	Positive	Positive

Free Exercise and Religious Freedom

The next analysis considers the effect of a constitutional provision guaranteeing freedom of religion, much like the U.S. free exercise clause. The effect of this analysis is somewhat limited by the broad prevalence of free exercise clauses. More than 94 percent of the nations in my sample had such provisions. Table 6.2 presents the poisson regression results for my variables.

For the RAS scores, all the variables were statistically significant. Legal infrastructure provided a statistically significant positive effect, and all the other variables were consistent with the expected results. Legal infrastructure did not show these benefits for the RFF and Pew scores. On the Pew scale, only democracy had a statistically significant positive effect. The lack of statistical significance, though, may be due to the limited differentiation provided by this scale.

The presence of a free exercise clause in a constitution plainly had a positive effect on religious freedom. The magnitude of this effect is displayed in Figure 6.3, a box plot showing the RAS scores for countries with a constitutional provision promising religious freedom and those without such a guarantee

The size of the difference and the statistical significance (illustrated by the placement of the boxes) is also plain. Because the vast majority of nations have such clauses, this finding is perhaps not one of great practical significance. However, the relatively low RAS scores for the vast majority of nations with such a promise is instructive and

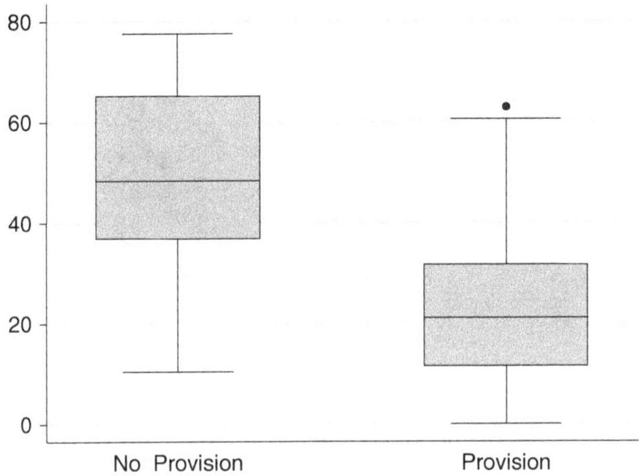

Figure 6.3 RAS Religious Freedom by Free Exercise Clause

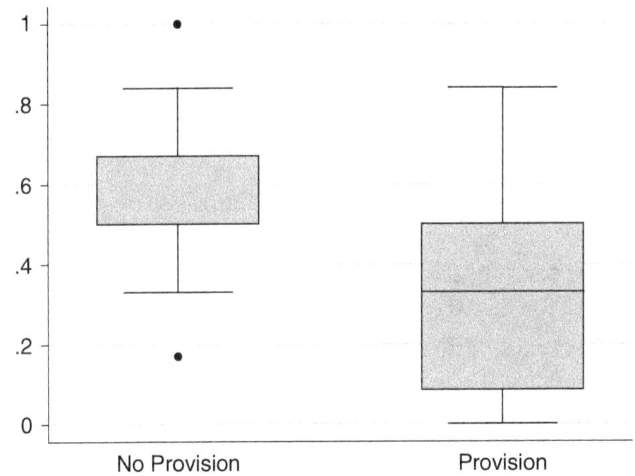

Figure 6.4 Pew Religious Freedom by Free Exercise Clause

indicates its value in protecting religious freedom. To check these results, I ran the same box plot using the Pew scores for religious freedom, displayed in Figure 6.4.

As before, the results are generally consistent with the RAS scores, but the effect is not so dramatic. The evidence indicates that

Table 6.3 *Establishment Clause and Religious Freedom*

	Overall RAS	RFF	Pew
Separation	Positive	Positive	Positive
Islamic Population	Negative	Negative	Negative
Log Per Capita GDP	Negative	Negative	Negative
Rule of Law	Negative	Positive	Negative
Legal Infrastructure	Positive	Negative	Negative
Democracy	Positive	Positive	Positive

a free exercise clause serves to promote religious freedom. While such a provision is no guarantee of religious freedom, the data suggest that it helps to some degree.

Establishment Clause and Religious Freedom

The next constitutional provision to be examined is the existence of something like the American establishment clause that calls for the separation of church and state. In the sample, 39 percent of the nations have such a provision. Table 6.3 displays the poisson multiple regression of my variables, including the establishment clause, on the different scales for religious freedom.

The results for the RAS overall score are strong, with nearly all variables statistically significant and in the expected direction. The Pew scores are roughly similar, though the presence of a separation clause was not a statistically significant determinant by that measure. The clause is a positive by all three scales. To illustrate the nature of the relationship and magnitude of the difference, Figure 6.5 provides a box plot of the overall RAS religious freedom scores for nations with and without such a constitutional provision.

A separation clause appears to provide for greater religious freedom, but those benefits seem relatively slight. A graph for the Pew scale shows a similar association, though slightly less difference for the presence of the clause. The establishment clause appears to have some beneficial effect on religious freedom, but only to a very

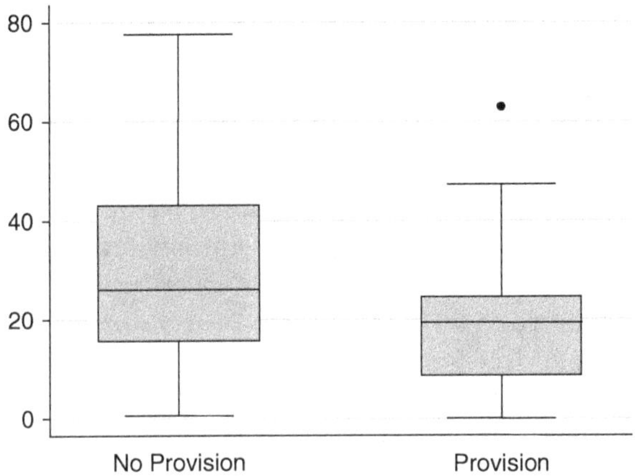

Figure 6.5 RAS Religious Freedom by Separation Clause

Table 6.4 *Separation of Church and State and Categories of Religious Freedom*

	Oppression	Regulation	Religious Laws
Constitutional Separation	Positive	Positive	Positive
Islamic Population	Negative	Negative	Negative
Log Per Capita GDP	Negative	Negative	Negative
Rule of Law	Negative	Negative	Negative
Legal Infrastructure	Positive	Positive	Positive
Democracy	Positive	Positive	Positive

marginal degree. It does not dramatically advance the protection of such freedom.

The most powerful results are found with the RAS scale. In addition to its overall measure, reported in the prior table, the RAS measures break down restrictions on religious freedom into subcategories, which I categorized as minority oppression, regulation, and the adoption of religious laws. I consider the relative effects of my variables for the subcategories in Table 6.4.

Presumably, our greatest concern over religious freedom might be the oppression of minority religions. Although the separation clause had a positive effect here, the only statistically significant results were for Islamic population and democracy. Perhaps this is to be expected. Such oppression is probably the practice of an authoritarian, even theocratic state, which might be expected to pay somewhat less mind to legal niceties. Judicial protection might be weaker or even ignored. The most powerful results are for religious legislation, where judicial protection might be anticipated to be stronger.

Next, I consider the Pew measure for constitutional content. One of the questions was whether the constitution or basic law of the nation provides for freedom of religion. This is not as clear a measure of constitutional content as the Elkins and Ginsburg coding. The meaning of religious freedom is not perfectly clear. Moreover, the answer to the question may be influenced, for example, by judicial interpretation. The direct coding of content says that several nations have text protecting freedom of religion (e.g., Algeria, Mauritania), while the Pew measure says that they do not. Perhaps this difference is because the text has been obliterated by interpretation. Indeed, as shown in Table 6.5, there is not a particularly high correlation between the Elkins and Ginsburg coding of religious freedom and the Pew coding for the same variable. The Pew scores might best be regarded as the national constitution in practice rather than the constitution on paper.

The Pew scale of constitutional protection repeatedly has a positive influence on religious freedom. Interestingly, the strength of the association is greater by the RAS measure than by the Pew measure of overall religious freedom. Islamic population and per capita GDP

Table 6.5 *Pew Constitution Measure and Religious Freedom*

	Overall RAS	RFF	Pew
Pew Measure	Positive	Positive	Positive
Islamic Population	Negative	Negative	Negative
Log Per Capita GDP	Negative	Negative	Negative
Rule of Law	Negative	Positive	Negative
Legal Infrastructure	Positive	Negative	Negative
Democracy	Positive	Positive	Positive

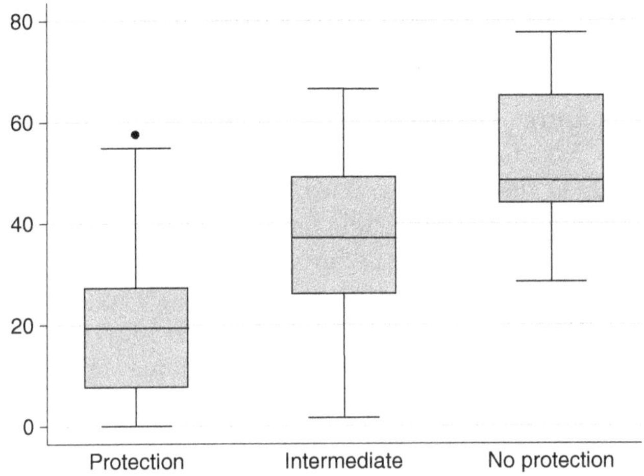

Figure 6.6 Pew Constitution Measure and RAS Overall

remain consistently negative in their effect on religious freedom. Democracy, by contrast, is always positive in its effect and statistically significant. The results for the Pew measures of constitutional content are fundamentally consistent with the Elkins and Ginsburg measures, which add confidence to our conclusions.

The Pew coding has three categories – the constitution protects religious freedom, the constitution does not specifically provide for freedom of religion but does offer some protection, and the constitution does not protect religious freedom. To illustrate the nature of their association, Figure 6.6 displays the RAS overall religious freedom scores, based on the category of constitutional protection of religious freedom from the Pew data.

The effect of constitutional protection on religious freedom is quite striking. Although nations with constitutional protection occasionally produce poor RAS scores, their typical religious freedom is clearly better than nations with intermediate protection, whose freedom is typically better than nations with no protection. None of the nations with no constitutional protection has truly good religious freedom. The highest level of freedom for any of these nations is distinctly worse than the average level of freedom for nations with constitutional protection.

The data seem to show that constitutional protections of religious freedom actually have a positive effect. The confidence in this conclusion is enhanced by the fact that the results are robust to two different measures of constitutional content and several different measures of religious freedom. The results vary in significance, depending upon the measures used, but they remain consistent in direction. Moreover, the preceding figures demonstrate the substantive significance of constitutional protections.

The data show that constitutional promises do not serve as guarantees. The degree of protection of religious freedom varies considerably among nations with given constitutional provisions. The constitutions do appear to push nations toward greater religious freedom in practice, depending upon other national factors. The degree to which nations conform to their constitutions is plainly dependent upon other factors. For example, democracy seems to be a very strong promoter of religious freedom. The variables plausibly associated with judicial protection, rule of law, and legal infrastructure do not show much effect. But the regressions did not distinguish such external effects depending on the nature of the constitution.

Up to this point, none of the analyses considers the interaction of constitutions with the other variables. James Madison's theory was that constitutions inspire democracies to protect the individual rights contained in those constitutions. To see if this is part of the explanation for democracy's positive effect on religious freedom, one must compare the role of democratic governance in countries that have constitutional protection with its effect in countries that do not. The following section explores whether constitutional protections operate in tandem with other factors to promote religious freedom.

Interaction of Constitutions and Social Factors

The analysis so far considers the various external social and legal factors and the constitutional measures in general. But this assumes the external factors operate the same in the presence or absence of a constitution. Perhaps the significance of a constitution is in how it influences the societal factors affecting religious freedom. Thus,

Table 6.6 *Interaction of Separation with Democracy and Legal Infrastructure*

	Overall RAS	RFF	Pew
Separation Clause	Positive	Negative	Positive
Islamic Population	Negative	Negative	Negative
Log Per Capita GDP	Negative	Negative	Negative
Rule of Law	Negative	Positive	Negative
Legal Infrastructure	Negative	Negative	Negative
Democracy	Positive	Positive	Positive
Democracy x Separation Clause	Negative	Negative	Negative
Legal Infrastructure x Separation Clause	Positive	Positive	Positive

Madison suggested that a constitution could inspire the democratic protection of such freedom. If this is true, the previous analyses would miss this effect.

The association of constitutions with the nonconstitutional factors can be captured through interaction effects. This is a process that produces a variable which combines the existence of a constitutional provision with the level of another variable, demonstrating the effect of the two variables together. I conduct my regression with interaction variables for democracy and legal infrastructure. This should provide information on whether a constitution encourages democratic protection of religious freedom and/or encourages legal protection of religious freedom. Table 6.6 displays the effect on religious freedom of the traditional variables, plus interaction variables for constitutional separation of religion and state with democracy and legal infrastructure.

The results of this analysis are quite striking. The interaction terms of democracy and legal infrastructure display their effect in the presence of a separation clause. The uninteracted terms of democracy and legal infrastructure show their effects in the absence of such a clause. Democracy, which was such a powerful creator of religious freedom, appears to have this effect due to the absence of such a constitutional protection. It offers little when such a provision is present. Legal infrastructure has the opposite effect. It advances religious freedom when a separation clause is present but does not when such a provision is absent.

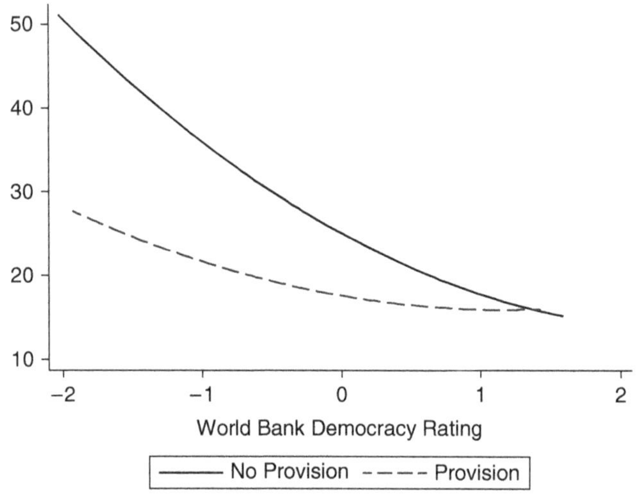

Figure 6.7 Democracy and Constitutional Separation Clause

The effect of democracy with and without constitutional provisions can be seen visually. For the separation clause, Figure 6.7 displays the effect of democracy for nations with and without a constitutional separation of church and state.

The presence of a separation clause means religious freedom is well protected, even at low levels of democracy, but more democracy improves the situation somewhat. In the absence of a separation clause, low democracy means much restriction of religious freedom. Only at very high levels of democracy is religious freedom well protected without a separation clause.

The depiction of legal infrastructure is equally informative. In the basic regressions earlier in the chapter, this variable did not appear to carry much weight in protecting religious freedom. But when interacted with the existence of a constitutional protection, it turned strongly positive. Given a legal constitutional provision, legal infrastructure enforces it.

Figure 6.8 displays the effect of higher levels of legal infrastructure on the overall RAS measure for religious freedom, with and without a constitutional separation clause.

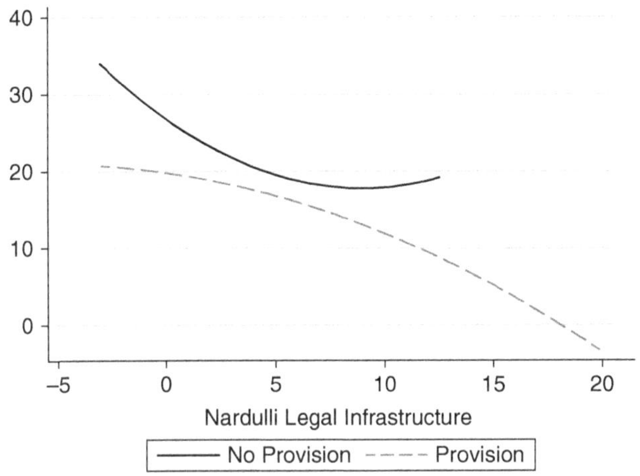

Figure 6.8 Legal Infrastructure and Constitutional Separation Clause

Nations with separation clauses consistently have more religious freedom. Without such a clause, legal infrastructure improves freedom somewhat. In the presence of a separation clause, though, more legal infrastructure improves religious freedom a great deal.

This effect is not limited to separation clauses. Consider a constitutional provision prohibiting a state religion and its effect on religious freedom. Figure 6.9 illustrates the effect of democracy on religious freedom, using the RAS scale, for nations with and without this constitutional provision.

Here we see that democracy has a very dramatic effect in promoting religious freedom where there is no prohibition on national religion. More democracy means fewer laws limiting religious freedom. In the presence of the constitutional prohibition, though, democracy is irrelevant. Religious freedom is highly protected regardless of the degree of national democracy. It's not that democracy is not beneficial in the presence of this constitutional protection; it appears to be unnecessary.

Democratic governance and constitutionalism are often seen as in tension with one another (Bellamy & Castiglione 1997). This is clear from the fact that judges use constitutions to strike down

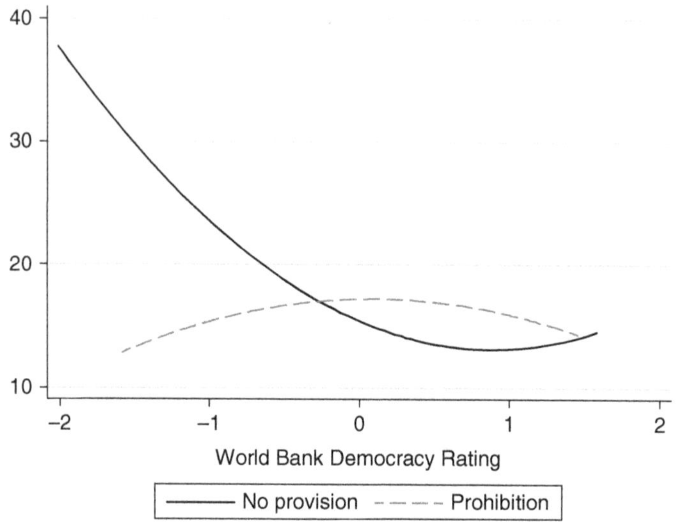

Figure 6.9 Effect of Democracy Depending on Constitutional Prohibition of National Religion

statutes that were adopted by the democratic branches. But the previous chapter showed that the judiciary is relatively majoritarian in nature, perhaps as much as the executive branches. And in the case of the furtherance of religious liberty, it appears that both serve to enhance it independently.

The constitutional provision and democracy are functional substitutes. Either such a provision or a high level of democracy will protect freedom. In contrast to Madison's view that constitutions will inspire democratic majorities, it appears that the people need no constitution to provide religious freedom. But such a constitutional provision will offer protection, even in the absence of democratic pressure.

The substantive nature of the association of legal infrastructure for a constitutional prohibition on state religion is shown in Figure 6.10.

This figure illustrates what the regression analysis with interaction effects showed. Without a constitutional provision of prohibition, legal infrastructure may be slightly beneficial but has little effect. In

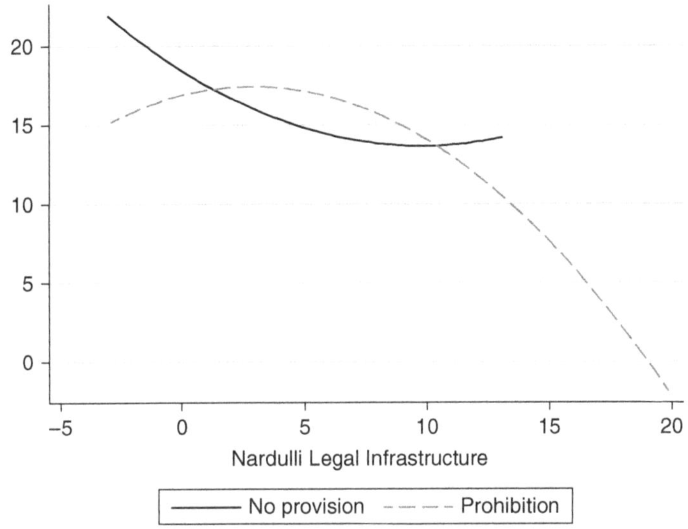

Figure 6.10 Effect of Legal Infrastructure Depending on Constitutional Prohibition of National Religion

the presence of a constitutional guarantee, however, greater legal infrastructure has a substantial effect in protecting religious freedom.

The results suggest that directionality is from democracy to religious freedom (otherwise one would see the association in the presence of constitutional protection). They illustrate the value of the judicial system in the enforcement of constitutional guarantees. With such guarantees and a strong legal infrastructure, religious freedom is protected independent of democracy.

Individual Laws and Actions

I have been relying on the RAS overall scale as a measure of religious freedom in a nation. This scale is comprised of dozens of individual state laws or actions. This section considers the effect of constitutional provisions on the individual cases. I begin by considering free exercise clauses. Running a logistic regression using the presence or absence of a free exercise clause with the societal variables invariably showed that the constitutional provision had a positive effect. Indeed, the positive effect was statistically significant for numerous measures, including:

- Restrictions on public observance of religious services, festivals, and/or holidays
- Restrictions on building, repairing, and/or maintaining places of worship
- Restrictions on access to places of worship
- Forced observance of religious laws of other groups
- Restrictions on formal religious organizations
- Restrictions on the ability to make and/or obtain materials necessary for religious rites
- Restrictions on conversion to minority religions
- Restrictions on proselytizing
- Restrictions on other types of observance of religious law
- Restrictions on the publication or dissemination of written religious material
- Restrictions or prohibitions on the sale of alcoholic beverages
- Restrictions on conversions away from the dominant religion
- Restrictions on interfaith marriages
- Mandatory closing of some or all business during religious holidays
- Other restrictions on activities during religious holidays
- Mandatory religious education in public schools
- Government funding of religious schools or religious educational programs in secular schools
- Official government positions, salaries, or other funding for clergy
- Certain religious officials become government officials by virtue of their religious position
- Some or all government officials must meet certain religious requirements in order to hold office
- Presence of religious courts with jurisdiction over some matters of law

- Religious organizations must register with the government to obtain official status
- Unspecified restrictions on women (such as on education and employment)

This is an impressive list of religious freedoms advanced, if not guaranteed, by free exercise clauses. However, the difficulty with this measure is the commonality of such clauses. The analysis can test only a limited number of nations that do not have them.

Using the same procedure, I considered specific laws or actions that were affected by a nation's establishment clause, which are far less common internationally. Statistically significant associations promoting religious freedom existed for the following categories in the RAS data:

- Forced conversions
- Restrictions or prohibitions on the sale of alcoholic beverages
- Laws of inheritance defined by religion
- Restrictions on interfaith marriages
- Mandatory religious education in public schools
- Government funding of religious schools or religious educational programs in secular schools
- Government funding of religious charitable organizations
- Some or all government officials must meet religious requirements in order to hold office
- Presence of religious courts with jurisdiction over some matters of law
- Prohibitive restrictions on abortion

This is a less impressive list of benefits than the one for the free exercise clause. Moreover, there was no significant effect for some measures where one would clearly expect an establishment clause to have such an effect, such as providing official government positions to clergy.

Unlike the free exercise clause, some of the outcomes for the establishment clause ran in the opposite direction expected, with establishment clauses associated with less freedom. In general, though, such clauses operated as one might expect legally, with the strongest effect found in religious laws. Establishment clauses were consistently associated with less religious legislation, with multiple unlisted laws and policies nearing a statistically significant association, if not reaching it, which would explain why the overall combination had a statistically significant positive association. The establishment clause had less effect on measures for oppression of minority religions.

As already observed, the effect of an establishment clause is affected by a nation's legal infrastructure. When the interaction clause for infrastructure was added to the analysis, the associations with religious freedom were somewhat stronger but still largely limited to religious legislation. This is where the effect of the establishment clause is primarily seen.

Proportionality

Some national constitutions promise religious freedom but qualify that promise with conditions. They may permit limitations on religious freedom in the interest of national security or public morality or some other standard. This is commonly known as proportionality doctrine. While such qualifications seem like obvious loopholes for a government to deny freedom, the relevance of such express qualifying language is uncertain. Proportionality is the most common approach today (Sweet & Mathews 2008). But Fox (2011,61) suggests that the balancing process means that "individual clauses taken in isolation are not necessarily reliable indicators of government policies" and that national security clauses are commonly used to override other constitutional guarantees.

Even when constitutional language appears to be absolute, in application it is typically qualified by governmental institutions. Even such a strong statement as "Congress shall make no law" in the U.S. First Amendment has produced judicial recognition of various exceptions, laws that can be made even though they limit free speech.

Ginsburg and Elkins did not code constitutions for the presence of such qualifications. The Pew study did ask the question: "Does the constitution or basic law include stipulations that appear to qualify or substantially contradict the concept of 'religious freedom'?" This appears to be asking for the presence of qualifying language of proportionality. It is imperfect because it is not clear that the question is referring to the language of the constitution itself or its application in practice. But it is the best data available on proportionality.

The Pew question admitted of four answers:

- No (scored 0)
- Yes, there is a qualification (scored .33)
- Yes, there is a substantial contradiction and only some religious practices are protected (scored 0.67)
- Religious freedom is not provided in the first place (scored 1)

The intermediate answers appear to reflect a situation where the constitution explicitly provides for proportionality in its protection of religious freedom. Figure 6.11 displays a dot plot of the average overall RAS score by each category. As always, lower scores mean more religious freedom.

Once again, the constitution appears to make a practical difference. The most religious freedom is found in nations with no

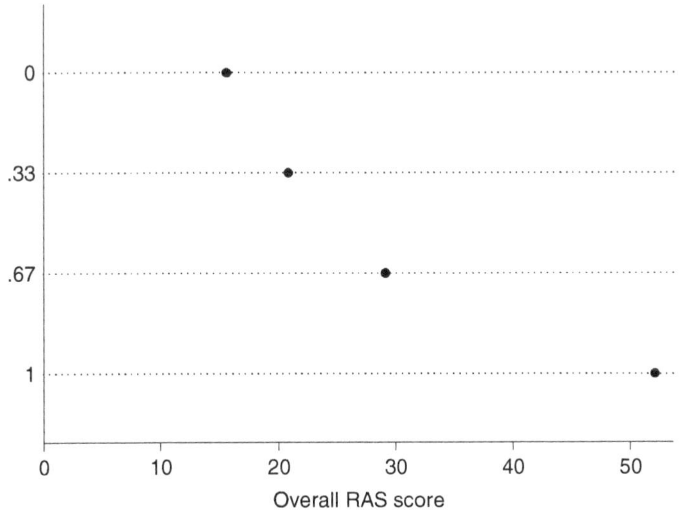

Figure 6.11 Religious Freedom by Proportionality

Table 6.7 *Proportionality and Religious Freedom*

	Overall RAS	RFF	Pew
Free Exercise	Positive	Positive	Positive
Proportionality	Negative	Negative	Negative
Islamic Population	Negative	Negative	Negative
Log Per Capita GDP	Negative	Negative	Negative
Rule of Law	Negative	Positive	Negative
Legal Infrastructure	Positive	Negative	Negative
Democracy	Positive	Positive	Positive

constitutional proportionality. The least religious freedom is found in nations that do not provide for it constitutionally. Nations with constitutional freedom and proportionality have an intermediate level of religious freedom.

To analyze the effect of proportionality, including the other variables, I run a regression using the background social variables, the Pew proportionality measure, and the presence of a free exercise clause, which the proportionality typically conditions. Table 6.7 reports the associations and their statistical significance.

Again, the constitutional provisions appear to have a beneficial effect on religious freedom. For the RAS scale, both the presence of a free exercise clause and the lack of proportionality qualifications were beneficial for religious freedom and statistically significant. For the RFF and Pew overall measures, both were positive and one or the other had statistical significance in this relationship. Although all nations qualify religious and other freedoms, the presence of express proportionality language appears to produce relatively more restrictions on freedoms.

Government Assistance

Some of the RAS individual measures involved government financing of religions, such as in the area of educational activities. The Pew scale has a different measure for government support of religions.

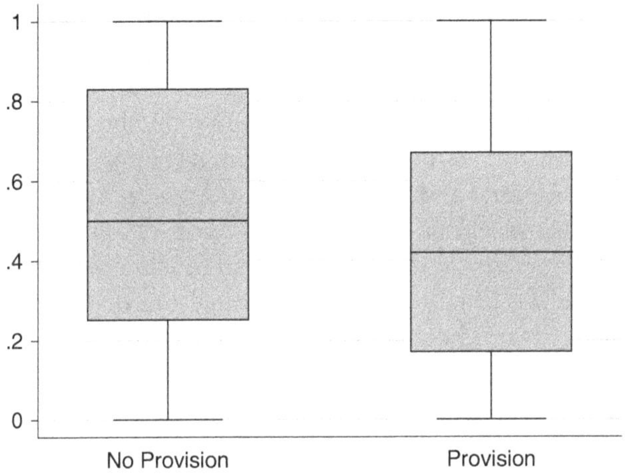

Figure 6.12 Establishment Clause and Government Funding of Religion

The question was: "Does any level of government provide funds or other resources for religious property (e.g., buildings upkeep, repair or land)?" Answers could be 0 for no assistance, 0.5 for such assistance with no obvious favoritism for a particular group or groups, or 1 for yes with obvious favoritism. The scores have closer gradations, but the first half of the scale apparently reflects the theory that government may favor religions, so long as they don't play favorites among religions.

One might expect a separation clause to have an effect here. But in the regression with the background societal variables, there is no effect. The directionality of the relationship is correct, but the association is a weak one. Figure 6.12 shows the association of an establishment clause with the Pew scores for government funding.

The two categories are virtually identical. Countries with establishment clauses have on average only very slightly less government funding of religion. Dividing the scale into the two halves does not alter this. Nor does a freedom of religion clause show any effect.

This topic is where formal state religion comes into play. For nations with a state religion, the average score was around .8, showing considerable favoritism, and the lowest score was around .4. For nations in which such a state religion was forbidden or left to the political branches, the average score was below .5, and both had representative countries at zero. Interestingly, nations where a state religion was forbidden actually showed somewhat more favoritism than nations where it was left to the elected branches.

Religion provisions in constitutions do not appear to have much effect on government funding of religion generally. A formal national state religion is associated with much higher funding and favoritism. Other religious provisions have at best a slight effect on such funding. Of course, funding provides some favoritism but does not deny religious choice and could disadvantage the favored religion, with conditions placed on government funding. The most influential variable was democracy, which was associated with much less government funding of religion.

Registration

One significant regulation on religion in the world is some registration requirement, as discussed in Chapter 2. To obtain recognition and benefits, religions must register with the government and be approved. At best, this provision merely imposes some additional costs on religious groups, but at worst it can be used to control and manipulate their practices. The RAS has a category it calls registration, but it does not truly capture this government licensing process. The Pew group, though, had a question: "Does any level of government ask religious groups to register for any reason, including to be eligible for benefits such as tax exemption?" Again, this is not a yes/no question. Answers could be 0 for no registration, .33 for registration but in a nondiscriminatory way, .67 for registration that adversely affects the ability of some religious groups to operate, or 1 for a process that clearly discriminates against some religious groups. This enables a test of whether constitutional provisions affect such a registration process.

As with the matter of government funding, neither an establishment clause nor a free exercise clause shows any effect on the existence of government registration requirements or their severity. Nor did the presence of a state religion or a clause forbidding a state religion. In each case, the registration scores were virtually identical for nations with constitutional protections and those without. Although one might think that such registration systems might interfere with the free exercise of one's religion or be associated with an establishment of religion, the data do not suggest this is occurring. Nor do the interaction variables show much effect, though legal infrastructure does appear to reduce the severity of registration requirements. Again, the most powerful determinant was democracy, which reduced registration requirements.

Conclusion

The analyses in this chapter present some clear results. Constitutional protection of religious freedom matters. Different constitutional provisions all show a positive effect on religious freedom. This effect persists with the introduction of third variables. It also survives different measures for religious freedom. While the results among these measures are not perfectly consistent, the constitutional provisions inevitably reveal some positive benefit for religious freedom.

Different constitutional provisions have different effects. Forbidding a national religion has some positive effect but little additional benefit over leaving the question to nonconstitutional decision making. A formal state religion, though, plainly has a negative effect. Free exercise clauses seem to have a plain benefit, but nearly all nations have them, and some of these still do not offer strong protection to religious freedom. A separation clause shows some clear benefits and is not so common. Express constitutional proportionality language qualifying religious freedom has a negative effect, as would be expected if the language of constitutions was important. However, constitutions don't appear to have much effect on other issues, such as government funding of religion or registration requirements.

The results also say much about how and why constitutions matter. Constitutions are not essential to protect religious freedom. Very high levels of democracy protect such freedom in the absence of constitutions. However, constitutions are a valuable protection of religious freedom in nations with lower levels of democracy. This is especially true when a nation has sufficient judicial infrastructure to facilitate the courts as a protector, consistent with Epp's theory of how such resources can activate constitutional protections. James Madison, it appears, was half right. The judiciary can protect religious freedom even in the absence of democracy. And while democracy is very important to the protection of religious freedom, it is not the result of constitutional inspiration. Even without such inspiration, democratic governance strongly promotes religious freedom.

7 Religious Freedom and Society

The last chapter answered the fundamental question of the book – do constitutions matter? It appears that they do provide greater religious freedom, though not universally. Their benefits are seen in some practices but not others. And the effect of constitutions depends on other circumstances of the state, such as legal infrastructure. This chapter examines the effect of such religious freedom on society, in an attempt to answer some of the questions posed by Chapter 1 of the book.

One argument for freedom of religion is that it promotes religious faith among a nation's people. Laycock (2011) argues alternatively for a religion-neutral case for religious liberty built more on individual freedom than faith. This chapter explores the operation of religious freedom and how it has conformed to the two visions.

I begin by examining the association of religious freedom, and constitutional protections, with various measures of national religious belief. These include religious diversity and religiosity, which freedom is hypothesized to enhance. I also examine the association of religious freedom with national levels of atheism, for which the relationship might be more contested.

I proceed to consider the association of religious freedom with other societal measures. These include the effect of a constitutional provision on a society's religious diversity and overall religiosity. The effect on atheism is also relevant. I also consider the effect of religious freedom on levels of expressed happiness and on the interests of women, which religion may undermine.

Religious Diversity

The economic theory of religion discussed in Chapter 1 suggests that different faiths will compete for followers. State regulation of religion plainly may discourage this competition, favoring a prevailing monopoly religion. Conkle (2011) suggests, however, that very high levels of religious diversity may become wild and seen as dangerous and undermine governmental protection of religious liberty. In this section, I consider whether greater religious freedom promotes greater religious diversity, as expected.

The value of greater religious diversity is certainly debatable. If everyone in a nation shared a religion, one might expect greater social cooperation. Barro and McCleary (2006) suggest that sharing a common religion facilitates communication and that individuals may lose utility when others have different faiths. Religious commonality could produce greater social capital. Religious diversity potentially could produce internal religious conflict that might become violent. Reynal-Querol (2002) found that differing religious beliefs produced greater conflict, but Fearon and Laitin (2003) found no association between religious diversity and domestic conflict. Rummel (2002) found that the relationship was contingent on a lack of democracy.

Gruber (2005) studied the effect of greater market density and found that it was associated with higher religious participation and other benefits, including education, income, marriage, and less reliance on welfare. The study covered only the United States, though, where religions are freely chosen. Any market density was the product of individual choices, not state action. This does illustrate the limitations of findings on density, though. It may be crucially important whether the density is chosen or forced. Moreover, diversity has the fundamental benefit of offering expanded freedom of choice.

A common measure of religious diversity uses a Herfindahl-style index. This takes the percentage of people for each religion, squares that number, and then adds the squared totals. The more diverse a nation, the lower these scores will be. The index was designed to measure competition, with scores ranging from zero to one, the latter representing a monopolistic lack of competition. When a religion approaches monopoly status, the scores will approach one. The data for this measure is taken from McCleary and Barro (2006a, 2006b).

The Herfindahl measures for the nations of the world vary considerably. Some nations have extremely high scores, such as Tunisia (.98) and Yemen (.98). High scores are not limited to Middle Eastern nations, though. South American nations, such as Columbia (.89) and Ecuador (.87), often have very high scores, as do some European nations, such as Poland (.85) and Greece (.85). The lowest scores are commonly found in Africa, with nations such as Ghana (.22) and Kenya (.22), though some European nations, Canada, and Australia also are on the low end of the scores.

Most of the religious Herfindahl scores would be considered high concentrations by the economic concentration standards of the index, but religion is different from most markets and probably has very high barriers to entry. There are more cultural pressures to adopt a religion than a particular product, and the government may add to those pressures, making minority religions more difficult.

To test the effect, I again conduct a regression using my broad societal measures and the scales of religious freedom. I eliminated percentage Muslim from the independent variables, because this is a component of the religious diversity measure that is the dependent variable, and legal infrastructure, which seems unrelated to the association. Table 7.1 reports the results of a regression on the determinants of religious diversity.

The societal control variables had no significant association with religious diversity. The only significant determinant was RAS religious liberty, which had a strong association with greater religious

Table 7.1 *Religious Freedom and Religious Diversity*

	Religious Diversity		
RAS Measure	Positive		
RFF Measure		Negative	
Pew Measure			Negative
Log Per Capita GDP	Negative	Negative	Negative
Rule of Law	Positive	Positive	Positive
Democracy	Negative	Negative	Negative

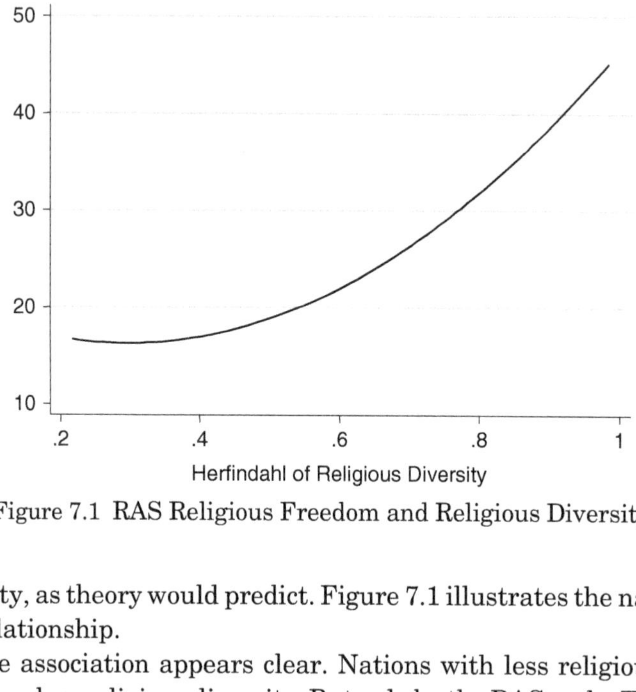

Figure 7.1 RAS Religious Freedom and Religious Diversity

diversity, as theory would predict. Figure 7.1 illustrates the nature of this relationship.

The association appears clear. Nations with less religious freedom have less religious diversity. But only by the RAS scale. The RFF and Pew measures showed no such effect. The other measures – democracy, rule of law, and per capita GDP – showed no real effect. The profound effect of the RAS measure, though, suggests that its scale for religious freedom is associated with greater religious diversity in a nation. RAS is the one source that measures direct legislative restrictions on religious freedom.

Religiosity

Religious freedom might result in more or less religiosity. If religious freedom encourages religious pluralism, which in turn produces a market in religions, one might expect it to produce greater religiosity, as consumers were better able to find a program of beliefs that they liked. Conkle (2011) suggests that the relationship goes both ways; that religiosity supports religious liberty. This is the economic theory of religion described in Chapter 1. However, the program that individuals select may not be highly religious. Some consumers might select religious programs that didn't require much commitment of them. North and Gwin (2004) found that greater state involvement with religion was associated with less religiosity.

For a state religion, monopolistic status might be expected to discourage religiosity. However, state religion also may come with considerable cultural pressure to be highly religious or at least in the practice of saying one was highly religious. In some Islamic nations, there may be considerable political and cultural pressure to be a devout Muslim. It may be important to pragmatic success in society. Hence, it is unclear whether greater religious freedom should logically lead to greater religiosity.

There is no clear measure for a nation's religiosity, but various scales could be used. The Gallup poll provides one measure. It asked people in over one hundred countries: "Is religion an important part of your daily life?" The scores tended to be quite high, with several nations having more than 99 percent of the people giving an affirmative answer and nearly half the sample at 90 percent or greater. European nations had the lowest scores, as expected from the research on secularization.

A poll has obvious imperfections. The notion of "an important part" may have different meanings in different cultural circumstances. Simpler life circumstances may contribute to religious importance. In human history, religion was much more important in the past, dictating everything from who governed a society to medical practices. One might expect a person living in Europe of the Middle Ages to say religion was quite important because it was largely the organizing factor of the entire society. Moreover, the notion of "an important part" may have linguistically different meanings in different cultures, so the measure does not allow for precise comparison among nations. Nevertheless, the scale seems about as good as possible for measuring religiosity.

My societal and legal measures do not offer much explanation for a nation's level of religiosity. The economic hypothesis suggests that religious diversity should enhance religious belief, and the association is a positive one, but does not approach any standard of statistical significance. Of course, it is possible that diversity increases religious belief but not of the intensity measured. Increased religious liberty, whether by the RAS, RFF, or Pew scales, also has little effect on this measure of religiosity.

Since the measures of actual religious freedom do not closely correlate to national religiosity, it is unsurprising that the constitutional variables also lack any association. This is illustrated in Figure 7.2 in a box plot of religiosity levels for nations with and without separation of church and state clauses in their constitutions.

Nations with separation clauses appear to have slightly less religiosity by this measure, but the effect is obviously not a

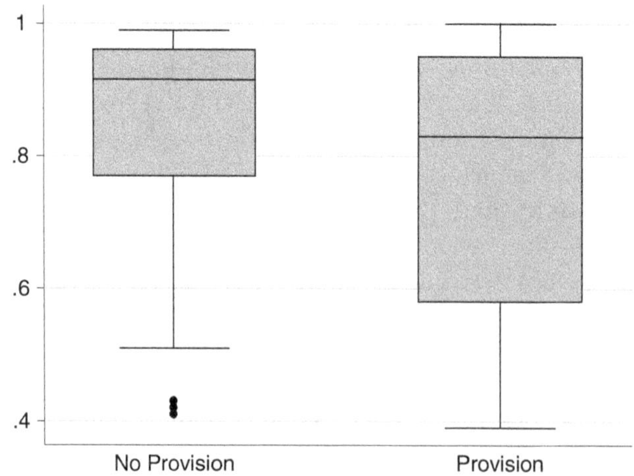

Figure 7.2 Establishment Clause and Religiosity

statistically significant one. Other constitutional provisions show similar effect. Government subsidization has no apparent effect on religiosity. Constitutional freedom of religion simply doesn't seem to be an important factor in driving the religious intensity of a nation's population.

Some geographic effect looks like a possible driver, for whatever reason. European nations had relatively low levels of religiosity, while much of the rest of the world, especially Africa and the Middle East, had very high levels. This may simply be wealth related. Per capita GDP had a statistically significant association with less religiosity, as secularization suggests. Interestingly, democracy also tended to be associated with less religiosity. But none of the legal variables had a significant effect.

Barro and McCleary (2003a) have conducted the leading cross-country study on determinants of relative religiosity. They found that economic growth tended to reduce religiosity, as suggested by the secularization hypothesis. The presence of an official state religion tended to increase religiosity by a substantial amount (nearly 50 percent), but the regulation of religion and reduced religious diversity tended to lower religiosity. Increased education actually tended to be associated with greater religiosity.

The measures for religiosity used in this research were church attendance and certain religious beliefs, such as expressed belief in God or the nature of the afterlife taken from the World Values Survey. These measures have their own difficulties. The data are available for a smaller number of countries that is not so representative of the world. Moreover, the meaning of the questions may vary by religion. Buddhism does not believe in a God, as do other religions. Buddhism and Hinduism have a belief in reincarnation, which is a different approach to the afterlife than found in Muslim or Christian beliefs. The church attendance measures seem like a valuable scale, though, so I will consider them.

While I do not attempt to precisely replicate the Barro and McCleary analysis, I do have the advantage of updated measures of religious freedom and constitutional protections. Those authors had only crude binary variables for state religion and state regulation of religion, taken from secondary sources. I will use my new information on religious freedom to examine a couple of these variables.

Before doing so, the comparison with the Gallup religiosity measure is instructive. Several nations have higher percentages attending church than say that religion is an important part of daily life. In Ireland, it is much higher. While this association is plausible, other nations have levels of church attendance less than half the percentage who speak of the importance of religion to daily life (India, Greece, Latvia, Romania, Turkey), a less plausible finding. It seems odd that a person who finds religion so important to his or her daily life would not attend church. This surely speaks to the imperfection of the Gallup measure.

For the measure of church attendance, none of the variables I use showed much effect. Unlike for the Gallup expressed preferences, greater per capita GDP and democracy were not associated with less religiosity, contrary to secularization theories. Freedom of religion clauses could not be evaluated, as all the nations in this smaller sample had them. Separation clauses were not statistically significant, but certainly did not discourage church attendance. Figure 7.4 shows attendance rates in nations with and without establishment-type clauses.

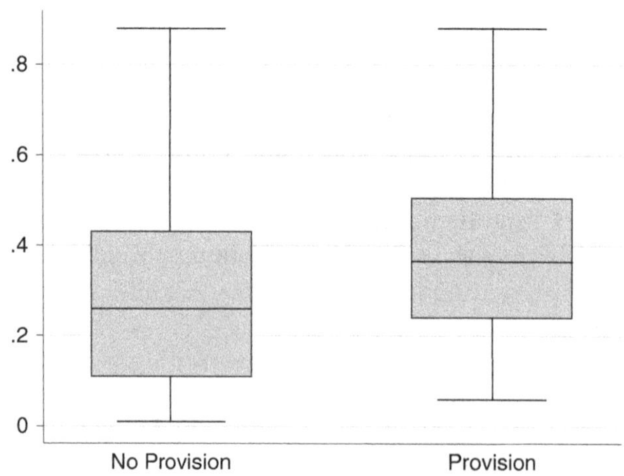

Figure 7.3 Establishment Clause and Church Attendance

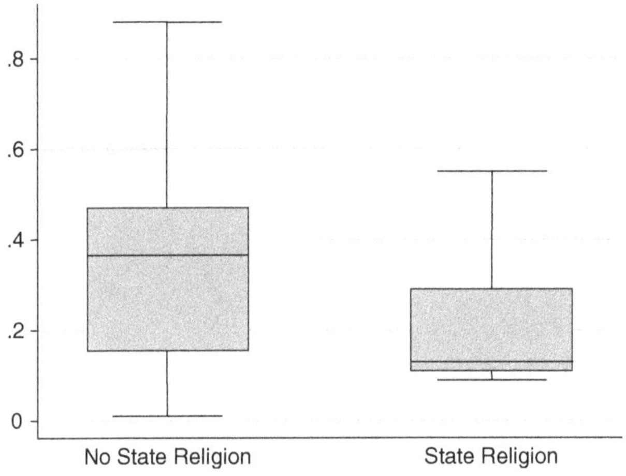

Figure 7.4 State Religion and Church Attendance

There is not statistically significant effect, as the boxes overlap, but establishment clauses do not appear to harm church attendance. Nations with such clauses tend to have somewhat higher church attendance rates than nations without such clauses, indicating that such provisions do not particularly secularize a society.

For state religions, the results were interesting. They fell short of having a statistically significant effect, but the numbers were nonetheless intriguing. Figure 7.4 displays relative attendance rates in nations with a formal state religion, as opposed to all other nations.

The average church attendance in nations with a formal state religion was less than half that in nations without such a national religion. The 95th percentile high attendance rates in nations with a state religion were lower than the average in nations without. It seems quite clear that a state religion does not encourage religious faith but instead appears to have a contrary effect, as the economic theories of religious belief would suggest. One suspects that a state religion is more for the benefit of the state than of religion. The highest average rate of attendance was in nations in which a state religion was forbidden. Such nations had attendance rates that averaged nearly 15 percent higher than other nations. A formal forbidding

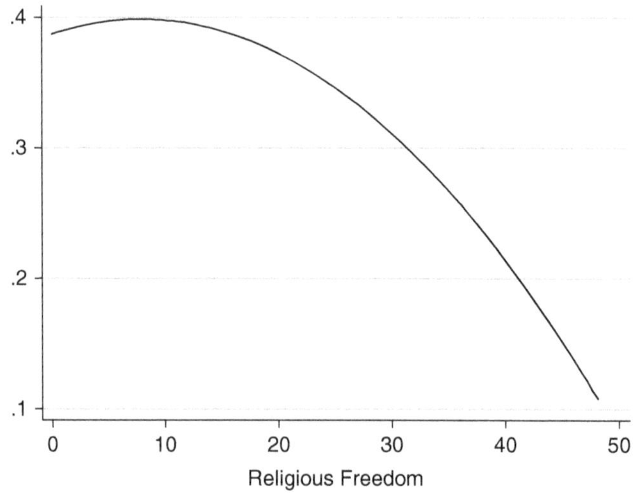

Figure 7.5 Religious Freedom and Church Attendance

of a state religion seems to encourage church attendance, further making the case for separation of church and state.

With respect to actual religion and church attendance, there was no statistically significant association, and the coefficients tended to be positive. The nature of the relationship between the RAS score and church attendance rates can be illustrated by Figure 7.5, with the church attendance on the vertical axis.

At high levels of government restriction of religious freedom at the right side of the graph, church attendance tends to be quite low. Where religious freedom is relatively protected, church attendance tends to be higher. This seems logical and is consistent with the economic theories. When free religion is allowed to blossom, church attendance will be higher. Moreover, the church attendance measure could understate the association between freedom and religion. Some believers in a religious marketplace might reject organized religion and its emphasis on regular church attendance.

The association of attendance with the Herfindahl index is contrary to expectations. While not nearly significant, nations with higher religious concentrations also had higher church attendance. Religious diversity was not associated with this measure of religiosity, as economic theories suggest. Perhaps this shows one shortcoming of the attendance measure – people may attend church out of a community expectation. When everyone in a community is a member of a given religion, absence from church may be more noticeable.

The results using the Barro and McCleary data should be viewed with some caution for other reasons. They are a much smaller sample size than that of the earlier research, and the nations contained in the sample are not representative but weighted toward richer nations. They should be viewed with this caveat. But they should not be dismissed. The smaller sample means that one is less likely to find statistical significance for relationships that would prove statistically significant with a larger sample of nations assessed. They carry the strong suggestion that religious freedom and separation of church and state are associated with greater church attendance.

Atheism

The next analysis considers disbelief. As discussed in Chapter 1, granting express recognition to religious freedom seems to elevate religion. Consequently, it could discourage the irreligious. In practice, though, freedom of religion arguably has had a secularizing effect, empowering the courts to discourage any promotion of religion. Freedom of religion could also promote freedom of atheism, as some cases have in fact held. This section considers the association of constitutional religious freedom and atheistic beliefs.

The data on atheism were taken from Zuckerman (2007). The accuracy of this data may be questioned, as it comes from various different sources for different countries, which may have used different standards or tools of measurement. However, it corresponds reasonably well to the Gallup numbers on the importance of religion, which is confirmatory. The sample is large, but differs from the Gallup sample, so it serves as an additional check.

The majority of nations have very low atheism numbers, commonly 0.5 percent. This is especially true for the nations of Africa and the Middle East and to a lesser degree those of South America. A few nations have relatively high numbers of atheists. Japan has a remarkably high rate of atheism, and several European nations also have high rates. A glance at the data shows a clear association of atheism with higher income.

The simple analysis of constitutional provisions shows no association with atheism. Having a state religion, or a forbidden state religion, or an establishment clause reveals no correlation. Nations without constitutional guarantees of freedom of religion never have high atheism levels, but this may simply be a function of the few nations lacking such guarantees. Most nations with such clauses also have very low atheism levels.

In a multiple regression, atheism is strongly affected by the societal control variables. Greater per capita GDP and rule of law have a statistically significant association with more atheism, while a larger Muslim population and democracy have a negative association. Adding the varying measures for religious freedom was revealing as shown in Table 7.2.

The regression was highly predictive of atheism levels. Whereas greater GDP was associated with more atheism, democracy was associated with less (though the correlation between these two variables makes the latter finding more uncertain). All my measures of religious freedom showed a strong positive association with higher levels of national atheism. The results are strong and consistently show that greater religious freedom is associated with higher levels of atheism. The nature of this association, and its size, can be seen in Figure 7.6, with atheism rates on the vertical axis compared with the RAS overall measure for religious freedom.

Table 7.2 *Religious Freedom and Atheism*

		Atheism	
RAS Measure	Positive		
RFF Measure		Positive	
Pew Measure			Positive
Islamic Population	Negative	Negative	Negative
Log Per Capita GDP	Positive	Positive	Positive
Rule of Law	Positive	Positive	Positive
Democracy	Negative	Negative	Negative

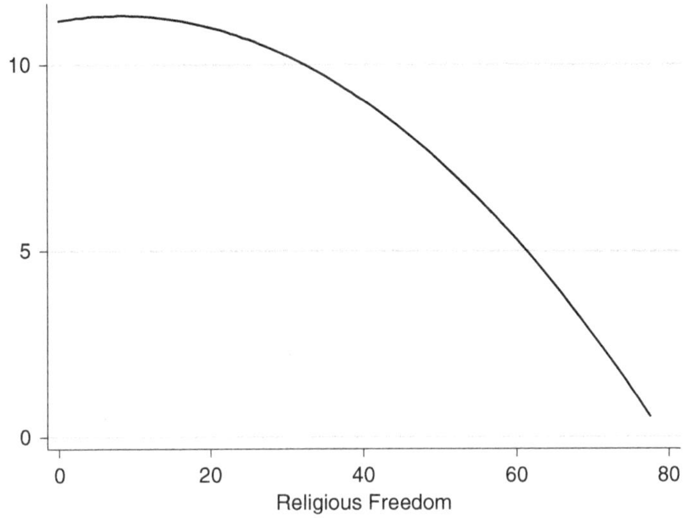

Figure 7.6 Religious Freedom and Atheism

Nations with the highest level of oppression of religious freedom have virtually no atheism in their societies. However, nations with the lowest levels of such oppression and the highest religious freedom have about 10 percent of the population as atheist. Freedom of religion also appears to yield the freedom to be irreligious, as suggested by the analysis in Chapter 1.

When I put the constitutional variables into the same multiple regression analysis, they were all associated with greater national atheism rates. Freedom of religion clauses did not have a statistically significant association, though it was associated with much higher atheism; establishment clauses did, and they were associated with 16 percent higher rates of atheism. Having a state religion was statistically significantly associated with 26 percent lower atheism rates, whereas forbidding such a religion had 6 percent higher atheism rates. Leaving the matter to other branches showed no association.

The analysis of atheism also adds a wrinkle to the earlier findings. Although democracy was strongly associated with higher levels of religious freedom, it had a statistically significant negative association with atheism rates. This may be some suggestion of majoritarian tyranny. The presence of constitutional protections counteracted the democratic effect, perhaps due to the secularizing effect of empowering the judiciary, as described in Chapter 1. The constitutional protections for religious freedom appear to benefit the irreligious as well as the religious.

Government Subsidies

Some governments provide subsidies to religions. The Pew study examined and measured the extent of such subsidies and the degree to which they favored one religion over another. Such subsidies are a very small part of the general religious freedom indices but could have a substantial effect on national religious culture.

The effect of government subsidies for religious belief are ambiguous. Barro and McCleary (2003a) find that subsidies enhance religiosity because subsidies enhance religions and perhaps make belief cheaper. Alternatively, though, subsidies distort religious market, preventing efficiency and religious pluralism that promotes greater religious belief.

Figure 7.7 shows the association between government subsidization of religion and religiosity.

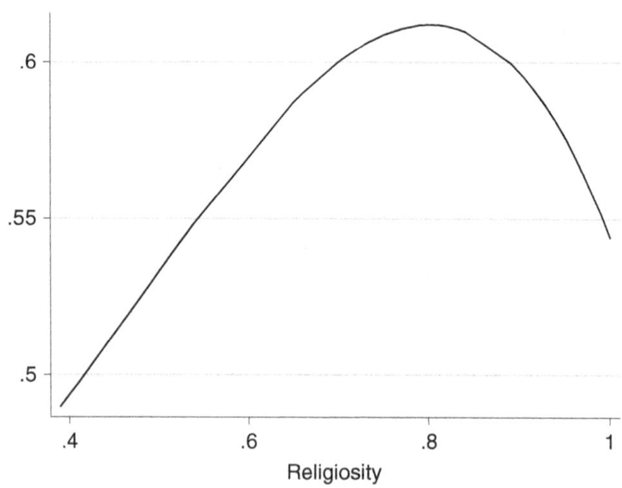

Figure 7.7 Government Subsidies and Religiosity

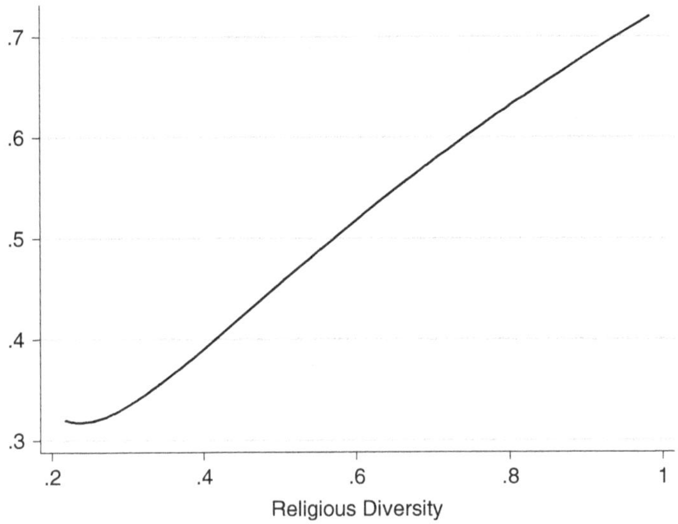

Figure 7.8 Government Subsidies and Religious Diversity

One might think that subsidies would have an effect on religious diversity, especially if such subsidies had favoritism. The graph in Figure 7.8 displays the association between the answers on government subsidies and religious diversity, as measured by the Herfindahl scale.

The effect is stark. Higher numbers on the Herfindahl scale of religious diversity show greater monopolistic concentration of religion. There clearly is a close association between government subsidization and less religious diversity. This connection might be expected, given the government favoritism, but the graph provides supportive evidence.

Well-Being

If religion is an important part of life for many people, greater freedom of religion could be associated with greater personal well-being. Chapter 1 presented some evidence of such a positive association. Some of the research has involved happiness. Gruber and

Mullainathan (2002) found that self-reported happiness jumped dramatically with increasing church attendance rates. For some at least, religiosity seems important to personal happiness.

Independent of the extent of religious belief, simple freedom of religion could be valuable. Thucydides suggested that the secret of happiness was freedom. Inglehart, Foa, Peterson, and Welzel (2008) demonstrate that more freedom of choice in general is associated with greater happiness. Verme (2009) found that freedom of choice predicted happiness better than any other major determinant. Elliott and Hayward (2009) found that government regulation of religion was associated with less happiness, using the GRI scores of government regulation of religion.

Happiness, now commonly studied, is a fairly obscure quality, though. It may not be measuring what we wish to promote. Measures are blunt and influenced by different expectations of different cultures. Disadvantaged people (perhaps untouchables in India) could be quite happy, because they believe they have everything to which they are entitled. Perhaps an authoritarian could make his or her people happier by beating them down so badly they believe this to be the best of all possible worlds. Rising expectations, while presumably good, may counteract human happiness (Verme 2009, Haybron 2007).

Nor is it clear that it is valid to compare survey responses across different nations. As noted with the question on the importance of religion, language differences may create problems. Other languages may not have a word that corresponds closely with the English word for happiness. Wierzbicka (2004) observes that it is an illusion to think that happiness has equivalent expressions in the languages of the world, which undermines any comparison of self-reports among countries.

Individuals may also have different standards for happiness. Some may evaluate themselves in isolation, while others by comparison to peer groups. The latter group obviously creates problems for evaluating happiness research, because it could suggest that reducing the welfare of the most successful peer groups could increase overall happiness. Even for individuals, expressed happiness is variable and the same person will produce very different estimates depending on question phrasing (Hagerty 2003). Haybron (2007) questions the degree to which we are even aware of our affective states and that this awareness may vary by culture and country.

Moreover, happiness, at least as expressed, may have little to do with any external events. A person's happiness may be genetic, a trait inherent to certain groups of people. Given the same external circumstances, different people will give very different reports of happiness. This is also evidenced from the research on adaptation. Given a great benefit or detriment, reported happiness will respond immediately. The lottery winner will be especially happy. The person suffering a disability will lose happiness. Yet in both cases, the individuals will return to their pre-event happiness level after a period of time. This may be because of adaptation, inherent traits, or changed expectations.

This problem was illustrated by Jones et al. (2011), who examined patients who had suffered brain injuries. Their research found that those who had suffered brain injuries remained well-satisfied but that those who had suffered the most severe injuries had the highest life satisfaction. If we were to use greater happiness as a guide to policy, this would suggest that we should strive to make brain injuries as bad as possible, in the long run happiness interests of the patient.

Notwithstanding all these reasons to question research on reported happiness, considerable research exists, and its findings are quite plausible. Greater wealth increases happiness, though not so much as some would suppose. Marriage and companionship increase happiness, as does individual freedom. All these findings have facial validity. Investigation of relative happiness has some potential (Norrish & Vella-Brodrick 2007).

Various measures are available, and I will use Gallup's survey because of the breadth of its international coverage, though it slightly postdates my measures for religious freedom. In this survey, individuals across the globe were asked to reflect on their overall satisfaction score and how they had felt the previous day. From this, the researchers calculated the percent of individuals in each nation who were thriving. The numbers tend to be rather low. While Denmark was first, with 82 percent of its people thriving, a majority of nations had

Table 7.3 *Religious Freedom and Happiness*

		Atheism	
RAS Measure	Positive		
RFF Measure		Negative	
Pew Measure			Negative
Log Per Capita GDP	Positive	Positive	Positive
Rule of Law	Negative	Negative	Negative
Democracy	Positive	Positive	Positive

less than 25 percent of their citizens thriving, by this measure. Though other continents have low scores, African nations are consistently among the lowest on this scaling.

I use my traditional model in a regression for the effects of my different measures of religious freedom (excluding Islamic population which has no theoretical basis for this score). Results are reported in Table 7.3.

The results were dominated by per capita GDP, which had by far the strongest effect on Gallup's measure of personal thriving in each country. Greater democracy was quite positive, as expected, and rule of law was curiously negative. Again, this may be due to its high correlation with democracy. Controlling for these variables, the RAS measure of religious freedom had a statistically significant association with greater happiness. The RFF and Pew measures had a negative association, though neither appeared statistically significant. The variables obviously capture different measures of religious freedom. The RAS measure of legislation and government action appeared to be the one relevant to personal thriving.

The association between the RAS scale of religious freedom and the relative happiness of national populations is illustrated in Figure 7.9.

At relatively high levels of religious freedom, more than 25 percent of the population was considered thriving, while at the lowest levels the average was only about half that. The graph is fairly flat at relatively high levels of religious freedom, suggesting that the more severe religious repression is associated with lessened happiness.

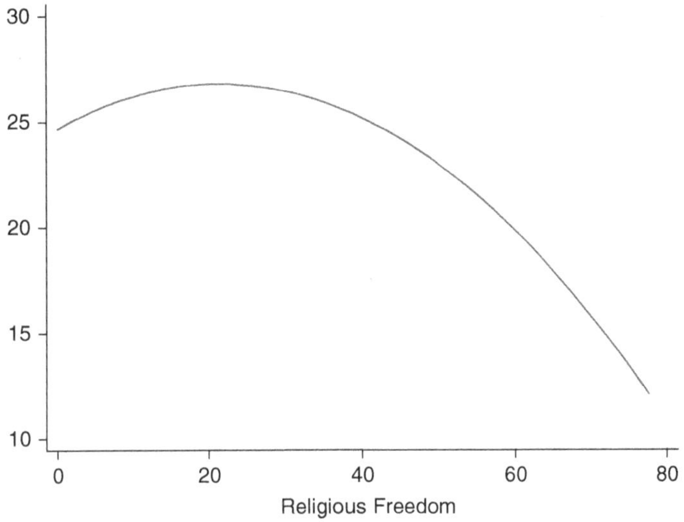

Figure 7.9 Religious Freedom and Happiness

There was no association with my constitutional variables. The presence of freedom of religion was plainly negative, though this is compromised by the small number of countries without such a provision. Whatever effect such constitutional provisions have on happiness is only channeled through an effect on producing religious freedom, on the RAS scale.

I conducted the same regression analysis for the variables on national religion analyzed earlier in this chapter. Greater religious diversity, as measured by the Herfindahl scale, had a statistically significant association with greater happiness. Atheism also had a statistically significant positive association, though overall religiosity was negative. The associations of diversity and atheism reveal that greater religious choice is clearly correlated with personal thriving.

This result is somewhat confirmatory of Elliott and Hayward (2009), insofar as religious freedom measured by the RAS scale is associated with higher levels of personal thriving. This is theoretically plausible, as one would expect individuals to be happier if they had greater freedom of religion, which is important to at least some.

This is confirmed by the results for religious diversity and atheism. While secondary to per capita GDP, at least the RAS measure of freedom seems to yield greater personal happiness.

Gender

One common criticism of religion is its negative association with the rights of women. This is especially pronounced in Islam, where women may be beaten for refusing to wear a burqa or for having sex (even if they were raped). Women lack the freedom to travel without spousal permission, and women in Saudi Arabia may not drive automobiles. In many countries, women have fewer rights with respect to marriage, divorce, education, occupation, and financial matters.

Criticism of religion over gender equality is by no means limited to Muslims. The Council of Europe has recognized that women's rights are often curtailed or violated in the name of religion. Religious institutions have been characterized as "male-dominated patriarchal institutions that continue to perpetuate discrimination against women" (Stuart 2010, 439). Religions commonly involve male control, hierarchy, and a family division of labor that calls upon women to be wives and mothers first. Only males may become Catholic priests, and constitutional freedom of religion prevents any state action requiring equal opportunity. Some research (Heaton and Cornwall 1989) indicates, though, that Catholics are relatively egalitarian with respect to women.

Research has shown that the religious are less supportive of gender equality and more likely to endorse traditional conservative views of women's role in society (Hoffman & Miller 1997, Zuckerman 2009). Conservative Protestants and others who participate more regularly in religious activity tend to be less egalitarian with respect to women's rights (Heaton & Cornwall 1989). Religions commonly try to exercise control over women's reproductive freedom. Gioso, Sapienza, and Zingales (2003) report that the religious have less progressive attitudes toward women than do atheists. Moreover, they find this effect is much more pronounced with religious diversity and not with a dominant religion (though they suggested that this might simply be due to nonbelievers attending church in the presence of a dominant religion).

The critics of religion's general discrimination against women must come to grips with the fact that women are consistently more religious than men. No matter how religiosity is measured, the research indicates that women are more religious (Francis 1997). Women show much higher levels of religious attendance and prayer. In America, men make up about three quarters of those who consider themselves to be atheist or agnostic (Zuckerman 2009). Various reasons have been hypothesized for this effect, ranging from different risk-taking preferences to socialization to childrearing responsibilities (Roth & Kroll 2007). The affinity of women for religious belief surely calls into question the conflict between such belief and womens' rights and interests. This association is not the product of societal indoctrination of women because the association exists even for those without traditional gender role stereotypes (Miller & Stark 2002). The affinity of women for religion surely makes it difficult to maintain that religion is intrinsically antifeminist. Even a patriarchal religion may provide benefits for women – one study found that young women from conservative Protestant backgrounds who attended church frequently attained more education than those who were less observant (Lehrer 2004a).

Some argue that religion, and specifically the Bible, has promoted gender equality out of its recognition of human equality. It is in Christian cultures that the status of women has improved the most and where women are recognized as most equal. Hackett (2004) explains how the religious have shown an inherent commitment to human dignity and associated rights, though the emphasis varied among different religions. One study in western Europe, though, found that religion was unrelated to support for women's rights (Wilcox 1991). In some countries, Catholics were relatively more supportive, in others, less so. Those with no religion tended to show greater support for women's rights in some countries and less support in others.

This section evaluates the effect of religious freedom upon the interests of women. There are numerous possible ways to assess the interests of women in society and a variety of global gender indices.

The best one contemporaneous with my data on religious freedom is probably the United Nations gender empowerment measure. This is a measure of women legislators and managers, female professional and technical workers, and the ratio of female-to-male income. It measures the political and economic standing of women in a nation, which seems a reasonable scale for their relative status. For the year 2002, coverage is reasonably broad but misses many less developed nations.

I first consider the effect of relative religious belief on the status of women in society. Given the stereotypes, one might expect nations with greater religiosity to be associated with less gender equality. Religious diversity has uncertain implications, but one might expect it to have some positive association with women's interests, as faiths compete for women followers. Given the record of Islam with respect to women, it merits use as a control variable. I also include the traditional control variables for per capita GDP, democracy, and rule of law. Greater wealth might be expected to be associated with greater gender equality, and democracy should promote such equality. The results of the multiple regression are reported in Table 7.4.

The results are not intuitive but they are also not meaningful. None of the associations even remotely approached statistical significance. Whatever determines the status of women in society, religious variables do not appear to be important. Replacing the larger sample measure for religiosity with the data for church attendance does not change the results or produce any significant determinants.

Table 7.4 *Religious Belief and Gender Status*

	Gender Empowerment Index
Religiosity	Positive
Diversity	Negative
Islamic Population	Negative
Log Per Capita GDP	Positive
Rule of Law	Positive
Democracy	Negative

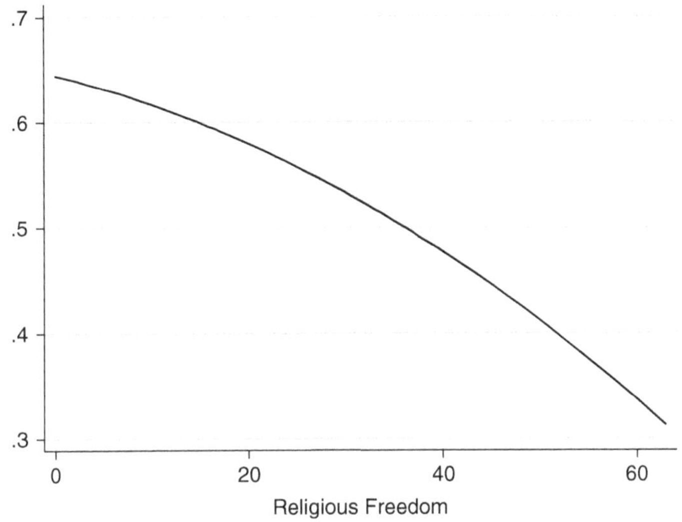

Figure 7.10 Religious Freedom and Gender Empowerment

There was little direct association between the constitutional provisions I examined and the gender empowerment index. The same multiple regression analysis was run with the various measures of religious freedom I have considered (RAS, RFF, and Pew). All measures of religious freedom were correlated with a higher gender empowerment index score, but none approached statistical significance. However, Figure 7.10 offers an intriguing graphic look at the association for the RAS score.

This is a pattern we have seen before. At high levels of religious freedom, gender empowerment is at its highest. As religious freedom declines, gender empowerment steadily declines along with it. Because the association was not a statistically significant one, with the other control variables, one should be cautious about concluding that greater religious freedom promotes gender equality. However, the very positive association revealed in the figure should give us some confidence that it does not undermine the rights and interests of women. As noted, data for the gender empowerment index were limited for less developed nations, and more data might have helped find a significant relationship.

Conclusion

This chapter illustrates some of the societal effects of religious freedom. Within the sphere of religion itself, greater freedom, at least as measured by the RAS scale, yields increases in religious pluralism and choice, as would naturally be expected. The effects of freedom on people's religiosity are not overwhelming, with the exception of church attendance, which freedom appears to encourage. However, the effect on atheism is a clearly profound one, with greater religious freedom associated with more atheism. It appears that religious freedom furthers the freedom *not* to believe, as well as the choice among religions.

In broader society, there is a clear association between the RAS measure of religious freedom and human thriving. Significant restrictions on religious freedom plainly reduce overall happiness. This may not be causal, and religious freedom may well be associated with other freedoms that contribute to the result, but it suggests a value of recognizing freedom of religion. Given all of the factors that would be expected to influence happiness in a given nation, the association with religious freedom is a striking one, which would seem to support constitutionally singling out the importance of such freedom.

Religious belief has been criticized for undermining the interests of women. However, there was no negative association between the degree of national religiosity and the UN measure of gender equality. Moreover, there was some indication that greater religious freedom may tend to enhance gender empowerment.

Bibliography

Abel, C. F. and Hans J. Hacker. 2006. Local Compliance with Supreme Court Decisions: Making Space for Religious Expression in Public Schools. *Journal of Church and State*. **48**: 355–377.

Ackerman, Bruce A. 1995. *We the People: Foundations*. Cambridge, MA: Harvard University Press.

Ackerman, Bruce A. 1985. Beyond Carolene Products. *Harvard Law Review*. **98**: 713–746.

Alon, Ilan and Gregory Chase. 2005. Religious Freedom and Economic Prosperity. *Cato Journal*. **25**: 399–406.

Apodaca, Clair. 2004. The Rule of Law and Human Rights. *Judicature*. **87**: 292–299.

Arjomand, Said Amir. 2003. Law, Political Reconstruction, and Constitutional Politics. *International Sociology*. **18**: 7–33.

Armstrong, David Alan. 2009. Measuring the Democracy-Repression Nexus. *Electoral Studies*. **28**: 403–412.

Asad, Talal. 1993. *Genealogies of Religion: Discipline and Reasons of Power in Christianity and Islam*. Baltimore: Johns Hopkins Press.

Babie, Paul and Neville Rochow. 2010. Feels Like Déjà vu: An Australian Bill of Rights and Religious Freedom. *Brigham Young Law Review*. **2010**: 821–858.

Bainbridge, William S. 1989. The Religious Ecology of Deviance. *American Sociological Review*. **54**: 288–295.

Barclay, Scott and Thomas Birkland. 1998. Law, Policymaking, and the Policy Process: Closing the Gaps. *Policy Studies Journal*. 227–243.

Barrett, David B. and Todd M. Johnson. 2001. *World Christian Trends*. Pasadena, CA: William Carey Library.

Barro, Robert and Rachel McCleary. 2006. Which Countries Have State Religions? *The Quarterly Journal of Economics*. **120**: 1331–1370.

Barro, Robert and Rachel McCleary. 2003a. Religion and Economic Growth Across Countries. *American Sociological Review*. **68**: 760–781.

Barro, Robert J. and Rachel M. McCleary. 2003b. International Determinants of Religiosity. National Bureau of Economic Research Working Paper No. 10147.

Baum, Lawrence. 2006. *Judges and Their Audiences*. Princeton, NJ: Princeton University Press.

Baum, Lawrence. 2003. The Supreme Court in American Politics. *Annual Review of Political Science*. **6**: 161–180.

Beatty, David M. 2001. The Forms and Limits of Constitutional Interpretation (National Approaches to Religious Freedom. *American Journal of Comparative Law*. **49**: 79–120.

Beit-Hallahmi, Benjamin. 2007. Atheists: A Psychlogical Profile. In Michael Martin ed. *The Cambridge Companion to Atheism*. New York, NY: Cambridge University Press.

Bellamy, Richard and Dario Castiglione. 1997. Constitutionalism and Democracy – Political Theory and the American Constitution. *British Journal of Political Science*. **27**: 595–618.

Berger, Julia. 2004. Religious Nongovernmental Organizations: An Exploratory Analysis. *VOLUNTAS: International Journal of Voluntary and Nonprofit Giving*. **14**: 15–39.

Berggren, Niclas. 1997. Rhetoric or Reality? An Economic Analysis of the Effects of Religion in Sweden. *Journal of Socio-Economics*. **26**: 571–596.

Beyer, Peter. 2003. Constitutional Privilege and Constituting Pluralism: Religious Freedom in National, Global, and Legal Context. *Journal for the Scientific Study of Religion*. **42**: 333–339.

Birkby, Robert H. 1966. The Supreme Court and the Bible Belt: Tennessee Reaction to the "Schempp" Decision. *Midwest Journal of Political Science*. **10**: 304–319.

Board of Education of Kiryas Joel v. Grumet. 1994. 412 U.S. 687.

Bodenhamer, David J. 2012. *The Revolutionary Constitution*. Oxford: Oxford University Press.

Boyle Kevin and Juliet Sheen. 1997. *Freedom of Religion and Belief: A World Report*. London: Routledge.

Braithwaite, Robert and Andrew Bramsen. 2011. Reconceptualizing Church and State: A Theoretical and Empirical Analysis of the Impact of Separation of Religion and State on Democracy. *Politics and Religion*. **4**: 229–263.

Breault, Kevin D. 1989. New Evidence on Religious Pluralism, Urbanism, and Religions Participation. *American Sociological Review*. **54**: 1048–1053.

Brent, James C. 1999. An Agent and Two Principals: U.S. Court of Appeals Responses to Employment Division Department of Human Resources v. Smith and the Religious Freedom Restoration Act. *American Politics Quarterly*. **27**: 236–266.

Brest, Paul. 1985. Who Decides? *Southern California Law Review*. **58**: 661–670.

Brooks, Arthur C. 2005. *Gifts of Time and Money*. Lanham, MD: Rowman & Littlefield Publishers, Inc.

Brooks, Arthur C. 2003. Religious Faith and Charitable Giving. *Policy Review*. **121**: 39–48.

Brown v. Board of Education, 1954. 347 U.S. 483, 490.

Bruce, Steve. 2002. *God Is Dead: Secularization in the West*. Malden, MA: Blackwell Publishing.

Bruce, Steve. 1993. Religion and Rational Choice: A Critique of Economic Explanations of Religious Behavior. *Sociology of Religion*. **54**: 193–205.

Buchanan, James M. 1988. Contractarian Political Economy and Constitutional Interpretation. *The American Economic Review*. **78**: 135–139.

Bueno de Mesquita, Bruce, Feryal Marie Cherif, George Downs, and Alistair Smith. 2005. Thinking Inside the Box: A Closer Look at Democracy and Human Rights. *International Studies Quarterly*. **49**: 439–458.

Carey, John M. 2000. Parchment, Equilibria, and Institutions. *Comparative Political Studies*. **33**: 735–761.

Chaves, Mark. 1994. Secularization as Declining Religious Authority. *Social Forces*. **72**: 749–774.

Chaves, Mark and David E. Cann. 1992. Regulation, Pluralism, and Religious Market Structure. *Rationality & Society*. **4**: 272–290.

Chaves, Mark and Philip S. Gorski. 2001. Religious Pluralism and Religious Participation. *Annual Review of Sociology*. **27**: 261–281.

City of Boerne v. Flores. 1997. 521 U.S. 507.

Clark, Tom S. 2011. *The Limits of Judicial Independence*. New York, NY: Cambridge University Press.

Cohen, Adam B. 2002. The Importance of Spirituality in Well-Being for Jews and Christians. *Journal of Happiness Studies*. **3**: 287–310.

Conkle, Daniel O. 2011. Religious Truth, Pluralism, and Secularization: The Shaking Foundations of American Religious Liberty. *Cardozo Law Review*. **32**: 1755–1780.

Connolly-Ahern, Colleen and Guy J. Golan. 2007. Press Freedom and Religion: Measuring the Association Between Press Freedom and Religious Composition. *Journal of Media & Religion*. **6**: 63–76.

Cooter, Robert and Thomas Ginsburg. 2003. Leximetrics: Why the Same Laws Are Longer in Some Countries Than Others. University of Illinois Law & Economics Research Paper No. LE03.

Corley, Felix. 2008. The Former Soviet Union. In Paul A. Marshall, ed. *Religious Freedom in the World*. Lanham, MD: Rowman & Littlefield Publishers, Inc.

Correa, Alfredo Qispe. 1998. The Evolution of Religious Belief in a Constitutional Text. *Brigham Young University Law Review*. **1998**: 357–367.

Corwin, Edwin S. 1936. The Constitution as Instrument and as Symbol. *American Political Science Review*. **30:** 1071–1079.

Corwin, Edwin S. 1934. *Twilight of the Supreme Court*. New Haven, CT: Yale University Press.

Cross, Frank B. 2007. *Decision Making in the U.S. Courts of Appeals*. Stanford, CA: Stanford University Press.

Cross, Frank B. 2005. Law and Trust. *Georgetown Law Journal*. **93**: 1457–1543.

Cross, Frank B. 2000. Institutions and Enforcement of the Bill of Rights. *Cornell Law Review*. **85**: 1529–1608.

Cross, Frank. 1999. The Relevance of Law in Human Rights Protection. *International Review of Law & Economics*. **19**: 87–98.

Cross, Frank B. and Blake J. Nelson. 2001. Strategic Institutional Effects on Supreme Court Decisionmaking. *Northwestern University Law Review*. **95**: 1437–1493.

Dahl, Robert A. 1967. *Pluralist Democracy in the United States: Conflict and Consent*. Chicago: Rand McNally & Company.

Dahl, Robert A. 1957. Decision-Making in a Democracy: The Supreme Court as a National Policy-Maker. *Journal of Public Law*. **6**: 279–295.

Darrow, Mac and Philip Alston. 1999. Bills of Rights in Comparative Perspective. In Philip Alston, ed. *Promoting Human Rights Through Bills of Rights*. Oxford University Press: New York.

Davenport, Christian. 1996. Constitutional Promises and Repressive Reality: A Cross-National Time-Series Investigation of Why Political and Civil Liberties Are Suppressed. *Journal of Politics*. **58**: 627–654.

Dawson, John W. 2003. Causality in the Freedom-Growth Relationship. *European Journal of Political Economy*. **19**: 479–495.

De Figueiredo, Rui J. P. 2002. Electoral Competition, Political Uncertainty, and Policy Insulation. *American Political Science Review*. **96**: 321–333.

Devins, Neal. 2007. The D'oh! of Popular Constitutionalism. *Michigan Law Review*. **105**: 1333–1351.

Dinan, John J. 1998. *Keeping the People's Liberties*. Lawrence, KS: University Press of Kansas.

Doestoevsy, Fyodor. 1990. *The Brothers Karamazov*. San Francisco, CA: North Point Press.

Dotan, Yoav. 2005. The Spillover Effect of Bills of Rights: A Comparative Assessment of the Impact of Bills of Rights in Canada and Israel. *American Journal of Comparative Law*. **53**: 293–341.

Downs, Anthony. 1957. *An Economic Theory of Democracy*. New York, NY: Harper and Row.

Driessen, Michael D. 2010. Religion, State, and Democracy: Analyzing Two Dimensions of Church-State Arrangements. *Politics and Religion*. **3**: 55–80.

Driver, Justin. 2010. Why Law Should Lead. *The New Republic*. April 2, 2010. Retrieved from http://www.newrepublic.com/article/books-and-arts/why-law-should-lead

Durlauf, Steven N., Andros Kourtellos, and Chih Ming Tan. 2005. How Robust Are the Linkages Between Religiosity and Economic Growth. Tufts Economics Department Discussion Paper No. 510.

Dworkin, Ronald. 1986. *Law's Empire*. Cambridge, MA: Harvard University Press.

Easterbrook, Frank H. 1992. Bills of Rights and Regression to the Mean. *Harvard Journal of Law & Public Policy*. **15**: 71–83.

Edelman, Paul H., David E. Klein, and Stefanie A. Lindquist. 2008. Measuring Deviations from Expected Voting Patterns on Collegial Courts. *Journal of Empirical Legal Studies*. **5**: 819–852.

Edgell, Penny, Joseph Gerteis, and Douglas Hartmann. 2006. Atheists as "Other": Moral Boundaries and Cultural Membership in American Society. *American Sociological Review*. **71**: 211–234.

Eisgruber, Christopher and Lawrence Sager. 2007. *Religious Freedom and the Constitution*. Cambridge, MA: Harvard University Press.

Eisgruber, Christopher and Lawrence Sager. 1994. The Vulnerability of Conscience: The Constitutional Basis for Protecting Religious Conduct. *University of Chicago Law Review*. **61**: 1245–1315.

Elkins, Zachary, Tom Ginsburg, and James Melton. 2009. *The Endurance of National Constitutions*. Cambridge: Cambridge University Press.

Elliott, Marta and R. David Hayward. 2009. Religion and Life Satisfaction Worldwide: The Role of Government Regulation. *Sociology of Religion*. **70**: 285–310.

Ellison, Christopher G. 1998. The Religion-Health Connection: Evidence, Theory, and Future Directions. *Health Education & Behavior*. **25**: 700–720.

Ellison, Christopher G. 1991. Religious Involvement and Subjective Well-being. *Journal of Health and Social Behavior*. **32**: 80–99.

Elster, Jon. 1979. *Ulysses and the Sirens*. New York, NY: Cambridge University Press.

Employment Division, Department of Human Resources of Oregon v. Smith. 1990. 494 U.S. 872.

Engel, Christoph. 2011. Law as a Precondition for Religious Freedom. Electronic copy available at: http://papers.ssrn.com/sol3/papers.cfm?abstract_id=1803254.

Engel v. Vitale. 1962. 370 U.S. 421.

Epp, Charles R. 1998. *The Rights Revolution: Lawyers, Activists, and Supreme Courts in Comparative Perspective*. Chicago, IL: University of Chicago Press.

Epp, Charles R. 1996. Do Bills of Rights Matter? The Canadian Charter of Rights and Freedoms. *American Political Science Review*. **90**: 765–779.

Epperson v. Arkansas. 1968. 393 U.S. 97.

Eskridge, William N., Jr. and John Ferejohn. 1994. Virtual Logrolling: How the Court, Congress, and the States Multiply Rights. *Southern California Law Review*. **68**: 1545–1564.

Everson v. Board of Education. 1947. 330 U.S. 1.

Fajnzylber, Papblo, Daniel Lederman, and Norman Loatza. 2002. Inequality and Violent Crime. *Journal of Law and Economics*. **45**: 1–37.

Farber, Daniel, 2002. Rights as Signals. *Journal of Legal Studies*. **31**: 83–98.

Farnsworth, Ward. 2007. *The Legal Analyst: A Toolkit for Thinking About the Law*. Chicago, IL: University of Chicago Press.

Faure, Bernard. 2003. *The Power of Denial: Buddhism, Purity, and Gender*. Princeton, NJ: Princeton University Press.

Fearon, James D. and David D. Laitin. 2003. Ethnicity, Insurgency, and Civil War. *American Political Science Review*. **97**: 75–90.

Feofanov, Dmitry N. 1994. Defining Religion: An Immodest Proposal. *Hofstra Law Review*. **23**: 309–405.

Ferejohn, John and Lawrence Sager. 2003. Commitment and Constitutionalism. *Texas Law Review*. **81**: 1929–1962.

Ferejohn, John and Pasquale Pasquino. 2010. The Countermajoritarian Opportunity. *University of Pennsylvania Journal of Constitutional Law*. **13**: 353–394.

Finke, Roger. 1990. Religious Deregulation: Origins and Consequences. *Journal of Church and State*. **32**: 609–626.

Finke, Roger and Rodney Stark. 1988. Religious Economies and Sacred Canopies: Religious Mobilization in American Cities. *American Sociological Review*. **53**: 41–49.

Finkelman, Paul. 1990. James Madison and the Bill of Rights: A Reluctant Paternity. *The Supreme Court Review*. **1990**: 301–347.

Finnis, John. 2009. Does Free Exercise of Religion Deserve Constitutional Mention? *American Journal of Jurisprudence*. **54**: 41–66.

Fish, M. Steven. 2002. Islam and Authoritarianism. *World Politics*. **55**: 4–37.

Fisher, Louis. 1998. *Constitutional Dialogues*. Princeton, NJ: Princeton University Press.

Fox, Jonathan. 2011. Out of Sync: The Disconnect Between Constitutional Clauses and State Legislation on Religion. *Canadian Journal of Political Science*. **44**: 59–81.

Fox, Jonathan. 2008a. *A World Survey of Religion and the State*. New York: Cambridge University Press.

Fox, Jonathan. 2008b. State Religious Exclusivity and Human Rights. *Political Studies*. **56**: 928–948.

Fox, Jonathan. 2004. The Rise of Religious Nationalism and Conflict: Ethnic Conflict and Revolutionary Wars. *Journal of Peace Research*. **41**: 715–731.

Fox, Jonathan and Ephraim Tabory. 2008. Contemporary Evidence Regarding the Impact of State Regulation of Religion on Religious Participation and Belief. *Sociology of Religion*. **69**: 245–271.

Fradkin, Hillel. 2000. Does Democracy Need Religion? *Journal of Democracy*. **11**: 87–94.

Francis, Leslie. 1997. The Psychology of Gender Differences in Religion: A Review of the Empirical Research. *Religion*. **27**: 81–96.

Frazee v. Illinois Department of Employment Security. 1989. 489 U.S. 829.

Freedom from Religion Foundation, Inc. v. Obama. 2011. 641 F.3d. 803.

Freeman, Richard B. 1986. Who Escapes? The relation of Churchgoing and Other Background Factors to the Socioeconomic Performance of Black Male Youths from Inner-City Tracts. In Richard B. Freeman and Harry J. Holzer, eds. *The Black Youth Employment Crisis*. Chicago: University of Chicago Press.

Friedman, Barry. 2009. *The Will of the People*. New York: Farrar Straus & Giroux.

Fukuyama, Francis. 2011. *The Origins of Political Order*. New York: Farrar, Straus & Giroux.

Fuller, Lon. 1969. *The Morality of Law*. New Haven, CT: Yale University Press.

Garlicki, Leszek Lech. 2001. Perspectives on Freedom of Conscience and Religion in the Jurisprudence of Constitutional Courts. *Brigham Young University Law Review*. **2**: 467–510.

Garvey, John H. 1996a. An Anti-Liberal Argument for Religious Freedom. *Journal of Contemporary Legal Issues*. **7**: 275–292.

Garvey, John H. 1996b. *What Are Freedoms For?* Cambridge, MA: Harvard University Press.

Gash, Alison and Angelo Gonzalez. 1998. School Prayer. In Nathaniel Persily, Jack Citrin, and Patrick J. Egan, eds. *Public Opinion and Constitutional Controversy*. New York, NY: Oxford University Press.

Gey, Steven G. 2007. Atheism and the Freedom of Religion. In M. Martin, ed. *The Cambridge Companion to Atheism*. Cambridge: Cambridge University Press.

Gill, Anthony and Erik Lundsgaarde. 2004. State Welfare Spending and Religiosity: A Cross-National Analysis. *Rationality and Society*. **16**: 399–436.

Gill, Anthony. 2001. Religion and Comparative Politics. *Annual Review of Political Science*. **4**: 117–138.

Gill, Anthony. 1999. Government Regulation, Social Anomie, and Protestant Growth in Latin America. *Rationality and Society*. **11**: 87–316.

Gill, Anthony. 1994. Rendering Unto Caesar? Religious Competition and Catholic Political Strategy in Latin America, 1962–1979. *American Journal of Political Science*. **38**: 435–456.

Ginsburg, Tom. 2010. Constitutional Specificity, Unwritten Understandings and Constitutional Agreement. Andras Sajo and Renata Uitz. *Constitutional Topography*. The Hague: Eleven International Publishing.

Gioso, Luigi, Paola Sapienza, and Luigi Zingales. 2003. People's Opium? Religion and Economic Attitudes. *Journal of Monetary Economics*. **50**: 225–282.

Goderis, Benedict and Mila Versteeg. 2009. Human Rights Violations After 9/11 and the Role of Constitutoinal Constraints. Presented at the Fourth Annual Conference on Empirical Legal Studies. Los Angeles, CA.

Gogineni, Rajaji Ramanadha Babu and Lars Gule. 2004. Humanism and Freedom from Religion. In Tore Lindholm, W. Cole Durham, Jr., Bahia G. Tahzib-Lie, Elizabeth Sewell, and Lena Larson, eds. *Facilitating Freedom of Religion or Belief: A Deskbook*. Leiden: Martinus Nijhoff Publishers.

Goldwin, Robert A. 1997. *From Parchment to Power: How James Madison Used the Bill of Rights to Save the Constitution*. American Enterprise Institute: Washington, DC.

Goodman, Josh. 2009. Divine Judgment: Judicial Review of Religious Legal Systems in India and Israel. *Hastings International and Comparative Law Review*. **32**: 477–528.

Gorski, Philip S. and Ates Altinordu. 2008. After Secularization? *Annual Review of Sociology*. **34**: 55–85.

Green, Donald P., Peter M. Aronow, Daniel E. Bergan, Pamela Greene, Celia Paris, and Beth I. Weinberger. 2011. Does Knowledge of constitutional Principles Increase Support for Civil Liberties? *Journal of Politics*. **73**: 463–476.

Greenawalt, Kent. 2008. *Religion and the Constitution 2*. Princeton, NJ: Princeton University Press.

Greenberg, Anna. 2000. The Church and the Revitalization of Politics and Community. *Political Science Quarterly*. **115**: 377–394.

Greene, Kenneth V. and Bong Joon Yoon. 2004. Religiosity, Economics, and Life Satisfaction. *Review of Social Economy*. **62**: 245–261.

Grim, Brian J. 2009. Religious Freedom and Social Well-Being: A Critical Appraisal. *International Journal of Religious Freedom*. **2**: 37–46.

Grim, Brian J. 2004. The Cities of Good Versus the Countries of Earth: The Restriction of Religious Freedom (RFF) Index.

Grim, Brian J. and Roger Finke. 2011. *The Price of Freedom Denied*. New York, NY: Cambridge University Press.

Grim, Brian J. and Roger Finke. 2006. International Religion Indexes: Government Regulation, Government Favoritism, and Social Regulation of Religion. *Interdisciplinary Journal of Research on Religion*. **2**: 1–40.

Grim, Brian J. and Richard Wike. 2010. Cross-Validating Measures of Global Religious Intolerance: Comparing coded State Department Reports with Survey Data and Expert Opinion. *Politics and Religion*. **3**: 102–129.

Gruber, Jonathan H. 2005. Religious Market Structure, Religious Participation, and Outcomes: Is Religion Good for You. *Advances in Economic Analysis & Policy*. **5**: 1–30.

Gruber, Jonathan and Sendhil Mullainathan. 2002. Do Cigarette Taxes Make Smokers Happier? NBER Working Paper No. 8872.

Guiso, L. P., P. Sapienza, and L. Zingales. 2003. People's Opium? Religion and Economic Attitudes. *Journal of Monetary Economics*. **50**: 225–282.

Gunn, T. Jeremy. 2005. Deconstructing Proportionality in Limitations Analysis. *Emery International Law Review*. **19**: 465–498.

Gunn, T. Jeremy. 2004. Religious Freedom and Laïcité: A Comparison of the United States and France. *Brigham Young University Law Review*. **2004**: 419–506.

Habermas, Jurgen. 2006. Religion in the Public Sphere. *European Journal of Philosophy*. **14**: 1–25.

Hackett Rosalind I. J. 2004. Human Rights: An Important and Challenging New Field for the Study of Religion. In Peter Antes, Armin W. Geertz, and Randi R. Warne, eds. *New Approaches to the Study of Religion*. Berlin: Walter de Gruyter GmbH & Co.

Hagerty, Michael R. 2003. Was Life Better in the "Good Old Days"? Intertemporal Judgments of Life Satisfaction. *Journal of Happiness Studies*. **4**: 115–139.

Halik, Habib C. 2008 Christians of the Middle East: A Story of Accelerating Erosion. In Paul A. Marshall, ed. *Religious Freedom in the World*. Lanham, MD: Rowman & Littlefield Publishers, Inc.

Hall, Matthew E. K. 2011. *The Nature of Supreme Court Power*. New York: Cambridge University Press.

Hamilton, Marci. A. 2005. *God vs. the Gavel: Religion and the Rule of Law*. New York, NY: Cambridge University Press.

Hanburger, Philip. 2003. Separation and Interpretation. *Journal of Law & Politics*. **18**: 7–64.

Hand, Learned. 1960. *The Spirit of Liberty: Papers and Addresses of Learned Hand*. New York, NY: Alfred A. Knopf Publishing.

Handberg, Roger and Harold F. Hill, Jr. 1980. Court Curbing, Court Reversals, and Judicial Review: The Supreme Court Versus Congress. *Law & Society Review*. **14**: 309–322.

Hansford, Thomas G. and James F. Spriggs II. 2006. *The Politics of Precedent on the U.S. Supreme Court*. Princeton, NJ: Princeton University Press.

Hardin, Russell. 1999. *Liberalism, Constitutionalism, and Democracy*. New York, NY: Oxford University Press.

Harris, Fredrick C. 1994. Something Within: Religion as a Mobilizer of African-American Political Activism. *Journal of Politics*. **56**: 42–68.

Harvey, Anna and Barry Friedman. 2006. Pulling Punches: Congressional Constraints on the Supreme Court's Constitutional Rulings. *Legislative Studies Quarterly*. **31**: 533–562.

Haybron, Daniel M. 2007. Do We Know How Happy We Are? On Some Limits of Affective Introspection and Recall. *Nous*. **3**: 394–428.

Heath, W. C., M. S. Waters, and J. K. Watson. 1995. Religion and Economic Welfare: An Empirical Analysis of State Per Capita Income. *Journal of Economic Behaviour and Organization*. **27**: 129–142.

Heaton, Tim B. and Marie Cornwall. 1989. Religious Group Variation in the Socioeconomic Status and Family Behavior of Women. *Journal for the Scientific Study of Religion*. **28**: 283–299.

Henderson, Conway. 1991. Conditions Affecting the Use of Political Repression. *Journal of Conflict Resolution*. **35**: 120–142.

Henderson, Lynne. 1990. Authoritarianism and the Rule of Law. *Indiana Law Journal*. **66**: 379–446.

Hendley, Kathryn. 1996. *Trying To Make Law Matter*. Ann Arbor: The University of Michigan Press.

Hiebert, Janet L. 2005. Interpreting a Bill of Rights: The Importance of Legislative Rights Review. *British Journal of Political Science*. **35**: 235–255.

Hirschl, Ran. 2010. *Constitutional Theocracy*. Cambridge, MA: Harvard University Press.

Hirschl, Ran. 2006. The New Constitutionalism and the Judicialization of Pure Politics Worldwide. *Fordham Law Review*. **75** (2006): 721–752.

Hoffman, John and Alan Miller. 1997. Social and Political Attitudes Among Religious Groups: Convergence and Divergence. *Journal for the Scientific Study of Religion*. **36**: 52–70.

Holmes, Stephen. 1995. *Passions and Constraint: On the Theory of Liberal Democracy*. London: The University of Chicago Press.

Horwitz, Morton. 1977. The Rule of Law: An Unqualified Human Good? *Yale Law Journal*. **86**: 561–566.

Hoyos, Viviane A. Morales. 1999. Religious Liberty and Cultural and Ethnic Pluralism in the Columbian Constitution of 1991. *Brigham Young Law Review*. **1999**: 561–579.

Hummer, Robert, Richard Rogers, Charles Nam, and Christopher Ellison. 1999. Religious Involvement and U.S. Adult Mortality. *Demography*. **34**: 273–285.

Huntington, Samuel P. 1996. *The Clash of Civilizations and the Remaking of the Modern World*. New York, NY: Simon & Schuster.

Husa, Jaakko. 2000. Guarding the Constitutionality of Laws in the Nordic Countries: A Comparative Perspective. *The American Journal of Comparative Law*. **48**: 345–381.

Iannaccone, Laurence R. 1998. Introduction to the Economics of Religion. *Journal of Economic Literature*. **36**: 1465–1496.

Iannaccone, Laurence R. 1995. Voodoo Economics? Reviewing the Rational Choice Approach to Religion. *Journal for the Scientific Study of Religion*. **34**: 76–88.

Iannaccone, Laurence R. 1991. The Consequences of Religious Market Regulation: Adam Smith and the Economics of Religion. *Rationality and Society*. **3**: 156–177.

Iannaccone, Laurence R. and Eli Berman. 2006. Religious Extremism: The Good, the Bad, and the Deadly. *Public Choice*. **128**: 109–129.

Iannaccone, Laurence R., Roger Finke, and Rodney Stark. 1997. Deregulating Religion: The Economics of Church and State, *Economic Inquiry*. **35**: 350–364.

Inglehart, Ronald, Roberto Foa, Christopher Peterson, and Christian Welzel. 2008. Development, Freedom, and Rising Happiness: A Global Perspective (1981–2007). *Perspectives on Psychological Science*. **3**: 264–285.

International Religious Freedom Report: Saudia Arabia. Bureau of Democracy, Human Rights, and Labor. US Department of State.

Ignagni, Joseph A. 1993. U.S. Supreme Court Decision-Making and the Free Exercise Clause. *Review of Politics*. **55**: 511–529.

Jackson, Lynne M. and Bruce Hunsberger. 1999. An Intergroup Perspective on Religion and Prejudice. *Journal for the Scientific Study of Religion*. **38**: 509–523.

Jones, Janelle M., S. Alexander Haslam, Jolanda Jetten, W. Huw Williams, Richard Morris, and Sonya Saroyan. 2011. That Which Doesn't Kill Us Can Make Us Stronger (and More Satisfied with Life): The Contribution of Personal and Social Changes to Well-Being After Acquired Brain Injury. *Psychology & Health*. **26**: 353–369.

Kammen, Michael. 1986. *A Machine That Would Go of Itself: The Constitution in American Culture*. New York, NY: Alfred A. Knopf Publishing.

Kapiszewski, Diana. 2011. Tactical Balancing: High Court Decision Making on Politically Crucial Cases. *Law and Society Review*. **45**: 471–505.

Kaufman, Daniel, Aart Kraay, and Massimo Mastruzzi. 2004. Governance Matters III: Governance Indicators for 1996, 1998, 2000, and 2002. *World Bank Economic Review*. **18**: 253–287.

Keith, Linda Camp. 2010. Human Rights Instruments. In Peter Cane and Herbert Kritzer, eds. *The Oxford Handbook of Empirical Legal Research*. New York, NY: Oxford University Press.

Keith, Linda Camp. 2002. Constitutional Provisions for Individual Human Rights (1977–1996): Are They More Than Mere "Window Dressing." *Political Research Quarterly*. **55**: 111–143.

Keith, Linda Camp, C. Neal Tate, and Steven C. Poe. 2009. Is the Law a Mere Parchment Barrier to Human Rights Abuse? *The Journal of Politics*. **71**: 644–660.

Kelly, James B. 2011. Judicial and Political Review as Limited Insurance: The Functioning of the New Zealand Bill of Rights Act in 'Hard' Cases. *Commonwealth and Comparative Politics*. **49**: 295–317.

Kleinerman, Benjamin A. 2009. "The Court Will Clean It Up": Executive Power, Constitutional Contestation, and War Powers. In Steven Kautz, Arthur Melzer, Jerry Weinberger, and M. Richard Zinman, eds. *The Supreme Court and the Idea of Constitutionalism*. Philadelphia, PA: University of Pennsylvania Press.

Koenig, Harold G., Linda K. George, Keith G. Meador, and Dan G. Blazer. 1994. Religious Practices and Alcoholism in a Southern Adult Population. *Hospital & Community Psychiatry*. **45**: 225–231.

Kokkinakis v. Greece. 1993. App. No. 14307/88, 260 Eur. Ct. H.R. § 31.

Koppelman, Andrew. 2010. How Shall I Praise Thee? Brian Leiter on Respect for Religion. *San Diego Law Review*. **47**: 961–986.

Kramer, Larry D. 2004. *The People Themselves: Popular Constitutionalism and Judicial Review*. New York, NY: Oxford University Press.

Kritzer, Herbert M. and Mark J. Richards. 2005. The Influence of Law in the Supreme Court's Search-and-Seizure Jurisprudence. *American Political Research*. **33**: 33–55.

Lambert, Yves. 1999. Religion in Modernity as a New Axial Age: Secularization or New Religious Forms? *Sociology of Religion*. **60**: 303–333.

Landman, Todd and Edzia Carvalho. 2010. *Measuring Human Rights*. New York, NY: Routledge.

Law, David S. 2010. Constitutions. In Peter Cane and Herbert Kritzer, eds. *The Oxford Handbook of Empirical Legal Research*. New York, NY: Oxford University Press.

Law, David S. and Mila Versteeg. 2011. The Evolution and Ideology of Global Constitutionalism. *California Law Review*. **99**: 1163–1249.

Laycock, Douglas. 2011. Reviews of a Lifetime. *Texas Law Review*. **89**: 949–965.

Laycock, Douglas. 1996. Religious Liberty as Liberty. *Journal of Contemporary Legal Issues*. **7**: 313–356.

Laycock, Douglas. 1993. The Religious Freedom Restoration Act. *Brigham Young University Law Review*. **1993**: 221–257.

Lee, Matthew R. 2006. The Religious Institutional Base and Violent Crime in Rural Areas. *Journal of the Scientific Study of Religion*. **45**: 309–324.

Lehrer, Evelyn L. 2004a. Religion as a Determinant of Economic and Demographic Behavior in the United States. *Population and Development Review*. **30**: 707–726.

Lehrer, Evelyn L. 2004b. Religion as a Determinant of Educational Attainment: The Case of Servative Protestant Women in the United States. *Review of Economics of the Household*. **2**: 203–219.

Leibiger. 1993. James Madison and Amendments to the Constitution, 1787–1789: "Parchment Barriers". *Southern History*. **59**: 441–468.

Leiter, Brian. 2010. Foundations of Religious Liberty: Toleration or Respect? *San Diego Law Review*. **47**: 935–959.

Leiter, Brian. 2008. Why Tolerate Religion? *Constitutional Commentary*. **25**: 1–27.

Lemon v. Kurtzman. 1971. 403 U.S. 602.

Leung, Beatrice. 2005. China's Religious Freedom Policy: The Art of Managing Religious Activity. *The Chin Quarterly*. **184**: 894–913.

Levinson, Daryl. 2011. Parchment and Politics: The Positive Puzzle of Constitutional Commitment. *Harvard Law Review*. **124**: 657–746.

Lindholm, Tore, W. Cole Durham, Jr., Bahia G. Tahzib-Lie, Elizabeth Sewell, and Lena Larson. 1998. *Facilitating Freedom of Religion or Belief: A Deskbook*. Leiden: Martinus Nijhoff Publishers.

Lindquist, Stefanie A. and David E. Klein. 2006. The Influence of Jurisprudential Considerations on Supreme Court Decisionmaking: A Study of Conflict Cases. *Law & Society Review*. **40**: 135–162.

Liviatan, Ofrit. 2011. Faith in the Law – The Role of Legal Arrangements in Religion-Based Conflicts Involving Minorities. *Boston College International and Comparative Law Review*. **34**: 53–89.

Lupu, Ira C. 1996. To Control Faction and Protect Liberty: A General Theory of the Religion Clauses. *Journal of Contemporary Legal Issues*. **7**: 357–384.

Lynn, Richard, John Harvey, and Helmuth Nyborg. 2008. Average Intelligence Predicts Atheism Rates Across 137 Nations. *Intelligence*. **37**: 11–15.

Macedo, Stephen. 1994. "The Rule of Law, Justice, and the Politics of Moderation." In Ian Shapiro, ed. *The Rule of Law: Nomos XXXVI*. New York, NY: New York University Press.

Madison, James. (1961a). "The Federalist No. 48." In Roy P. Farifield, ed. *The Federalist Papers*. Garden City, NY: Anchor Books. 146–151.

Madison, James. (1961b). "The Federalist No. 51." In Roy P. Farifield, ed. *The Federalist Papers*. Garden City, NY: Anchor Books. 158–164.

Madison, James. (1789). Speech placing the proposed Bill of Rights Before the U.S. House of Representatives.

Malloch, Theodore. 2008. Free to Choose: Economics and Religion. In Paul A. Marshall, ed. *Religious Freedom in the World*. Lanham, MD: Rowman & Littlefield Publishers, Inc.

Mahmud, Tayyab. 1995. Freedom of Religion and Religious Minorities in Pakistan: A Study of Judicial Practice. *Fordham International Law Journal*. **19**: 40–100.

Marshall, Paul A. 2008. *Religious Freedom in the World*. Lanham, MD: Rowman & Littlefield Publishers, Inc.

Marshall, Paul A. 2009. The Range of Religious Freedom in 2008: Results of a Global Survey. *International Journal of Religious Freedom*. **2**: 25–36.

Marshall, Thomas R. 2008. *Public Opinion and the Rehnquist Court*. Albany, NY: State University of New York Press.

Marshall, Thomas R. 1989. *Public Opinion and the Supreme Court*. Boston: Unwin Hymen.

Marshall, Thomas R. and Joseph Ignani. 1994. Supreme Court and Public Support for Rights Claims. *Judicature*. **78**: 146–151.

Marshall, William P. 1996. Religion as Ideas: Religion as Identity. *Journal of Contemporary Legal Issues*. **7**: 385–406.

Marshall, William P. 1991. In Defense of Smith and Free Exercise Revisionism. *University of Chicago Law Review*. **58**: 308–328.

Marty, Martin E. 1996. Religious Dimensions of Human Rights. In John Witte, Jr. and Johan D. Van der Vyver, eds. *Religious Human Rights in Global Perspective: Religious Perspectives*. The Hague: Martinus Nijhoff Publishers.

Mattis, Jacqueline S. 2001. Religion and African American Political Life. *Political Psychology*. **22**: 263–278.

McCann, Michael W. 1994. *Rights at Work: Pay Equity Reform and the Politics of Legal Mobilization*. Chicago, IL: University of Chicago Press.

McCleary, Rachel M. and Robert J. Barro. 2006a. Religion and the Economy. *Journal of Economic Perspectives*. **20**: 49–72.

McCleary, Rachel M. and Robert J. Barro. 2006b. Religion and Political Economy in an International Panel. *Journal of the Scientific Study of Religion*. **45**: 149–175.

McClosky, Herbert and Alida Brill. 1983. *Dimensions of Tolerance: What Americans Believe About Civil Liberties*. New York, NY: Russell Sage Foundation.

McConnell, Michael W. 2000. The Problem of Singling Out Religion. *DePaul Law Review*. **50**: 1–48.

McConnell, Michael W. and Richard A. Posner. 1989. An Economic Approach to Issues of Religious Freedom. *University of Chicago Law Review*. **56**: 1–60.

McDaniel v. Paty. 1978, 435 U.S. 618.

McDaniel, Stephen W. 1989. The Use of Marketing Techniques by Churches: A National Survey. *Review of Religious Research*. **31**: 275–182.

McGuire, Kevin T. 2009. Public Schools, Religious Establishments, and the U.S. Supreme Court. *American Politics Research*. **37**: 50–74.

McGuire, Kevin T. 1998. Explaining Executive Success in the U.S. Supreme Court. *Political Research Quarterly*. **51**: 505–526.

McGuire, Kevin T. and James Stimson. 2004. The Least Dangerous Branch Revisited: New Evidence on Supreme Court Responsiveness to Public Preferences. *Journal of Politics*. **66**: 1018–1035.

Miller, Alan S. and Rodney Stark. 2002. Gender and Religiousness: Can Socialization Explanations Be Saved? *American Journal of Sociology*. **107**: 1399–1423.

Miller, Kent D. 2002. Competitive Strategies of Religious Organizations. *Strategic Management Journal*. **23**: 435–456.

Miner, Christopher J. 1998. Losing My Religion: Austria's New Religion Law in Light of International and European Standards of Religious Freedom. *Brigham Young University Law Review*. **1998**: 601–646.

Mishler, William and Reginald S. Sheehan. 1993. The Supreme Court as a Countermajoritarian Institution? The Impact of Public Opinion on Supreme Court Decisions. *American Political Science Review*. **87**: 87–101.

Mitchell, Neil J. and James M. McCormick. 1988. Economic and Political Explanations of Human Rights Violations. *World Politics*. **40**: 476–498.

Nagel, Stuart. 1965. Court Curbing Periods in American History. *Vanderbilt Law Review*. **18**: 925–944.

Nardulli, Peter F., Budd Peyton, and Joseph Bajjalieh. 2010. Institutions and Economic Growth: An Empirical Assessment of the Post WWII Era, presented at the Annual Meeting of the American Political Science Association.

Nasr, S. V. R. 1995. Democracy and Islamic Revivalism. *Political Science Quarterly*. **110**: 261–285.

Neuhaus, Richard John and Peter L. Berger. 1977. *To Empower People: The Role of Mediating Structures in Public Policy*. Washington, DC: American Enterprise Institute.

Neumeyer, Eric. 2002. Do We Trust the Data? On the Validity and Reliability of Cross-National Environmental Surveys. *Social Science Quarterly*. **83**: 332–340.

Noland, Marcus. 2003. Religion, Culture, and Economic Performance. KDI School of Public Policy & Management Paper No. 03-13.

Norris, Pippa and Ronald Inglehart. 2004. *Sacred and Secular: Religion and Politics Worldwide*. New York, NY: Cambridge University Press.

Norrish, Jacolyn M. and Dianne A. Vella-Brodrick. 2007. Is the Study of Happiness a Worthy Scientific Pursuit? *Social Indicators Research*. **87**: 393–407.

North, Charles M. and Carl R. Gwin. 2004. Religious Freedom and the Unintended Consequences of State Religion. *Southern Economic Journal*. **71**: 103–117.

Nowak, Manfred and Tanja Vospernik. 1998. Permissible Restrictons on Freedom of Religion or Belief. In Tore Lindholm, W. Cole Durham, Jr., Bahia G. Tahzib-Lie, Elizabeth Sewell, and Lena Larson, eds. *Facilitating Freedom of Religion or Belief: A Deskbook*. Leiden: Martinus Nijhoff.

Nussbaum, Martha. 2008. *Liberty of Conscience*. New York, NY: Basic Books.

O'Brien, David. 1996. *Storm Center: The Supreme Court in American Politics*. New York, NY: W. W. Norton & Company.

Opfinger, Matthias. 2010. Religiosity and Personal Well-Being: People Can Be Happy With or Without Religion. Kiel Advanced Studies in International Economic Policy Working Paper No. 455.

Page, Benjamin I. and Robert Y. Shapiro. 1983. Effects of Public Opinion on Policy. *American Political Science Review*. **77**: 175–190.

Paul, Gregory S. 2005. Cross-National Correlations of Quantifiable Social Health with Popular Religiosity and Secularism in the Prosperous Democracies. *Journal of Religion and Society*. **7**: 1–17.

Peretti, Terri Jennings. 1999. *In Defense of a Political Court*. Princeton, NJ: Princeton University Press.

Persily, Nathanial. 2008. Introduction. In Nathaniel Persily, Jack Citrin, and Patrick J. Egan, eds. *Public Opinion and Constitutional Controversy*. New York, NY: Oxford University Press.

Peterson, Steve. 1992. Church Participation and Political Participation: The Spillover Effect. *American Politics Research*. **20**: 123–139.

Pew Forum on Religion & Public Life. 2009. *Global Restrictions on Religion*. Washington, DC: Pew Research Center.

Philpott, Daniel. 2007. Explaining the Political Ambivalence of Religion. *American Political Science Review*. **101**: 505–525.

Pinker, Steven. 1997. *How the Mind Works*. New York, NY: Norton.

Planned Parenthood v. Casey. 1992. 505 U.S. 833.

Podoprigora, Roman. 2004. Freedom of Religion and Belief and Discretionary State Approval of Religious Activity. In Tore Lindholm, W. Cole Durham, Jr., and Bahia G. Tahzib-Lie, eds. *Facilitating Freedom of Religion or Belief: A Deskbook*. Leiden: Martinus Nijhoff Publishers.

Poe, Steven C. and C. Neal Tate. 1994. Repression of Human Rights to Personal Integrity in the 1980s: A Global Analysis. *American Political Science Review*. **88**: 853–872.

Poe, Steven C., C. Neal Tate, and Linda Camp Keith. 1999. Repression of the Human Right to Personal Integrity Revisited: A Global Cross-National Study Covering the Years 1976–1993. *International Studies Quarterly*. **43**: 291–313.

Porter, Roy. 2000. *The Creation of the Modern World*. New York, NY: W. W. Norton & Company.

Powe, L. A. 2005. Are "The People" Missing in Action (and Should Anyone Care)? *Texas Law Review*. **83**: 855–895.

Pryor, Frederic L. 2007. Are Muslim Countries Less Democratic? *The Middle East Quarterly*. **14**: 53–58.

Putnam, Robert D. 2000. *Bowling Alone: The Collapse and Revival of American Community*. New York, NY: Simon and Schuster.

Rabban, David M. 1997. *Free Speech in Its Forgotten Years*. New York: Cambridge University Press.

Raday, Frances. 2009. Secular Constitutionalism Vindicated. *Cardozo Law Review*. **30**: 2769–2798.

Rawls, John 1996. *Political Liberalism*. New York, NY: Columbia University Press.

Rawls, John. 1979. *A Theory of Justice*. Cambridge, MA: Harvard University Press.

Rebell, Michael and Arthur R. Block. 1982. *Educational Policy Making and the Courts: An Empirical Study of Judicial Activism*. Chicago, IL: University of Chicago Press.

Resnik, Judith. 2000. Trial as Error, Jurisdiction as Injury: Transforming the Meaning of Article III. *Harvard Law Review*. **113**: 924–1038.

Reynal-Querol, Marta. 2002. Ethnicity, Political Systems, and Civil Wars. *Journal of Conflict Resolution*. **46**: 29–54.

Richardson, James T. 2006. Religion, Constitutional Courts, and Democracy in Former Communist Countries. *The Annals of the American Academy of Political and Social Science*. **603**: 129–138.

Riker, William H. 1982. *Liberalism Against Populism*. Prospect Heights, IL: Waveland Press Inc.

Riker, William H. 1976. Comments on Vincent Ostrom's Paper. *Public Choice*. **27**: 13–19.

Roe v. Wade. 1973. 410 U.S. 113.

Rosen, Jeffrey. 2006. *The Most Democratic Branch: How the Courts Serve America*. New York, NY: Oxford University Press.

Rosenberg, Gerald N. 1991. *The Hollow Hope*. Chicago, IL: University of Chicago Press.

Ross, Michael L. 2008. Oil, Islam, and Women. *American Political Science Review*. **102**: 107–123.

Roth, Louise Marie and Jeffrey C. Kroll. 2007. Risky Business: Assessing Risk Preference Explanations for Gender Differences in Religiosity. *American Sociological Review*. **72**: 205–220.

Rummel, Rudolph J. 2002. Is Collective Violence Correlated with Social Pluralism? *Journal of Peace Research*. **34**: 163–175.

Saeed, Abdullah and Hassan Saeed. 2004. *Freedom of Religion, Apostasy, and Islam*. Burlington, VT: Ashgate Publishing.

Sager, Lawrence G. 2005. Courting Disaster. *Fordham Law Review*. **73**: 14361–1376.

Sager, Lawrence Gene. 1978. Fair Measure: The Legal Status of Underenforced Constitutional Norms. *Harvard Law Review*. **81**: 1212–1264.

Samaha, Adam M. 2008. Dead Hand Arguments and Constitutional Interpretation. *Columbia Law Review*. **108**: 606–680.

Schwadel, Philip. 2005. Individual, Congregational, and Denominational Effects on Church Members' Civic Participation. *Journal of the Scientific Study of Religion*. **44**: 159–171.

Scolnicov, Anat. 2011. *The Right to Religious Freedom in International Law*. London: Routledge.

Sedler, Robert A. 1988. The Constitutional Protection of Freedom of Religion, Expression, and Association in Canada and the United States: A Comparative Analysis. *Case Western Reserve Journal of International Law*. **20**: 577–621.

Segal, Jeffrey A. and Harold J. Spaeth. 1993. *The Supreme Court and the Attitudinal Model*. New York, NY: Cambridge University Press.

Segal, Jeffrey A., Chad Westerland, and Stefanie A. Lindquist. 2010. Congress, the Supreme Court, and Judicial Review: Testing a Constitutional Separation of Powers Model. *American Journal of Political Science*. **55**: 89–104.

Sheehan, Coleen A. 2005. Public Opinion and the Formation of Civic Character in Madison's Republican Theory. *The Review of Politics*. **67**: 37–48.

Sheiman, Bruce. 2009. *An Atheist Defends Religion*. New York, NY: Penguin Press.

Sherkat, Darren E. and Christopher G. Ellison. 1999. Recent Developments and Current Controversies in the Sociology of Religion. *Annual Review of Sociology*. **25**: 363–394.

Sidel, John T. 2006 *Riots, Pogroms, Jihad: Religious Violence in Indonesia*. Ithaca, NY: Cornell University Press.

Sisk, Gregory C. 2005. How Traditional and Minority Religions Fare in the Courts: Empirical Evidence from Religious Liberty Cases. *University of Colorado Law Review*. **76**: 1021–1054.

Sisk, Gregory C. 2004. Searching for the Soul of Judicial Decision Making: An Empirical Study of Religious Freedom Decisions. *Ohio State Law Journal*. **65**: 491–614.

Smidt, Corwin E. 2008. *Pews, Prayers, and Participation*. Washington, DC: Georgetown University Press.

Smidt, Corwin E. 1999. Religion and Civic Engagement: A Comparative Analysis. *Annals of the American Academy of Political Science*. **1**: 176–192.

Smilde, David. 2005. A Qualitative Comparative Analysis of Conversion to Venezuelan Evangelicalism: How Networks Matter. *The American Journal of Sociology*. **111**: 757–796.

Smith, Ian. 1993. The Economics of Church Decline in Scotland. *International Journal of Social Economics*. **20**: 27–36.

Smith, Rogers M. 2009. Judicial Power and Democracy: A Machiavellian View. In Steven Kautz, Arthur Melzer, Jerry Weinberger, and M. Richard Zinman, eds. *The Supreme Court and the Idea of Constitutionalism*. Philadelphia, PA: University of Pennsylvania Press.

Smith, Steven D. 1991. The Rise and Fall of Religious Freedom in Constitutional Discourse. *University of Pennsylvania Law Review*. **140**: 149–240.

Songer, Donald R. and Susan J. Tabrizi. 1999. The Religious Right in Court: The Decisionmaking of Christian Evangelicals in State Supreme Courts. *Journal of Politics*. **61**: 507–526.

Sorauf, Frank J. 1976. *The Wall of Separation: The Constitutional Politics of Church and State*. Princeton, NJ: Princeton University Press

Spann, Girardeau. 1993. *Race Against the Court*. New York, NY: New York University Press.

Stark, Rodney. 1971. Psychopathology and Religious Commitment. *Review of Religious Research*. **12**: 165–176.

Stark, Rodney and Laurence Iannaccone. 1994. A Supply-Side Reinterpretation of the "Secularization" of Europe. *Journal for the Scientific Study of Religion*. **33**: 230–252.

Stark, Rodney and James C. McCann. 1993. Market Forces and Catholic Commitment: Exploring the New Paradigm. *Journal of the Scientific Study of Religion*. **32**: 111–124.

Stuart, Alison. 2010. Freedom of Religion and Gender Equality: Inclusive or Exclusive? *Human Rights Law Review*. **10**: 429–459.

Sullivan, Kathleen M. 1992. Religion and Liberal Democracy. *University of Chicago Law Review*. **59**: 195–224.

Swatos, William H. and Kevin J. Christiano. 1999. Secularization Theory: The Course of a Concept. *Sociology of Religion*. **60**: 209–228.

Sweet, Alec Stone and Jud Mathews. 2008. Proportionality Balancing and Global Constitutionalism. *Columbia Journal of Transnational Law*. **47**: 72–164.

Sweet, Martin J. 2010. *Merely Judgment*. Charlottesville, VA: University of Virginia Press.

Tebbe, Nelson. 2011. Nonbelievers. *Virginia Law Review*. **97**: 1111–1180.

Toma, Eugenia F. 1996. A Contractual Model of the Voting Behavior of the Supreme Court: The Role of the Chief Justice. *International Review of Law & Economics*. **16**: 433–447.

Torcaso v. Watkins. 1961. 367 U.S. 488.

Traunmuller, Richard and Marcus Freitag. 2011. State Support of Religion: Making or Breaking Faith-Based Social Capital? *Comparative Politics*. **43**: 253–269.

Tushnet, Mark. 1999. *Taking the Constitution Away from the Courts*. Princeton, NJ: Princeton University Press.

Tutu, Desmond. 1996. Preface. In John Witte, Jr. and Johan D. Van der Vyver, eds. *Religious Human Rights in Global Perpsective: Religious Perspectives*. The Hague: Martinus Nijhoff Publishers.

Twining, William. 2009. *General Jurisprudence: Understanding Law from a Global Perspective*. New York, NY: Cambridge University Press.

United States v. Seeger. 1965. 380 U.S. 163.

Van der Vyver. 2004. The Relationship of Freedom of Religion or Belief Norms to Other Human Rights. In Tore Lindholm, W. Cole Durham, Jr., and Bahia G. Tahzib-Lie, eds. *Facilitating Freedom of Religion or Belief: A Deskbook*. Leiden: Martinus Nijhoff Publishers.

Vanberg, Georg. 2006. "John Marshall Has Made His Decision." In James R. Rogers, Roy B. Flemming, and Jon R. Bond, eds. *Institutional Games and the U.S. Supreme Court*. Charlottesville: University of Virginia Press.

Vanberg, Georg. 2000. Establishing Judicial Independence in West Germany: The Impact of Opinion Leadership and the Separation of Powers. *Comparative Politics*. **32**: 333–355.

Venter, Francois. 2010. *Global Features of Constitutional Law*. Nijmegan: Wolf Legal Publishers.

Verme, Paolo. 2009. Happiness, Freedom, and Control. *Journal of Economic Behavior & Organization*. **71**: 146–161.

Verweij, Johan, Peter Ester, and Rein Nauta. 1997. Secularization as an Economic and Cultural Phenomenon: A Cross-National Analysis. *Journal for the Scientific Study of Religion*. **36**: 309–324.

Voas, David, Daniel V.A. Olson, and Alisdair Crockett. 2002. Religious Pluralism and Participation: Why Previous Research Is Wrong. *American Sociological Review*. **67**: 212–230.

Voigt, Stefan. 2009. Explaining Constitutional Garrulity. *International Review of Law and Economics*. **29**: 290–303.

Waldron, Jeremy. 2005. Compared to What? Judicial Activism and New Zealand's Parliament. *New Zealand Law Journal*. **December**: 441–445.

Wallace v. Jaffree. 1985. 472 U.S. 38.

Way, Frank and Barbara J. Burt. 1983. Religious Morality and the Free Exercise Clause. *American Political Science Review*. **77**: 652–665.

Weber, Max. 1930. *The Protestant Ethic and the Spirit of Capitalism*. New York, NY: Charles Scribner's Sons.

Weisberg, Richard H. 1992. *Poethics, and Other Strategies of Law and Literature*. New York, NY: Columbia University Press.

Whittington, Keith E. 2009. Constitutional Constraints in Politics. In Steven Kautz, Arthur Melzer, Jerry Weinberger, and M. Richard Zinman, eds. *The Supreme Court and the Idea of Constitutionalism*. Philadelphia, PA: University of Pennsylvania Press.

Wierzbicka, Anna. 2004. "Happiness" in Cross-Linguistic and Cross-Cultural Perspective. *Daedalus*. **133**: 36–43.

Wilcox, Clyde. 1991. Support for Gender Equality in West Europe. *European Journal of Political Research*. **20**: 127–147.

Wilson, James G. 1993. The Role of Public Opinion in Constitutional Interpretation. *Brigham Young University Law Review*. **1993**: 1037–1138.

Wisconsin v. Yoder. 1972. 406 U.S. 205.

Witte, John, Jr. 2005. Religion and the American Constitutional Experiment. Boulder, CO: Westview.

Woods, Patricia J. and Lisa Hilbink. 2009. Comparative Sources of Judicial Empowerment: Ideas and Interests. *Political Research Quarterly*. **62**: 745–752.

Wright, Charles Alan. 1997. A Bill of Rights: Does It Matter? *Texas International Law Journal*. **32**: 381–391.

Wybraniec, John and Roger Finke. 2001. Religious Regulation and the Courts: The Judiciary's Changing Role in Protecting Minority Religions from Majoritarian Rule. *Journal for the Scientific Study of Religion*. **40**: 427–444.

Yarnold, Barbara M. 2000. Did Circuit Courts of Appeals Judges Overcome Their Own Religions in Cases Involving Religious Liberties? *Review of Religious Research*. **42**: 79–86.

Yousif, Ahmad. 2000. Islam, Minorities, and Religious Freedom: A Challenge to Modern Theory of Pluralism. *Journal of Muslim Minority Affairs*. **20**: 29–41.

Zorn, Christopher. 2006. Institutions and Independence in Models of Judicial Review. In James R. Rogers, Roy B. Flemming, and Jon R. Bond, eds. *Institutional Games and the U.S. Supreme Court*. Charlottesville: University of Virginia Press.

Zuckerman, Phil. 2009. Atheism, Secularity, and Well-Being: How the Findings of Social Science Counter Negative Stereotypes and Assumptions. *Sociology Compass*. **3**: 949–971.

Zuckerman, Phil. 2007. Atheism: Contemporary Numbers and Patterns. In M. Martin, ed. *The Cambridge Companion to Atheism*. Cambridge: Cambridge University Press.

Index

Note: An *f* following a page number indicates a figure; a *t* following a page number indicates a table.

abortion, 21, 23–24, 48–49, 123, 139, 141, 146
Ackerman, Bruce, 85, 112
ACLU, 148
adultery, 48
affirmative action, 87, 139
Afghanistan, 35, 48, 67
Africa
  atheists in, 195–196
  government subsidization of religion in, 54
  oppression of minority religions in, 38–39
  regulation of religion in, 51
  religiosity in, 191
  religious diversity in, 187
  religious laws in, 49
  social regulation of religion in, 67
  struggles between Muslims and Christians in, 6, 7
  See also *individual country*
African American churches, 13
African Americans, and activism, 20, 21
afterlife, belief in, 191
agnostics, 26, 27, 29, 31, 205
Albanian constitution, 156
alcoholic beverages
  abuse of, religion effect on, 13, 14
  restriction on consumption of, 48–49
  restriction on sale of, 35, 48
Algeria, oppression of minority religions in, 36
Alston, 121
altruism, 11–12, 13
American Bar Association, 119
Amish people, 28

Index

Amnesty International, 73
Animism, 43, 80–81
apartheid, World Council of Churches role in demise of, 22
apostasy, 39, 79–80
Argentina, 43, 156, 163
Arjomand, 157, 159–160
Armenia, 44
Armstrong, 87
Asad, 2
Asia
  oppression of minority religions in, 39–42
  regulation of religion in, 51
  religious education in, 55
  religious laws in, 48–49
  See also *individual country*
Association of Religion Data Archives (ARDA), 65–68
  comparison with RAS overall score, 70–73, 72*f*
  comparison with RAS scores, 69–73
  correlation matrix of religious freedom measures, 71*t*
  limitations of, 77
  and social regulation of religion, 67–68, 70
  and state religion, 161–162
  See also government favoritism of religion (GFI); government regulation of religion (GRI); Pew survey data on religious freedom; Religion and State (RAS) scores on religious freedom; RFF scores on religious freedom
atheism, 195–198
  China as officially atheist, 39
  and democracy, 84, 196*t*
  and gender equality, 204–205
  and happiness, 203
  and national income, 195–196, 196*t*
  and religious freedom, 197, 197*f*
  Supreme Court on, 26–27
  in Sweden, 23
  United Nations protection of, 27
  view toward, in United States, 26
attendance, church
  and establishment clause, 192–193, 192*f*, 193
  and establishment clauses, 192–193, 192*f*
  self-reported happiness effect on, 199–200
  state-controlled religion effect on, 16, 17
attitudinal studies on religion and economics, 10
attitudinal theory of judicial decisionmaking, 124–128
Australia, 96–97, 107–108, 187
Austria, 52–53, 131
authoritarian regime
  and happiness, 200
  and religious oppression, 168
  and resource curse, 79
  and rule of law, 90, 91
  state church opposition to, 20
  value of precommitment to, 112

Index

autocracy, religious suppression by, 7, 83
Azerbaijan, 38, 44–45, 155

backstop theory, 145
Baer, Harold, 129
Baha'i faith, 36, 37, 38
Bahrain, religious discrimination in, 37
Bajjalieh, 160–161
Bangladesh, 23, 41
Baptists, repression in Central Asia, 38
Barclay, 144
Barro, 10–11, 97, 186, 187, 191, 195, 198
Baum, Lawrence, 138–139
Belarus, registration requirements in, 44, 53
Belarus, religious repression in, 44
Belgium, government subsidization of religion in, 54
Berger, 20
Beyer, 34
Bhutan, 41, 158
Bible, on blasphemy, 79–80
Bill of Rights (U.S.), 1
  Americans' awareness of, 119–120
  and democracy, 114–121
  enforcement by courts, 144, 145
  James Madison on, 105
  and judicial enforcement, 114, 115, 121–122
  and religious toleration, 118–119
  uneven enforcement of, 107
bills of rights, 30
Birkby, 139–140
Birkland, 144
Black, Hugo, 26
blasphemy, 35, 48–49, 79–80
Board of Education of Kiryas Joel v. Grumet (1994), 26
Bosnia, religious harassment in, 46
brainwashing, 51
Braithwaite, 89
Bramsen, 89
Brazil, 151
Breault, 17
Brill, 8, 118–119
Britain. *See* United Kingdom
Brooks, 11
Brown v. Board of Education, 84, 139
Bruce, 94, 95, 96
Brunei, 48, 55
Buchanan, 121
Buddhism, 2
  beliefs of, 191
  discrimination in Vietnam, 42
  and religious freedom, 42, 81
  repression in Japan, 42
  repression in Nepal, 41
  repression in Tibet, 40
Bulgaria, 46, 50, 155
burial, religious restrictions on, 35
Burma, religious suppression in, 41, 42
Burt, 146–147

Cambodia, religious suppression in, 42
Canada
  free exercise clause in, 148–149

Canada (cont.)
judicial defense of human rights in, 153
religious diversity in, 187
secularization in, 96–97
Catholicism
and civil war in Yugoslavia, 6
and democratization, 19–20
economic effects of, 11
and fall of Polish communism, 22
favoritism toward wealthy in Latin American, 15–16
government support in Portugal, 53
pluralism effect on participation in, 17
and religious diversity, 16
and religious education in South America, 55
repression in China, 40
in South America, 43
suppression in Cuba, 44
suppression in Sri Lanka, 41
and women's rights, 204
Central Asia
direct oppression of minority religions in, 37–38
See also *individual country*
Chad, religious freedom in, 51
charity, 11–12
Charter of Rights and Freedoms (Canada), 153
China
crackdown on religious groups in, 22
Falun Gong in, 40
as officially atheist, 39
oppression of minority religions in, 39–40, 42
registration requirements in, 40
repression of Buddhists in Tibet, 40
restrictions on teachers and students in, 40
social regulation of religion in, 67
Christianity
growth of, 96
growth of fundamentalist, 96
and women's rights, 32
See also Catholicism; Christianity, repression of; evangelicalism; Protestantism
Christianity, repression of
in Burma, 41
in Central Asia, 37–38
in China, 39, 40
in Indonesia, 38
in Laos, 41–42
in Mauritania, 38–39
in Middle East, 36–37
in Vietnam, 42
church attendance
decline in Western Europe, 94–95
and establishment clause, 192–193, 192*f*, 193
and separation clauses, 192
state-controlled religion effect on, 16, 17
Church of Christian Science, recognition in Italy, 52
circuit courts, 127, 138
civic engagement, religious belief effects on, 12–13, 21

civil rights, 21, 87
Clark, 130
classical liberalism, 29
Colombia
  constitution of, 153
  religious discrimination in, 43
  religious diversity in, 187
  religious registration in, 51
Committee to Promote Virtue and Prevent Vice, 48
communist countries, former
  development of democracy in, 20
  religious suppression in, 44
  See also *individual country*
Comoros, oppression of minority religions in, 37
Congo, religiosity in, 23
Congress (U.S.), relationship with Supreme Court, 129–131
Conkle, 8, 186, 189
conscientious objection, 26
Constitution (U.S.)
  changes in meanings over time, 106–107, 112
  devotion to, 105
  and proportionality, 155–156
  See also Bill of Rights; constitutions
constitutional protection of religious freedom
  coding research on, 157–160
    difficulties with, 159–160
    elements of First Amendment, 159
    length of constitution, 157–158
    specificity of language used, 157
    state religion, 158–159
constitutional religions and religious freedom, 160–163
  ARDA scores on, 161–162
  no state religion as factor in, 162–163, 162*f*
  Pew scores on, 162, 163, 163*f*
  RAS scores on, 161, 163
  state religion as factor i, 161–163, 161*t*
establishment clause, 166–170, 166*t*
  constitutional content measures, 168–170
  effects of variables, 167, 167*t*
  oppression of minority religions measure on, 167–168
  Pew scores on, 166–167, 168–169, 168*t*, 169*f*
  RAS scores on, 166, 167, 167*f*, 169, 169*f*
free exercise clause, 164–166, 164*t*, 165*f*
  Pew scores on, 164, 165*f*
  RAS scores on, 164–166, 165*f*
government assistance, 180–182
  Pew scores on, 180
  Pew scores with establishment clause, 180–182, 181*f*
  RAS scores for educational activities, 180
individual laws and actions, 175–178
  establishment clause, 177–178
  free exercise clause, 175–177
interaction effects, 170–175
  democracy/legal infrastructure/ separation clause, 171, 171*t*

constitutional protection (cont.)
democracy/prohibition of national religion, 173–174, 174*f*
democracy/separation clause, 172, 172*f*
legal infrastructure/prohibition on state religion, 174–175, 175*f*
legal infrastructure/separation clause, 172–173, 173*f*
RAS scores on, 172, 173, 173*f*, 174*f*
proportionality, 178–180
free exercise clause, 180, 180*t*
Pew scores on, 178–179, 180
RAS scores for religious freedom by, 179–180, 179*f*, 180
provisions of constitutions, 154–157
establishment clauses, 156
establishment of state religion, 156
proportionality, 154–156
registration, 182–183
Pew scores on, 182
See also constitutions; establishment clause
constitutions
as aspirational, 107
devotion to, 105
popular constitutionalism, 116
provisions relevant to religious freedom, 27–28
creating or banning state religion, 27–28
freedom of religious belief, 28
separation of church and state, 28
reasons they matter, 108–113
coordinating function of, 108–110
precommitment function of, 110–113
structural provisions, 108
research on effect of protections, 149–151
as symbolic, 107
uneven enforcement of, 106–107
value of, 105–106
See also constitutional protection of religious freedom
contract law, precommitment theory on, 111
conversion, 200
away from Islam, 36
forced, 36, 39, 61
to other religion, consequences of, 67
Cooter, 158
Copts, 36
Corwin, 106, 144
Costa Rica, 55, 163
Council of Europe, 204
Council of the European Union, 73
countermajoritarianism, 123, 128–131, 133, 134, 135–136, 137, 138–139
See also Supreme Court (U.S.)
court-curbing (jurisdiction stripping), 129–130
criminal law, 139
Cross, 125, 132–133, 145, 149
Cuba, religious minorities in, 44
cults, 51, 52
Cyprus, constitutional court in, 131
Czech Republic, religiosity in, 23

Index

Dahl, Robert, 86, 139
Dahl, Ronald, 128
Darrow, 121
death penalty, 21
democracy
 effect on per capita GDP, 100
 effect on religious freedom, 100, 101, 161*t*
  and atheism, 84, 196*t*, 197–198
  and establishment clause, 166*t*
  and free exercise clauses, 164*t*
  and gender status, 206, 206*t*
  and happiness, 202, 202*t*
  Pew constitution measures on, 168*t*
  and Pew measure of GRI, 102–103, 103*t*
  and proportionality, 180*t*
  and RAS religious freedom measures, 82*f*, 100–103
  and religious diversity, 188*t*
  and RFF/GRI measures, 102, 102*t*
  and rule of law, 100
  and separation clause interaction with legal infrastructure, 171*t*
  and social factors, 83–89, 88*f*
 world democratization wave, 19–20
Democratic Republic of the Congo, religious suppression in, 43–44
Denmark
 government favoritism in, 70
 government subsidization of religion in, 54
 religiosity in, 23
 state religion in, 45, 54
deviant behavior, effect of religion on, 13–15
Devins, Neil, 119
dietary laws, 48–49
diversity, religious, 186–188, 188*t*
 and atheism, 196*t*, 197*f*
 and church attendance, 192–193, 192*f*, 194, 194*f*
 and gender status, 206, 206*t*, 207, 207*f*
 and government subsidization, 198–199, 198*f*, 199*f*
 RAS scores on, 188*f*
 and religiosity, 189–195, 190*f*
 and state religion/church attendance, 193–194, 193*f*
 and well-being, 188*f*, 199–204, 202*t*
divorce, 13, 32, 48, 111
Dostoyevsky, 9
Dotan, 122, 127
Douglas, William O., 124, 132–133
Driessen, 89
Driver, 129
Durlauf, 11
Dworkin, Ronald, 3, 84

Easterbrook, Frank, 105–106, 107
Eastern Europe, regulation of religion in, 53. See also *individual country*
Ecuador, 43, 187
Edelman, 126

education
  and government assistance, 55, 180–182
  of women, 205
  See also schools
Edwards, Thomas, 10
Egypt, 23, 36
Eisgruber, Christopher, 3
Elkins, Zach, 108, 158, 178
Elliott, 13–14, 200, 203
Ellison, 14
Employment Division, Department of Human Resources of Oregon v. Smith, 47, 155–156
Enlightenment, 7
environmental issues, 139
Epp, 106, 147, 148, 183–184
Equatorial Guinea, religious freedom in, 51
Eskridge, 145–146
establishment clause, 156
  and church attendance, 192–193, 192*f*, 193
  and constitutional content measures, 168–170
  effect on atheism, 197
  effects of variables on, 167, 167*t*
  and government assistance, 55, 180–182, 181*f*
  and individual laws and actions, 177–178
  and irreligious persons, 29–30
  and Islamic population, 166*t*
  and oppression of minority religions, 167–168
  Pew scores on, 166–167, 168–169, 168*t*, 169*f*
  RAS scores on, 166, 167, 167*f*, 169, 169*f*
  and state religions, 156
  violations of, 154
Estonia, 23, 44–45
Europe
  constitutional protection of minority religions in, 143
  effect of judicial review on compliance in, 142–143
  human rights in, 27, 53, 155
  pogroms against Jews in, 6
  religiosity in, 189, 191
  religious belief and life satisfaction in, 13
  religious diversity in, 187
  religious laws in, 49
  social regulation of religion in, 67
  See also *individual country*
European Convention on Human Rights, 155
European Court of Human Rights, 27, 53
evangelicalism
  and individual benefits of religious beliefs, 15
  prohibition against, 36, 37
  repression in Central Asia, 37–38
  repression in Greece, 45
  repression in Thailand, 41
  repression in Venezuela, 43
Evangelical-Lutheran religion, 156
Everson v. Board of Education (1947), 55

extremism
as argument against religious freedom, 8–9
as argument for religious freedom, 18–19

Falun Gong, 40
Farnsworth, 120
favoritism. *See* government favoritism of religion (GFI)
Fearon, 186
Federalist No. 10, 85
Feofanov, 2
Ferejohn, 145–146
Fiji, constitution of, 157, 159–160
Finke, 17, 84, 137
Finland, 45, 54
Finnis, 5
First Amendment, support by Americans, 120. *See also* Bill of Rights
First Amendment Center, 119, 120
Fish, 79
flag burning, 135
Foa, 200
forced conversions, 36, 39, 61
forced marriages, 39
Fox, Jonathan, 18, 60, 61, 88, 150–151, 155, 178
France
judicial review effect on compliance in, 142–143
regulation of religion in, 51–52
religious discrimination toward Muslims in, 45
religious freedom in, 45–46
See also Europe; Western Europe
Frazee v. Illinois Dept. Employment Sec. (1989), 26
Freedom House, 60
free exercise clause, effect on religious freedom, 164
in Canada, 148–149
and constitutional protections, 175–177
and democracy, 164*t*
and individual laws and actions, 175–177
and Islamic population, 164*t*
and legal infrastructure, 164*t*
Pew scores on, 164, 164*t*, 165*f*
and proportionality, 180, 180*t*
RAS scores on, 164–166, 165*f*
and rule of law, 164*t*
Freeman, 14
free press, 36, 79
free speech, 31, 43, 136, 178
Friedman, Barry, 128–129, 132
Fugitive Slave Act, 91
Fukayama, 25
Fuller, 90
fundamentalism
curbing, 31
effect on economic growth, 11
growth of, 96

Gallup poll
on constitutional religious issues, 119
on happiness, 201–202

Gallup poll (cont.)
on religiosity, 23, 189, 192, 195
on Ten Commandments monument, 135
game theory, on cooperation, 109
Garvey, 9
gay rights, 21
gender rights
religious freedom effect on, 204–207
Shari'a law and, 48
UN gender empowerment measure, 205–206
General Social Survey (2010), 135–136
generosity, 11–12
Georgia, 44, 53, 156
Germany
government subsidization of religion in, 54
and Holocaust, 6
regulation of religion in, 51–52
religious discrimination toward Muslims in, 45
religious education in, 55
See also Europe; Western Europe
Gey, 27
Ghana, religious diversity in, 187
Gill, 16, 17, 19
Ginsburg, Tom, 108, 158, 178
Gioso, 25, 204–205
Goderis, 146
good, religion as, 9–15
government favoritism of religion (GFI), 66, 70
and correlation matrix of religious freedom measures, 71*t*
and democracy, 89
in United States, 55
government regulation of religion (GRI), 49–53, 54–57, 66–67, 69
in Africa, 51
in Asia, 51
and correlation matrix of religious freedom measures, 71*t*
declaration of state religion as, 54
and democracy, 89
in Eastern Europe, 53
education, 55
financial support, 54
and law, 55
limits of, 56
in Middle East, 50–51
religious requirements for public office as, 54
in South America, 51
in United States, 53
in Western Europe, 51–53
See also *individual country*
government subsidies, 54, 198–199
effect on religiosity, 198*f*
effect on religious diversity, 199*f*
Great Britain. *See* United Kingdom
Greece
church attendance in, 192
constitution of, 159
minority religions in, 45
prohibition of proselytization in, 45, 46
regulation of religion in, 53
religious diversity in, 187
religious education in, 55
state religion in, 45, 54

Greek Orthodox Church, 45
Green, 120
Greenberg, 20
Grim, Brian, 11, 75, 84
Gruber, 186–187, 199–200
Guinea, religious registration in, 51
Gunn, 156
Gwin, 16–17, 189

Habermas, 21
Hackett, 205
Hall, 141
Hamilton, **(2005)**, 4
Hamilton, Alexander, 107, 114, 129, 138
Hanburger, Philip, 154
Hand, Learned, 105
happiness levels
  national income effect on, 202, 202*t*
  religious beliefs effect on, 24
  religious freedom effect on, 25
  See also well-being, and religious freedom
Hardin, Russell, 108–109
Harris, 20
Harvey, 132
Haybron, 201
Hayward, 13–14, 25, 200, 203
Henderson, 90, 93
Herfindahl scale, 187, 194–195, 199, 203
Herzegovina, religious harassment in, 46
Hiebert, 124, 154
Hinduism
  beliefs of, 191
  discrimination in Bangladesh, 41
  misogyny in, 32
  recognization in Italy, 52
  violence against in India, 6
Hindu Mahabharata, 32
Hirschl, Ran, 18, 30, 31, 33
historical case for religious freedom, 5–8
  Inquisition, 6
  oppression in name of religion, 5–7
  pogroms against Jews, 6
Holocaust, 6
Homicide rates, 23–24
Horwitz, 91
human rights
  in Australia, 107–108
  in Canada, 153
  and democracy, 87
  in Europe, 27, 53, 155
  in Latin America, 22
Human Rights Watch, 73
Hummer, 14
Huntington, 78–79

Iacconne, 13, 14
Iceland, state religion in, 45, 54
identity, and religion, 4, 5
Ignagni
Impeachment, 129
implied secularism, 29
India
  church attendance in, 192
  inter-religious violence in, 6

India (cont.)
religious freedom in, 40–41
secular courts in, 31
social regulation of religion in, 67
Indonesia
inter-religious violence in, 6
religiosity in, 23
religious repression in, 38, 42
Inglehart, 200
inheritance, religious restrictions on, 48–49
Inquisition, 6
International Covenant on Civil and Political Rights, 155
Iran
oppression of minority religions in, 36
value of judiciary in, 142
See also Islam; Islamic population
Iraq
oppression of minority religions in, 37
social regulation of religion in, 67
See also Islam; Islamic population
Ireland, 7, 192
irreligious persons, 25–31
atheists (*see* atheism)
equality of constitutional protection for, 28
and establishment clause, 29–30
growing reliance on constitutionalism, 30–31
and implied secularism, 29, 30–31
Islam
and apostasy, 39, 79
as authoritarian, 78–79
conversion away from, 36
effect on economic growth, 11
growth of fundamentalist, 96
recognization in Italy, 52
and women's rights, 204
See also Islamic population; Middle East; Shari'a law
Islamic population, effect on religious freedom, 100, 101, 161*t*
and atheism, 196, 196*t*
and establishment clause, 166*t*
and free exercise clause, 164*t*
and gender status, 206, 206*t*
and Pew constitution measures, 168*t*
Pew measure of GRI on, 102–103, 103*t*
and proportionality, 180*t*
RAS scores on, 101*t*
RFF/GRI measures on, 102, 102*t*
and separation clause/democracy/legal infrastructure interaction, 171*t*
social factors of, 81–82, 82*f*
and violent religious persecution, 80
Israel, bills of rights in, 127
Italy, religious regulation in, 52
Ivory Coast, religious education in, 55

Jackson, Andrew, 138
Jamaica, religious education in, 55
Japan
atheists in, 195–196
religious freedom in, 42
secularization in, 96–97
Jefferson, Thomas, 4–5, 138
Jehovah's Witnesses, 51, 52
Jews, 6

Jones, 201
Judaism
  and apostasy, 79–80
  economic effects of, 11
judges, effects of religious affiliation of, 125
judicial countermajoritarianism. *See* countermajoritarianism; Supreme Court (U.S.)
judicial majoritarianism. *See* majoritarianism
judicial overhang, 117–118
judicial supremacy, 117, 121
jurisdiction stripping (court-curbing), 129–130
justification for protecting religious freedom, 3–5

Kammen, 105, 119
Kapiszewski, 151
Kazakhstan, 38, 53
Keith, 87, 146, 147, 150
Kenya, 38, 187
Kirshas, 53
Klein, 126
Kokkinakis v. Greece (1993), 27
Koppelman, 2
Kourtellos, 11
Kramer, 116, 134–135
Krishnas, 37
Kritzer, 126
Kuwait, religious repression in, 36
Kyrgyz Republic, religious freedom in, 38
Kyrgyzstan, religious freedom in, 44–45

Laïcité, 45
Lambert, 97
Laos, religious suppression in, 41–42
lateral compliance, 141
Latin, 186
Latin America
  democratization by Catholic Church in, 20
  favoritism by Catholic Church in, 15–16
  pluralism effect on human rights in, 22
  See also *individual country*
Latvia, 44–45, 192
Law, 150
laws, religious, 48–53
  in Africa, 49
  in Asia, 48–49
  in Europe, 49
  Shari'a (*see* Shari'a law)
  in United States, 49
  See also legal infrastructure
Laycock, 7, 25–26, 185
legal infrastructure, and religious freedom, 160, 161, 161*t*, 162, 164
  and establishment clause, 166*t*
  and free exercise clause, 164*t*
  and interaction with separation clause/democracy, 171*t*
  and Pew constitution measures, 168*t*
  and proportionality, 180*t*
legal realism, 124
legitimation hypothesis, 115, 139
Leiter, Brian, 2, 3, 18, 25

Lemon v. Kurtzman (1971), 29–30
Levinson, 110, 112
Liberia, religious freedom in, 51
Libya, religious discrimination in, 37
Liechtenstein, state religion in, 45
life satisfaction. *See* well-being
Lincoln, Abraham, 21, 138
Lindholm, 53
Lindquist, 126, 132
Lithuania, religious freedom in, 44–45
Liviatan, 50
logrolling, 145–146
Louis XIV (France), 9–10
Lundsgaarde, 19
Lupu, 3
Lutherans, 45

Madison, James, 20, 85, 105, 135, 170–171, 184
majoritarianism, 128–129, 145
  and religious freedom, 84–85, 86–87
  tyranny of the majority, 84, 85, 90, 123
Malaysia, 42, 54
Mali, religious freedom in, 38
Malta, state church in, 54
Maoism, 39
marriage
  forced, 39
  religious restrictions on, 35, 37, 48–49
Marshall, 65, 140
Marty, 7
Marx, Karl, 91
Mattis, 20
Mauritania, religious repression in, 38–39
McCann, 16
McCleary, 10–11, 97, 186, 187, 191, 198
McClosky, 8, 118–119
McConnell, 30
McCormick Tribune Freedom Museum, 119
McDaniel v. Paty (1978), 30
McGuire, 140
measuring religious freedom
  difficulty of, 58–60
  and facial validity, 70
  See also Association of Religion Data Archives (ARDA); Pew survey data on religious freedom; Religion and State (RAS) scores on religious freedom; RFF scores on religious freedom
mediating institution, religion as, 20–21
Melton, 108
mental health benefits of religious belief, 14
Mexico, oppression of minority religions in, 43
Middle East
  atheists in, 195–196
  curbing fundamentalism in, 31
  discriminatory religious repression in, 36–37
  government subsidization of religion in, 54
  pogroms against Jews in, 6
  regulation of religion in, 50–51

religiosity in, 191
religious requirements for public office in, 54
See also Islam; Islamic population; Shari'a law, *individual country*
Miner, 27
minority religions
constitutional protection in Europe, 143
conversion to Christianity in Afghanistan, 35
direct oppression of, 35–47, 56 (See also *individual country*)
in Africa, 38–39
in Asia, 39–42
in Central Asia, 37–38
in China, 39–40
in communist countries, 44
in countries of two million or more people, 39
and Eastern Europe, 46
in India, 40–41
in Middle East, 36–37
in South America, 43
in states of former Soviet Union, 44–45
in Sub-Saharan Africa, 43–44
and United States, 46–47
and Western Europe, 45–46
and Supreme Court, 137
missionaries
in Africa, 43–44
prohibition in Kazakhstan, 53
prohibition in Nepal, 41
prohibition in Turkmenistan, 44
restrictions in Thailand, 42
modernization, effect on religion, 96
mootness, 139
Mormons, 46, 52, 53
Morocco, religious discrimination in, 37
Mozambique, relgious freedom in, 51
Muhammad, 48
Mullainathan, 199–200
multiple vetoes hypothesis, 145
Muslims
and civil war in Yugoslavia, 6
and religious discrimination, 45
violence against in India, 6
See also Islam; Islamic population

NAACP, 148
Nam, 14
Namibia, religious freedom in, 43–44
Nardulli, 160–161
national income, and religious freedom, 93–99, 99*f*, 100, 101, 161*t*
and atheism, 195–196, 196*t*
and establishment clause, 166*t*
and gender status, 206, 206*t*
and happiness, 202, 202*t*
and Pew constitution measures, 168*t*
Pew measure of GRI on, 102–103, 103*t*
and poorer nations, 100
and proportionality, 180*t*
RAS scores on, 82*f*, 99, 99*f*
religious freedom and religious diversity, 188*t*, 191

national income (cont.)
RFF/GRI measures on, 102, 102*t*
and secularization thesis, 93–95
and separation clause/democracy/ legal infrasturcture interaction, 171*t*
national religion. *See* state-controlled religion
Native Americans, 46, 138
Nazarenes, 53
Nazi Germany, 6, 90, 91
negative rights, protection of, 144
Nelson, 132–133
Nepal, religious suppression in, 41
Netherlands, public health protection in, 156
Neuhaus, 20
New Deal, 112
Newsweek poll on Bill of Rights, 119
New Zealand, 96–97, 118
Nicaragua, religious freedom in, 43
Nigeria, 39, 48, 54
noncompliance, 139–140
non-constitutional law, effect on religious freedom, 161–163, 161*t*
non-governmental organizations (NGOs), religious institutions as, 19, 20, 21
Noonan, John T., 4
North, 16, 189
North Korea, religious repression in, 42, 44
Norway
government subsidization of religion in, 54
mandatory Christian education in, 45
religiosity in, 23
religious freedom in, 45
religious requirements for public office in, 54
state religion in, 45, 54, 156
Nuremberg laws (1935), 6
Nussbaum, Martha, 28–29

O'Brien, David, 128
official religion. *See* state-controlled religion
Oman, religious freedom in, 38
Opfinger, 24
Orthodox Christianity
and civil war in Yugoslavia, 6
effect on economic growth, 11
growth of, 96
in Romania, 46
See also Greece; Russia
overhang, judicial, 117–118

Pakistan
constitutional change in, 107
fundamental Islam in, 37
Shari'a law in, 48, 55
social regulation of religion in, 67
Paraguay, religious registration in, 51
participation, religious, pluralism effect on, 17–18. *See also* attendance, church

Paul, 22
per capita GDP. *See* national income, and religious freedom
Peru, 43, 153
Peterson, 200
Pew Forum, 83
Pew survey data on religious freedom, 73–76
  and atheism, 196*t*
  and constitutions, 168*t*
  and establishment clauses, 166*t*
  and free exercise, 164*t*
  and government restrictions, 73–75
  and happiness, 202, 202*t*
  and law/policy effects, 75
  limitations of, 75
  reliability of, 77
  and religious diversity, 188, 188*t*
  and separation clause/democracy/legal infrastructure interaction, 171*t*
  and social hostilities, 73
  and specific content of constitutional protections, 73–74
  and state of religious freedom in practice, 74–75
  and state religion, 161*t*
  See also Association of Religion Data Archives (ARDA); constitutional protection of religious freedom; Religion and State (RAS) scores on religious freedom; RFF scores on religious freedom
peyote, 47
Peyton, 160–161
physical health benefits of religion, 14–15
Pilgrims, 7
Pinker, 25
Planned Parenthood v. Casey, 134
pluralism, religious
  benefits of, 16
  effect on human rights, 22
  effect on religious participation, 17–18
  effect on religious participation and belief, 18
  See also diversity, religious
Podoprigora, 49–53
Poe, 87, 150
pogroms, against Jews, 6
Poland, religious diversity in, 187
political role of religions, 19–22
  and African-American community, 20, 21
  and civil rights, 21
  as mediating institutions, 20–21
  and world democratization wave, 19–20
polygamy, 46
popular constitutionalism, 116, 134–135
Portugal, 53, 54
Powe, 116
precommitment theory, 110–113, 143
proportionality, 154–156
proselytization
  as competitive business, 95
  prohibition by Islam, 36, 37
  prohibition in Central Asia, 37–38
  prohibition in Greece, 45, 46

proselytization (cont.)
prohibition in Nepal, 41
prohibition in Switzerland, 45
restrictions in Asia, 42
in United States, 46
Protestantism
discrimination in Colombia, 43
discrimination in Vietnam, 42
effect on economic growth, 11
and gender equality, 204
and women's education, 205
Pryor, 79, 80
public dress, religious restrictions on, 35, 37, 41, 48–49
public morals
Puritans, 84
Putnam, 12, 21

Qatar, religious freedom in, 37
Qur'an, 79–80

racial segregation, 84, 139
Raday, 30
rape, 48, 204
rational choice religious economics, 95
Rawls, John, 28
Raz, 90
reapportionment, 139
reeducation camps, 40
registration requirements
in China, 40
in Indonesia, 51
in Singapore, 51
in Thailand, 51
in Vietnam, 42
reincarnation, 191
religion, overview of
benefits for individual believers, 13–15
benefits of, 32
definitional issues, 2–3
economic effects, 10–11, 24–25
and identity, 4, 5
and life satisfaction, 13–14
mental health benefits of, 14
negative effects of, 32
as not needing specific constitutional protection, 3–4
physical health benefits of, 14–15
societal effects of, 11–13, 23–24
as source of conflict, 7–8
Religion and State (RAS) scores on religious freedom, 60–65
advantages of, 64, 77
and atheism, 196–197, 196*t*
comparison of overall score with Pew score, 76*f*
comparison of scores with ARDA scores, 69–73, 72*f*
comparison with Pew score, 76*f*
composite score, 64, 64*f*, 69
disadvantages of, 65
distribution of overall scores, 64*f*
and establishment clause, 166*t*
and free exercise, 164*t*
and gender empowerment, 207, 207*f*
and happiness, 202–204, 202*t*
and Pew constitution measures, 168*t*
and religious diversity, 188*f*, 188*t*

and religious legislation, 62–63, 69
and religious regulation, 62, 69
and restrictions on minority religious practice, 61, 69
and separation clause/democracy/legal infrastructure interaction, 171*t*
and state religion, 161*t*
See also Association of Religion Data Archives (ARDA); constitutional protection of religious freedom; Pew survey data on religious freedom; RFF scores on religious freedom
religiosity, 189–195
diversity effect on, 189–195
gender differences in, 205
and gender status, 206, 206*t*
government subsidies effect on, 198*f*
and happiness, 203
religious freedom
as fundamental element to be protected, 1
link with individual freedom, 7
restrictions on, 35, 57
similarity to freedom of speech, 9
Religious Freedom Restoration Act (RFRA; 1993), 136–137
religious symbols in schools, 49
reproductive rights, 48, 204
resource curse, 79
Restrictions on Religious Freedom (RRF) index, 68, 70
Reynal-Querol, 186
RFF scores on religious freedom
and atheism, 196*t*
and establishment clause, 166*t*
and happiness, 202, 202*t*
and official religion effect, 161*t*
and Pew constitution measures, 168*t*
and religious diversity, 188, 188*t*
and rule of law, 102, 102*t*
and separation clause/democracy/legal infrastructure interaction, 171*t*
See also Association of Religion Data Archives (ARDA); Pew survey data on religious freedom; Religion and State (RAS) scores on religious freedom
RFRA (Religious Freedom Restoration Act; 1993), 136–137
Richards, 126
Riker, 106
Rogers, 14
Romania, 46, 192
Rosen, 128
Rosenberg, 122, 139, 141
Ross, 79
rule of law
effects on religious freedom, 27, 89–93, 100, 101, 161*t*
and atheism, 196, 196*t*
and authoritarian regime, 90, 91
and content of law, 91
and establishment clause, 166*t*
and free exercise, 164*t*
and gender status, 206, 206*t*
and happiness, 202, 202*t*

rule of law (cont.)
and Pew constitution measures, 168*t*
and Pew measure of GRI, 102–103, 103*t*
and proportionality, 180*t*
and RAS measures, 82*f*
and religious diversity, 188*t*
and RFF/GRI measures, 102, 102*t*
and separation clause, 167*t*, 171*t*
and tyranny of the majority, 90
World Bank measure compared with RAS measure, 92, 92*f*
as political control, 90–91
procedural definition of, 90
thin, 90
uncertainty of relation to religious freedom, 90–91
Rummel, 186
Russia, 6, 44, 54

Sabbath, compulsory, 48
Sager, Lawrence, 3, 141–142
Samaha, 109–110
Sapienza, 25, 204–205
Saudi Arabia
lack of religious freedom in, 72
religious laws in,
repression of minority religions in, 36–37
women's rights in, 204
See also Islam; Islamic population
school prayer, 27, 135–136
mandatory in Bhutan, 41
Supreme Court on, 46, 135–136, 139–140
schools
and Amish people, 28
ban on religious clothing in France, 45
and desegregation, 139
moment of silence in, 29
religious instruction in Austria, 52–53
religious instruction in Georgia, 53
religious instruction in Kuwait, 36
religious instruction in Norway, 45
religious instruction in Thailand, 41
school prayer, mandatory, in Bhutan, 41
Scientology, 2–3, 51–52, 53
Scotland, religious attendance in, 94
search and seizure, 149
secularization hypothesis, 191
Segal, 124, 126, 132
Senegal, religious freedom in, 38
separation clauses
and church attendance, 192
as constitutional provisions, 28
interaction with democracy/legal infrastructure, 171, 171*t*
and rule of law, 167*t*, 171*t*
separation of powers, 145
Shari'a law, 32, 36, 48
on apostasy, 39
and gender rights, 48
in Kenya, 38
in Malaysia, 38
in Nigeria, 39
in Pakistan, 48, 55

Shi'ites, war with Sunnis, 7
Shintoism, 42
Shouwang (church), 39
Sikhs, violence against in India, 6
Singapore, 49, 51
Sisk, 125, 137, 138
Slovakia, regulation of religion in, 53
Smidt, 13
Smith, **1991**, 8, 9, 27
Smith, Adam, 16, 19
social capital, 12, 13, 24
social factors and religious freedom
  democracy, 83–89
    future uncertainty and minority interests, 86
    and individual rights, 87
    and majoritarian institutions, 86–87
    and majority regard for rights of minority, 84–85
    and minority role in composition of majority, 85
    national comparison, 87–89, 88*f*
    and nonbelievers, 84
  and national income, 93–99, 99*f*
  Pew measure of GRI, 102–103, 103*t*
  RAS measures on, 82*f*
  religions attitude toward other religions, 78–82
    apostasy, 79
    freedom based on Islamic populations of nation, 81–82, 82*f*
    freedom by majority religion of nation, 80–81, 81*f*
    Islam, 78–82
  RFF/GRI measures on, 102, 102*t*
  SRI measures on, 102
social regulation of religion (SRI), 67–68, 70, 102
  and correlation matrix of religious freedom measures, 71*t*
Songer, 125
Sorauf, 125
Souter, David, 134
South Africa, religious freedom in, 43–44
South America
  atheists in, 195–196
  Catholicism in, 43
  direct oppression of minority religions in, 43
  regulation of religion in, 51
  religious diversity in, 187
  See also *individual country*
South Korea, religious freedom in, 42
Soviet Union, downfall of, 20
Soviet Union, former states
  oppression of minority religions in, 44–45
  religious education in, 55
  See also *individual countries*
Spaeth, 124, 126
Spain, 45, 54, 131
Spann, 87
Specter, A., 117
Sri Lanka, 23, 41
standing, 122, 139
Stark, 16, 17
State Administration for Religious Affairs

Index

state-controlled religion
  constitutional provisions for, 156
  effect on atheism, 197
  effect on religiosity, 189
  effect on religious attendance, 16, 17
  effect on religious freedom, 161*t*
  forbidden
    effect on atheism, 197
    effect on religious freedom, 161–163, 161*t*
  as inefficient/ineffective, 15–16
  as undermining religion, 18
state courts, and religious freedom, 145
State Department (U.S.), international religious freedom reports of, 65–66, 68, 73
STD infection rates, 23–24
Sub-Saharan Africa, religious suppression in, 43–44
subsidies. *See* government subsidies
Sudan, religious freedom in, 51
suffrage, 87
Sufis, banned from Chad, 51
suicide, 13
Sullivan, 2
Sunnis, war with Shi'ites, 7
supply-side approach to religious market, 96
Supreme Court (U.S.)
  on atheists, 26–27
  and attitudinal theory of judicial decisionmaking, 124–128
  and backstop theory, 145
  budgetary issues, 130–131
  and court-curbing (jurisdiction stripping), 129–130
  courts upholding constitutional rights, 123–138
  deference to other branches, 128–131
  deference to public opinion, 128–131, 133–135, 140
  enforcement and application of rulings, 121–122, 129, 138–143
    compliance, 140–142
    noncompliance, 139–140
  existing research on effect of constitutional protections, 149–151
  how courts could matter, 144–147
  and impeachment, 129
  implementation of decisions, 131–132
  and legitimation theory, 115
  and logrolling, 145–146
  and minority religions, 137
  necessary support structure for judicial role, 147–149
  on peyote use, 47
  and presidential election 2000, 142
  relationship with Congress, 129–131
  on school prayer, 135–136, 139–140
  on schools and secularism, 28
  veto power of, 144
Swaziland, government funding of religion in, 54
Sweden
  atheism in, 23
  religiosity in, 23

religious discrimination toward Muslims in, 45
religious education in, 55
Sweet, 139
Switzerland, 45, 89
Syria, regulation of religion in, 50–51

Tabory, 18
Tabrizi, 125
Taiwan, religious freedom in, 42
Tajikistan, religious freedom in, 38, 44–45
Tan, 11
Tate, 87, 150
teen pregnancy, 23–24
televangelism, 95
terrorism, 19, 23
Thailand, regulation of religion in, 42, 51
theocratic, 30, 31, 36, 70, 79, 142, 168
thin rule of law, 90
Thomas Justice, 124
Thucydides, 200
Tibet, repression of Buddhists in, 40
Tocqueville, 21, 22
Toma, 131
Torcaso v. Watkins, 26
Tunisia, religious diversity in, 187
Turkey, church attendance in, 192
Turkmenistan, 38, 44
Tushnet, Mark, 117, 120
Tutu, Desmond, 5
Twining, 34
tyranny of the majority, 84, 85, 90, 123

Ulysses analogy, 110–111
Unification Church, 42, 52
United Kingdom
religious discrimination toward Muslims in, 45
religious regulation in, 50
religious requirements for public office in, 54
religious tolerance in, 45
See also Europe; Western Europe
United Nations, protection of atheist beliefs by, 27
United Nations Declaration on the Elimination of All Forms of Intolerance and of Discrimination Based on Religion or Belief (1981), 1–2
United Nations gender empowerment measure, 205–206
United Nations International Covenant on Civil and Political Rights (1976), 1
United States (U.S.)
government favoritism of religion in, 55
government subsidization of religion in, 54
regulation of religion in, 53
religious belief and life satisfaction in, 13
religious belief effect on mortality in, 14
religious economics in, 95
religious laws in, 49

United States (U.S.) (cont.)
religious pluralism effect on rates of affiliation/practice, 16, 18
religious repression in, 46–47
view toward atheists in, 26
See also Bill of Rights; Supreme Court (U.S.)
United States v. Seeger (1965), 26
unreasonable search and seizure, 149
U.N. Special Rapporteur on Freedom of Religion or Belief, 73
U.S. Constitution. *See* Constitution (U.S.)
U.S.S.R., lack of enforcement of constitution, 106
U.S. State Department. *See* State Department (U.S.)
U.S. Supreme Court. *See* Supreme Court (U.S.)
Uzbekistan
religious freedom in, 72
religious registration in, 53
religious repression in, 37–38, 44

Vanberg, 142–143
Venezuela
constitution of, 155
discrimination against evangelicals in, 43
evangelicals in, 15
Verme, 200
Versteeg, 146, 150
vertical compliance, 141
veto power, of Supreme Court, 144, 145
Vietnam
oppression of minority religions in, 42
social regulation of religion in, 67
violence, religious, 19
voting rights, 46

Waldron, Jeremy, 112, 118
Wallace v. Jaffree (1985), 26, 29
Way, 146–147
Weber, Max, 10
welfare state, 94–95
well-being, and religious freedom, 199–204
and happiness, 202*t*
and life satisfaction, 13
mental health benefits of, 14
physical health benefits of religion, 14–15
and religious diversity, 188*f*
Welzel, 200
Westerland, 132
Western Europe
church attendance decline in, 94–95
regulation of religion in, 51–53
religious freedom in, 45–46
religious requirements for public office in, 54
See also Europe, *individual country*
White, Byron, 132–133
Whittington, 117
Wierzbicka, 200
women's rights
and Christianity, 32, 204

and education, 205
and Islam, 204
religious freedom effect on, 204–207
in Saudi Arabia, 204
and suffrage, 87
suppression of, 32
See also gender
World Bank, 88, 92
rule of law measure compared with RAS measure, 92, 92*f*
World Council of Churches, 22
World Values Survey, 16, 191
Wright, Charles Allen, 106
Wybraniec, 137
Yarnold, 125
Yemen
direct repression of minority religions in, 36
religious diversity in, 187
Yousif, 45, 80
Yugoslavia, civil war in former, 6

Zambia, religious freedom in, 51
Zimbabwe, religious suppression in, 43–44
Zingales, 25, 204–205
Zorn, 132
Zuckerman, 195

www.ingramcontent.com/pod-product-compliance
Lightning Source LLC
LaVergne TN
LVHW011523200926
848484LV00001B/122
9781107041448